LOST CHILDREN

Polly Toynbee, the journalist and author, spent three years researching and writing this investigation. It is not a 'sociological' work, in the narrow sense of that term, although she comes to some hard-hitting conclusions. Rather it is a series of thrilling stories which portray people at their most determined and their most vulnerable, engaged in a search of supreme importance. The results of their quests are often surprising, sometimes distressing, but they all agree that it is better to know the truth than be left in the dark.

Polly Toynbee's research led her to the conclusion that a searching look into the present adoption procedures was sorely needed.

About The Author

Polly Toynbee writes a regular weekly column in the *Guardian*. She was previously a feature writer on the *Observer*. In 1975 she won the Catherine Pakenham Memorial Prize for journalism, and she has twice received British Press Awards.

She is the author of THE WAY WE LIVE NOW (1983), HOSPITAL (1977), A WORKING LIFE (1971) and a novel, LEFTOVERS (1966). Polly Toynbee is married with four children and lives in Clapham, London.

'During her research for this in some ways controversial study of adoption since the passing of the 1975 Children's Act, Polly Toynbee interviewed over forty adults who have been adopted and who are seeking or have found their natural parents... The stories are all highly dramatic, encompassing moments of joyful reunion as well as the most chilling disappointments... The account is a tribute to the author's skill as an interviewer'

Times Literary Supplement

'Polly Toynbee has recorded the urgency and intensity of these searches, and the powerful emotions involved in their fulfilment: and her experience over the three years it took to research and write her book has changed her... The force of their feelings has drawn her, too, into waters deeper than she had bargained for'

Observer

'It has always been part of Polly Toynbee's unique talent that while she tells one story, she is somehow darkly hinting at another... Her tales seem to tell themselves at precisely the pace you want to read them, and it is only afterwards the undertow pulls you towards the obvious implications of her message'

Guardian

'Their stories are riveting; even though finding a parent doesn't necessarily mean a happy ending ... In her sympathetic and poignant book, she points to the present injurious effect on natural mothers and adopted children, whether or not they find each other; and rests her case'

New Society

'It is in the culmination of these desperate histories that Ms Toynbee is at her best. Her most persuasive and strongly argued conclusion points to the dishonesties inherent in our treatment of adoption'

The Listener

'Fascinating'

Sunday Telegraph

Lost Children

The story of adopted children searching for their mothers

Polly Toynbee

CORONET BOOKS
Hodder and Stoughton

To my children, Amy, Milly, Flora and Nathanial

First published in Great Britain in 1985
by Hutchinson & Co. Ltd
Coronet edition 1987

British Library C.I.P.

Toynbee, Polly
Lost children : the story of adopted
children searching for their mothers.
1. Birth parents — England —
Identification
I. Title
362.7'34 HV875.7.G7

ISBN 0-340-40574-0

Printed and bound in Great Britain for Hodder and Stoughton Paperbacks, a division of Hodder and Stoughton Ltd., Mill Road, Dunton Green, Sevenoaks, Kent (Editorial Office: 47 Bedford Square, London, WC1 3DP) by Richard Clay Ltd., Bungay, Suffolk.

Contents

Acknowledgements

I would like to thank all those who have given me so much of their time and expert advice to help with the research for this book. I am especially grateful to all those people who agreed to be interviewed and to talk in depth about themselves and their lives with such frankness and trust. I have here changed their names, and the towns where they live (with the exception of Georgina Enston) to protect their privacy and anonymity, but also to protect their natural mothers and their adoptive parents. I would also like to thank the many who spoke to me in depth, but whose stories do not appear here, for without their contribution I could not have used the stories in this book with the same confidence that they are reasonably typical of adopted people in search of their origins.

Particular thanks are due to John Stroud, Assistant Director of Hertfordshire Social Services, several Catholic adoption agencies, Norwich Social Services Department, Noel Timms, sociologist of Leicester University, Pamela Hopkins of NORCAP – the National Organisation for the Counselling of Adoptees and their Parents, The Crusade of Rescue, the British Agencies for Adoption and Fostering and especially to Diana Reich, adoption specialist and researcher.

1

Michael and Wayne

Most parents have nine months to contemplate the arrival of their child and to prepare themselves. But the Hensons had just five days. Within five days of being told officially that they had been accepted by a Catholic adoption society as suitable adopters, they found themselves bringing home their new son in his brand new carrycot.

Mark and Greta Henson had told no one, for they were not sure they would be accepted onto the waiting list. They did not know if they would have a child in months or years or never. Their friends and relatives knew nothing of the five long years of waiting and hoping for a child of their own, nor their application to adopt. While most couples are eased into parenthood, with nine months to anticipate the birth and with the support of their friends and relations, the Hensons were jolted into it alone and with startling speed.

It was on 17 September 1984 that the telephone rang. Mark and Greta were both waiting for the call and Greta picked up the receiver at once. A voice from the adoption society said, 'Yes, you have been accepted by the committee to be placed on our official list for a baby. And, by luck, there happens to be a baby waiting for you right now.' Nothing had quite prepared them for this. They had talked over the subject time and again, but it had always been a discussion about an event far in the future, something to get ready for once they knew they were on the list.

The baby, a boy named Wayne, had been born on 30

August 1984. He was eighteen days old already. His mother had cared for him in the hospital for six days, and since then he had been placed in a temporary foster home with a woman who frequently took in babies for the society while they awaited their new homes.

There was, however, one final obstacle to be overcome before they could take the child. The child's natural mother wanted to vet them first. She had been given information on several couples so that she could choose the ones she wanted her child to go to. She had picked out the Hensons – although she was not allowed to know their name or address, or even in what part of the country they lived. Now she wanted to meet them, to make sure she approved of them before she handed over her son. Were the Hensons willing to meet her and submit themselves to her scrutiny for final approval? Greta wanted to refuse. She hated the idea of meeting the woman at all. 'I didn't want to think about her. I didn't want to carry a picture of her in my mind. I wished she didn't exist.' Mark had a similar instinctive dislike of meeting Wayne's natural mother – but rationalized it by saying he was afraid that if she saw their faces, she might one day recognize them, find a way to trace them, and return to haunt them in years to come. But they could not refuse to see her if they wished to take her child, for she still had the right to veto them if she chose.

The next day the social worker from the society took them to the flat where the natural mother was staying – a shabby place, where she was living for a few weeks before she returned to Ireland where she had left her family. It was an uncomfortable interview for all of them. No one knew what to say, or what to ask. The social worker stayed with them and kept the conversation going as best she could. Greta and Mark expected to find a young girl, perhaps a slightly wild, dissolute character. Instead, they found a sad but respectable-looking woman of thirty-four. She had a strong Irish accent and looked, Greta said, very ordinary. Greta had the distinct impression that all the woman wanted was to get a look at them. She had nothing to say to them, but she stared long and hard. The social worker tried to get her to talk about herself and her family in Ireland, so that the Hensons would have a story to tell her son as he grew up.

She talked reluctantly, but she did tell them a little. She said she had another son in Ireland, also illegitimate, whom her family had accepted, but they wouldn't accept another one. Wayne's father had said he wanted to make her pregnant, wanted her to bear his child, and she had agreed, expecting marriage. But he had abandoned her when she was five months pregnant and had gone off with an older woman. She was bitter about him, but kept hoping until the last moment that he might change his mind and come back to her. He had visited her in hospital and proudly picked up his new son, carrying him around the ward to show him off to others. But he hadn't come back. He had promised her the money to get back to Ireland, but when they met after she came out of hospital he hit her and refused to give her money. She showed them the bruises on her arm. Was she sad to be giving up her child? 'She didn't seem to be,' Greta said guardedly. 'She never said so.'

Mark was disturbed to hear that her other son was half black. He said he would never tell their son that he had a half-brother, as he might not like to know his half-brother was half-caste. His friends at school might find out and tease him about it, he said.

This awkward interview lasted only twenty minutes. The Hensons wanted to get away as quickly as possible, and Greta felt the mother was ill at ease too. Greta says, 'I shall try to put her out of my mind from now on. I don't want to think about her, as he is our son now.'

The mother agreed that the Hensons should take her child. The social worker took them straight from this meeting to see the child at the foster home. Events seemed to be moving almost too fast for them. They felt they were being propelled along with hardly time to think. They found the foster mother's home chaotic. She had four adopted children, including twins, and one child of her own. There was an eighteen-month-old whom she was fostering temporarily, and Wayne, shortly to become theirs. The television was on the whole time and the noise level was high. There was also a cat and a dog, and the family's priest, who had happened to drop in for a visit.

However, they were found a quiet place to sit down and the baby was wheeled into the room in a pram, their first chance to look at him. They were nervous, for they had been told several times that they had to examine their feelings carefully when they first saw the baby. People sometimes find a particular baby unattractive or distasteful. If they had any such feelings about Wayne, then they should say so at once. They would not be struck off the list and would still get another chance. They were told to pick him up, which they did gingerly. How did he feel? How did they respond to him? They both said they took to him at once, and as soon as they were used to holding him they started to play with him and talk to him. 'But we were very careful, cautious, almost afraid of him at first,' Greta says.

They now had three days in which to prepare for taking him home. The foster mother advised them about what equipment they would need, and they went out at once and bought £500 worth of baby clothes, a pram and a cot. 'Friends offered us things, but we wanted everything for him to be brand new,' Greta says. She had to give abrupt notice at her insurance job, but luckily her employers were understanding. As she didn't intend to return, she had no entitlement to maternity leave. Each day for three days they went back to the foster home and learned to feed and change the child, to bath and care for him. The foster mother was expert at teaching inexperienced new adopters, and she guided them and reassured them.

Even so, the day they took him home was alarming. It was

21 September, and to them that is more like his birthday than the day he was born. They had been told by the social worker that they must keep a Baby Book for Wayne, in which they were to start on the first page with a photograph of his natural mother. Then they were to paste in a photograph of his being brought through the front door for the first time, the moment, as it were, of his adoption. Dutifully, they photographed themselves bringing him home. For the first few days they were told to be alone with him and not let strangers hold him. He had already had too much handling by so many different people – his mother, the nurses in the hospital and his foster parents. He needed time to get used to them.

They felt this was good advice in the first few days. The baby, Greta says, didn't seem to recognize them. 'It wasn't my imagination, because I know we saw a look of panic in his eyes when we went to pick him up. We were strangers to him. Little babies know more than people realize, and he certainly knew we were strangers. He had a look of fear on his face.' Perhaps it matched their own fear, for they often panicked. They would perpetually check to see if he was still breathing, and when he was sick they ran for the telephone to ask the foster mother what they should do.

The day they brought him home they changed his name from Wayne to Michael. They had always meant to call a son of their own Michael. Most adoptive parents change their new child's name, ostensibly because they don't like it, but also in order to wipe out the memory of his first mother who gave him that name. Even older children often get their names changed, all part of the desire to deny a child's own history.

After all, the Hensons had been told they must tell the child of his mother. He was to be brought up with his Baby Book always to hand, with the photograph of his natural mother. And yet they had been told as well that they must regard him absolutely as they would their own child.

When I met the Hensons, they had had the baby for six weeks, but even then, every five minutes, one or other of them would get up and go almost unconsciously to his pram in the corner of the room. Greta says, 'I must admit that at first I cried sometimes, and panicked, especially after Mark had to go back to work. I think what they call post-natal depression is exhaustion and anxiety, because that is what I suffered. Imagine, one day you are at work, getting on with your life, and almost at once you are a full-time mother.'

The society's social worker said to Greta, when it looked likely that the committee would accept them on the waiting list, 'Regard yourself as pregnant from today.' If, by any bad luck, the committee turned them down, the social worker said, Greta was to regard herself as having had a miscarriage. If, once they had taken Wayne home, his mother decided to take him back during the three months before the adoption papers were fully signed, then they were to regard this as equivalent to a cot death and mourn the departed child as they would a dead one. In other words, they were being encouraged into a belief that this was really their own son – and yet they were also to be open and honest with him about his real mother and his origins. How could they be expected to strike a balance between these opposite demands?

All this began five years ago, when the Hensons first married and wanted to have children. Eventually they went to their doctor and, after extensive tests, he told them that they would never have children of their own and suggested that they should consider adoption. They both reacted strongly against the idea at first. They were so shocked to have their infertility confirmed that they could not bear to think of taking in someone else's child. They had planned their whole lives around the children they hoped to have. They had bought a small suburban house on a mortgage and planned to fill it with children. They are both devout Catholics, Mark having been converted by Greta before they married. In their small front room hangs a large modern picture of Christ on the cross, and much of their spare time, before the adoption, was given to Catholic organizations.

They both said they could not understand the meaning of life without children. Their marriage and their vision of the future were centred around children. What would they be like in ten or twenty years with none, they asked each other? What were they working for, aiming for, without children? Emptiness, barrenness hung over them, oppressed them.

Finally they came to terms with their infertility and, a year later, began to discuss adoption. They knew it would be hard to get a child, but they hadn't realized quite how many couples apply and how few are chosen. Through their priest, they got in touch with a local large Catholic adoption society. Being Catholics, they had a better chance than many adopters since, for obvious good Catholic reasons, there are more unwanted Catholic babies brought into the world and given to Catholic adoption agencies. Even so, right at the outset, they were warned how difficult it would be.

Greta was thirty-two and Mark twenty-nine when they applied. They were told that the maximum age was thirty-five for adopting mothers, and time suddenly seemed short. The waiting list, they were told, was closed. The society tried to keep the number of people on the waiting list roughly equivalent to the likely number of babies so as not to raise false hopes. So their names were placed on the waiting list for the official waiting list. They were told it would be easier to get an older child, but they said firmly that they wanted a small baby. They were given long forms to fill out, and these made it clear just how thoroughly they would be checked and interviewed before being accepted on the official waiting list by the society's committee.

Fourteen months later they were told the waiting list was at last open and, together with other couples, they were called for an initial briefing. They would need a thorough medical, and the law required the police to check criminal records too. They would need written references from respectable people who had known them a long time. Their income and their living conditions would be scrutinized. If they passed this stage satisfactorily, the hardest part still lay ahead. One of the society's social workers would interview them, both separately and together, in an intensive series of meetings. They would find these interviews searching and difficult. They would be forced to examine their most profound feelings and divulge everything about themselves that the social worker deemed important.

The preliminary inquiries took a long time, but there were no problems. Then they were called by the social worker, who wanted to start the interviews.

The first meeting seemed to the Hensons surprisingly vague and directionless. They didn't understand what the social worker was getting at, as she engaged them both in general conversation. No doubt she was feeling her way. She saw each of them separately four times and both of them together three times. She was not only checking them out, but also probing deeply into their attitudes and motivations. She was confronting them with all the possible problems of adoption.

Greta says she found these sessions difficult. She wanted to be entirely open and honest, and thought they both had been, but then she very much wanted to give the 'right' answers too. But what were the 'right' answers? It was not always easy to tell.

Neither Mark nor Greta had any problems in talking about their family and their upbringing, nor in discussing how they would bring up the child. But there were uncertainties in Greta's mind. When she was asked whether she would agree to meet the child's mother, if the mother should want to meet her, Greta admitted her strong reservations. Though she promised they would tell the child all they knew about his adoption, she very much hoped she would not have to go through with this meeting. It is a fairly new practice in adoption to arrange such meetings, and it was certainly a surprise to Mark and Greta. They had thought only of the new baby, the prize at the end of this long grilling, not of its mother.

However, the social worker insisted and explained the reasons why it was advisable. First, it gave them a true picture to hand on to the child when he grew up. They would be able to make his mother real to him, and describe her. Second, it would help the mother herself come to terms with the loss of her child. She would at least know to whom the child had gone. Third, and perhaps most important, was the effect such a meeting would have on the Hensons themselves. Once they had met the mother they could not so easily delude themselves that this child was their own. They would have to admit to themselves that he had his own roots.

Like so many adopters, the Hensons started out by imagining their new tiny baby as if he were their own. They didn't look far into the future until the social worker forced them to. What were their prejudices? How much would the child's background matter? As he grew up, they would have to tell him he was adopted, and they would have to tell him all they knew about his natural mother and the circumstances of his birth. If he became troublesome in adolescence, would they wonder about this 'bad blood' coming out. Would they feel that the sins of the mother had been visited on the child? Would friends and relations look at this child, seeking out faults that came from his unknown parentage?

'She asked how we would feel about having the child of an incestuous relationship. We were a bit shocked, but we talked about it. I said I couldn't tell the child, but Mark said he thought we should if he asked. What about a subnormal mother? Would that affect how we saw him? Then she asked, "What about the child of a nun or priest?" and that really shocked me rigid. It was something that had never crossed my mind.'

They had to talk about their own upbringing, their

brothers and sisters, their marriage, their infertility. Had they come to terms with infertility? Could they in effect admit it to the world by telling the world their new child was adopted? If not, they would be likely to try to hide the fact of the adoption from others, from themselves and from the child, and this denial could in the end be deeply damaging.

They were questioned too about their values, but not in the way Greta had been expecting. Being deeply religious and devout, she was somewhat affronted when the social worker suggested that, in the course of the child's upbringing, they might have to alter their values. Greta retorted that theirs were good Catholic values and they had no intention of changing them. Perhaps the social worker, although she came from a Catholic agency, was testing the flexibility of their views, for she said, 'From now on your child must be the most important thing in the world to you, and not your religion.' But Greta protested that she could not imagine any circumstances in which a conflict could arise between her child and her religion. Presumably this was an acceptable answer.

The interviews were strange and strained, although they came to like and trust the social worker. But who could devise a questionnaire to test for perfect parenthood? Nature has arranged things so that there is no selection whatever in qualifying to become a parent, with the subnormal and the genius, beauty and the beast, saint and sinner alike permitted to bring children into the world. But not adopters. Yet what qualities should we look for? And, having chosen those qualities, how are we to identify those who have them? Can any social worker really tell who will provide the happiest home for a child? It may be that, apart from weeding out the utterly bizarre, this method in the end is almost as random as nature's own, a matter of the personal likes and dislikes of a particular social worker or a particular committee.

The sessions ended with a kind of written exam. Mark and

Greta each had to write five essays about themselves and their views, to be submitted to the committee together with the detailed report from the social worker. Then the committee would, in its wisdom, pronounce judgment upon them.

By the time I saw them, six weeks after they had taken the baby home, Greta was saying, 'He feels exactly the same now as if he was our own.' There was still the slight worry that his mother might take him away from them, but she had returned to Ireland and the society had no reason to think she would. The society had asked them to include his first name, Wayne, in the new names he was to be given at the font, in a religious ceremony of adoption. It would be better for him to keep that link, for his first mother had already baptized him. But no, they refused, and wiped out his first name altogether. Greta said that they wouldn't ever tell him what his first name had once been. From now on he was to be Michael, and no one else.

What of the future now? The law says that Michael can go in search of his natural parents once he is eighteen; he will be entitled to know all there is to know. The Hensons hope vehemently that he won't want to know. Thoughts of his mother have already faded from their minds. Perhaps she will always be there as a distant shadow, but probably, like many adoptive parents, they will manage to forget that she ever existed. Her Wayne has become their Michael, a new identity for their new child.

Will Michael be one of those adopted children who sets out to seek his lost roots? Or will he settle for what he has and never hunt out his natural mother? Will these strange beginnings, unnatural and abrupt, seem odd to him as he grows up and understands what happened to him in the first days of his life? Will he read the myths and legends, the many tales of adoption in the world's literature, from Oedipus to Oliver Twist, and believe he too has some fate, some identity, some natural destiny which drives him on to seek out his own origins? Will Michael ever set out in search of the lost Wayne?

In 1975 the Children's Act was passed. For the first time adopted people were given the legal right to discover who they were. The legal knot of secrecy surrounding adoption was cut. This change has caused a great upheaval in the way adoption is viewed.

It was a change that was greeted with much opposition at the time, a public outcry. Adopters protested that it would be unfair to them. They had brought up these children as their own, but now the law allowed their children to desert them and seek out their original parents who had abandoned them. The whole relationship between adopters and their adopted children was threatened. Adopters felt that the glue that bound them to their child depended on the absolute obliteration of that child's origins. It depended, almost, upon the pretence that the child was indeed their own. Acknowledging that a child had other origins than its upbringing seemed to them to belittle and undermine their role – an understandable fear. In addition, the natural parents might haunt both the child and the family.

Adoption agencies argued that this change in the law would be unfair to natural mothers who had given up their babies to adoption. Many of them might have kept their secret quiet all these years and would now live in terror of that knock on the door, the arrival of the child they thought they had given up for ever. The law, protesters complained, would be retrospective, yet mothers who had given up their babies had been guaranteed at the time that there would be no way to link them to their child: never would their child find out who his real mother was. Many of them would have married and would have new families of their own who would be horrified to discover the existence of a previous, unknown child. Families could be sundered by these shocking revelations, and irreparable damage done.

But the point of the Children's Act in its many provisions was to shift the emphasis of this and other laws, tilting it in favour of the rights of children. Children were no longer to be viewed as the mere chattels of adults, but their own interests, rights and wishes would be recognized. However uncomfortable adopters or natural mothers might feel, the rights of the adopted children would come first. Among its other provisions, the Act gave children the right to be represented on their own behalf in court, and emphasized that there should be greater consideration of their needs in custody, care and fostering. It also discouraged the adoption of children by stepfathers, following divorce.

In the provisions that concerned adoption, the new Act acknowledged that many adopted children grew up with a desperate longing to discover more about themselves and their roots. Even if their adoption had been successful and happy, many of them felt incomplete and unfulfilled without some knowledge of their blood origins. Under all previous legislation, they had no access to their original birth certificate unless they already knew their birth name which was kept in a separate register in Somerset House, now St Catherine's House, in London. They had no access to the files of information about their adoption or to the records of adoption societies. Once the adoption papers were signed, a child was cut off for ever from his natural parents and relatives. Those parents lost all rights and any chance of ever seeing their child again. An adoption order is the only final and absolute utterance a court can make. It separates mother and child and guarantees that a child's origins are kept secret for ever.

This secrecy in the early days of adoption was intended to benefit the child. In Victorian days orphanages were filled with illegitimate babies, whose death rate was a national scandal. Of those who were placed in such institutions from earliest infancy, more died than survived. Reformers wished, quite rightly, to get the children out of orphanages and give them the chance of a new life with a new family. But so strong was the stigma against bastard children that respectable families could not be found to take them in and treat them as their own.

To have a fair chance in life, these children had to be given a new name, a new identity. It had to be made impossible for anyone – for the adopters, the child itself, any outside inquirer or future employer – to discover anything whatever about where a child came from before being adopted. The adoption certificate became the only birth certificate. Only the Registrar General, in his special register, could link up the name of an adopted child with the name with which it had come into the world.

This process was the only hope for a baby born into a society where the fact of illegitimacy could be irretrievably damaging for life. It was a bold, imaginative idea, and it did indeed free vast numbers of children from the taint of disgrace. Adopted children became acceptable and accepted in life, for, so long as their origins were kept secret, they could assume the identity of their new families with little social stigma.

Since those days, however, illegitimacy has become far more socially acceptable. Certainly what stigma remains adheres mainly to the mother and no longer to the child. So the reason for surrounding an adopted child's origins with such secrecy are no longer seen primarily as being for the child's own good. It is justified now as protecting the adopting couple, giving them the emotional security of knowing that the natural mother has gone for ever, and they are entirely free to simulate natural parenting as best they can. A new baby arrives with them with very few strings attached, and no previous identity.

This secrecy is supposed to help bond new parents and adopted child, for they know that once those adoption papers are signed, the child has no one else anywhere in the world. It has nowhere to be sent 'back' to, any more than natural parents can stuff their baby back into the womb, were they suddenly to regret its arrival.

Adoption sounds as if it ought to be an easy and humane answer to the painful problems of unwanted children, and sad barren couples. But human emotions rarely fit so neatly into tidy compartments, especially where they deal with some of the most fundamental feelings about identity, heredity and lineage. Natural parents and their children seek in each other some clue to their own being. It is the strongest bond on earth, not lightly severed, or invented with the signing of an adoption paper.

It may not always be easy to graft a strange child onto new parents, particularly as it grows up. The evidence in the animal kingdom suggests that adoption of alien offspring with alien genes is virtually unknown. A male gorilla acquiring a new female into his group will automatically kill off her offspring by a previous male. A lion acquiring a new pride will kill off all the young progeny of a previous male. The instinct appears to be to multiply your own genes, not someone else's. There are cases where female animals will adopt the progeny of a dead female in the clan, but the young are always closely related by blood to their new mothers. Strange offspring from strange groups are likely to be killed. Western human beings are virtually the only creatures to adopt the children of total strangers. Natural selection does not select for such an instinct, say the zoologists. It is largely unknown among primitive human beings, who would absorb an orphan into a family group, but not one from some alien family.

Of course such comparisons with animals are crude, and an appeal to 'nature' and 'natural instincts' may be irrelevant to highly developed human experience. But I believe it gives us some idea of the obstacles we are attempting to overcome in grafting babies onto new families. A sense of alien, different, foreign, unknown blood and genes may not ever be totally obliterated from the relationship between new parents and child. All attempts at denying this fundamental difference may lead in the long run to more difficult relationships. Better to do away with secrecy, and openly acknowledge the true and difficult nature of the bond between a child and its adoptive parents.

With a high and growing divorce rate – one in three couples now divorcing – step-parents are becoming an important feature of many children's lives. But few researchers have made high claims for the success of the step-parent step-child relationship. I suspect it is not an insignificant fact that step-fathers are involved in a high proportion of cases of battered and murdered babies. Through social necessity and the convenience of adults, we may have become too willing to believe that children can easily be brought up by outsiders, as if they were their own. Perhaps some of the feelings expressed by adopted children in this book about the importance of blood ties may shed a little light also on the dark corner of step-parenting. For as step-parenting becomes more common, so it is assumed by many more people to be an easy, acceptable and even natural relationship. But the fact that there is a lot of it about does not mean that it necessarily works well. The whole theory behind adoption is somewhat the same. It has been assumed it really makes very little difference to the child, so long as the parents are good, and the child is adopted in early infancy. Because it has been socially convenient for adults to believe so, we have assumed that strange parents and children will bond to one another as if they were genuine blood kin. Perhaps many do. Perhaps even the majority do – yet the experiences of some of those who feel the lack of blood kinship raise uncomfortable questions.

The 1975 Act acknowledged for the first time that, for some people, adoption was not the simple, clear-cut issue it was originally thought to be. It lifted the corner of the stronger, darker emotions that lie beneath an apparently easy placing of an unwanted child. It gave back to any adopted child who wanted it an identity it had lost. It was a well-thought-out provision, hammered out in the face of fierce opposition, and designed to allay the worst fears about its possible consequences. Adopted children over the age of eighteen were given the absolute right to their original birth certificate. But before they could do so, they were obliged by law to undergo a counselling session with a social worker. It is the only example in law of the idea of compulsory counselling, a faintly ironical notion, but one which, in effect, seems to have worked well.

The system the new Act instituted is this: an adopted person, once they are eighteen, can apply either to the local authority social services where they live or where the adoption order was made or the original adoption agency that first arranged their adoption, or direct to the General Register Office. They will be given a long form to fill out, and a counselling session will be arranged for them. They will meet a social worker, from whichever agency they have approached.

The counsellor is supposed to warn the child of all the possible dangers that may lie ahead. Many adopted people have nourished some wildly unlikely and romantic image of their mother all their lives. Will they be strong enough to face the real and not the imaginary mother? (Very few of the adopted people I have talked to showed much interest in their fathers. Their natural mothers were the focus of their search for their identity. Most seemed to have written their fathers off as bad hats, assuming, usually correctly, that their mothers had been abandoned by them in pregnancy or shortly afterwards.) At this first stage on the long search for their mothers, many of the adopted people are looking only for the most basic information contained in their birth certificates. For many the knowledge of their first name, and their mother's name, appears to be enough, and they do not feel the need to look further, or they are too fearful to do so.

But others intend from the beginning to seek out a meeting with their mother.

The counselling session was built into the law to ensure that the child had some preparation for what might turn out to be shocking revelations ahead. At least they have this one time to stop and think realistically about what they are embarking upon, where it might lead, and what it might do to others. Is the adopted child ready and able to cope with possible rejection? They may find their mother, but their mother may refuse to meet or speak to them. Is the seeker ready for anything – including the sad and the sordid. I have come across cases where the seeker needed superhuman strength to overcome the shock of finding their mother. One, for instance, found her mother was severely mentally handicapped and had lived all her life in an institution. Then there are the difficult social problems. Few adopted people are likely to find their mothers in better social circumstances than their own, usually far worse. How will they cope with the social chasm that there may be between them? Will they be overwhelmed by guilt, or shame?

The quality of the counselling that these adopted people get seems to vary enormously, though mainly it appears to be well done. Some social services departments seem to regard these sessions as unimportant formalities. They offer no follow-up, and little further help beyond the statutory minimum. But others regard this first interview as just the beginning in a longer relationship with their client. They offer help with the tracing itself, and once the parent is found, they suggest that they act as go-between, to lessen the shock to the mother. Some social services departments assign specialist social workers who understand the likely problems of adopted people, while others allocate no time or money, beyond a brief homily, a rapid hand-shake. Most of the adoption agencies, though, appear to take delight in welcoming back their far-flung children. They take a special interest and can be particularly helpful. Nothing in the law obliges them to reveal anything in their files, but the law has had a profound effect upon their thinking, and most seem prepared to tell a child as much as they know. A few agencies, though, some of the adopted children report, still regard their real clients as either the adopters or the natural mothers, and are wary of the returning child seeking out its origins.

What caused this sudden change in thinking about adopted children? For the 1975 Act broke very new ground, and many of the agencies fought hard against altering the adoption practices of generations. Their duties, they felt, lay not only with adopters and natural mothers of the future, but in protecting those of the past, for whom this retrospective Act would have a profoundly unsettling effect. They thought their duty to the child had been adequately met by placing it with a good family, and that it had no rights, no need-to-know, beyond the bare fact of its adoption.

One of the events that most profoundly altered thinking about the status of adopted children was the publication of John Triseliotis' book, *In Search of Origins*. In it he argued forcibly for adopted children's rights and emotional needs. He conducted a careful study of adopted children in Scotland who had gone in search of their parents. By a *curious anomaly*, Scottish law had always allowed adopted children access to their original birth certificates. This, it is thought, had more to do with rights to inherit, and sprang not from any especially enlightened Scots attitude.

Dr Triseliotis studied a number of Scottish cases where children had used this access to their records to trace their roots. From his survey, he concluded that only a small number of adoptees made the initial step of gaining information about themselves. Of these, even fewer went on actually to try to trace their mothers, and a very small number indeed succeeded. There is no doubt that his heavy emphasis on the tiny number of adopted people likely to avail themselves of such a change in the law helped to smooth the way to the passing of the Act. It greatly reassured the opposition to feel that most adopted children apparently showed no interest.

Since the passing of the 1975 Act there has been no proper research into how many adoptees have in fact set out in search of their roots. The Registrar General does keep a note of the number of adopted people who apply for their original birth certificates. These figures suggest that less than 10 per cent of adopted children start out on the search.

But from the interviews I have conducted, I suspect that there are far more adopted people in search of their parents than the Registrar General has records of. For one of the effects of the Act was not just in the technical provision of access to birth certificates. It rapidly changed the attitudes of most agencies and social workers concerned with adoption. Once the law was changed, information was far more readily available. Adoptive parents themselves sometimes became more open. Realizing that a child could set out and find out for itself, many parents actually divulged what they knew, including the child's original name, obviating the need for the official request to be made to the Registrar General. At least half of the adopted children I spoke to had found either their birth certificate, or information about their name and their mother's name, while they were still children. Even when adopters spoke little of the adoption and kept their records tucked well away, adopted children appeared to be remarkably good at finding them in secret drawers and boxes under their parent's bed. In fact, it was so common an occurrence, that I wonder whether there might be some unconscious wish on the part of some adopters to reveal to a child all it needs to know about its birth. Perhaps they find the subject too painful to discuss, and instead allow the child to 'discover' for itself.

Many adoptees know which agency they came from, and make their way back there, already armed with their birth certificate information. Many make no official contacts at all. But there has been no official collection of statistics from all these various sources. Officially I was told over and over again the accepted 'truth' in the adoption world – 'Very few adopted children show any interest in their origins. Only a few unsettled, disturbed ones need to search out their mothers.' 'Fewer than ten per cent,' people said, time and time again.

If 10 per cent is the number officially recorded, I would make an estimate that at least twice, and probably three times that number have been in search of their parents, without the fact being known to the authorities. But until some research body turns their attention to the subject, that has to remain an informed guess.

Also, the law gives no right to the natural mother to set out in search of her child – and yet I have come across many cases where she has done so, and succeeded. Sometimes, peculiar practice of a slapdash kind in years gone by meant she was allowed to know the name of the family who had taken her child. In other cases, some agencies, some social services departments have looked with sympathy on some mothers' sad stories, and deep longings to see their lost child, and despite the law, have helped them – though most of course turn them away.

The methods I have used in this book to contact adopted people would naturally tilt my findings towards those who had gone through official channels, rather than those who didn't bother, and went ahead on their own. Social services departments and adopting agencies have been my main source for contacting people who are looking for or who have found their natural mothers. Even so, I estimate that only half of those I have spoken to would have been registered as seeking out their origins in the Registrar General's records.

This book does not purport to be a sociological survey. It is a collection of stories from those adopted children who have sought out their natural parents. What drove them to look for their origins? Why was the identity given them by their adoptive families not enough? In the course of writing the book, I have accumulated the stories of over forty adopted people, all adults, who are seeking or who have sought out their natural parents. I have chosen eight of the most typical, yet varied accounts to describe in full in the following chapters. Where possible I have included the natural mothers' stories, and their feelings on being reunited with their children.

I spent most of my time talking to adopted people who desperately wanted to find or who had found their mothers. I then turned my attention to those who claimed they had no interests at all in searching, and those who had reasons for denying themselves the desire to find out. In other words, those who according to official statistics, and in all probability, are the majority of adopted people.

What of *their* feelings? Why did they feel so differently about their adoption? I listened carefully to what they had to say. It is, of course, harder to talk about emotions you don't have than ones that you feel strongly. I was asking them a rather loaded negative question – Why don't you care who your natural parents are? Why don't you want to know who you really are? Why don't you wonder how you came into the world?

I found decoding their answers sometimes puzzling. Some of them just shrugged and said they'd never been interested, scarcely given it a thought. It wasn't important to them. 'She's only my biological mother,' one said, and others echoed the sentiment. I made him repeat that answer, to see if he heard anything strange about it himself. 'Only my birth mother,' said another as casually, like dropping a hammer on Freud's head from a great height. How could they dismiss the idea of motherhood so lightly? After all, for better or worse, fairly or unfairly, it forms the basis of our most powerful myths, religions, symbols, icons. It's the fount of all life, the image of life, nature and identity. Yet some of these adopted people denied any such notion.

Perhaps it is presumptuous, but having listened to the agonizings of those who felt the loss of their first mother so keenly, I simply could not accept at face value that the image of their natural mothers meant nothing at all to them – a neutral, irrelevant force in their lives. I talked to various psychiatrist and psychologist friends, including Dr Anthony Storr, the distinguished Oxford writer and teacher. They all agreed that it was almost impossible that original parents could be of no importance, or that the idea of their natural mothers could be wiped out altogether.

Look at mythology, look at literature, where the mystery surrounding lost children and lost parents is a perpetual, powerful theme. Start with Oedipus himself, infant abandoned and left on the mountainside to die, adopted, all unknowingly, by a king. That poor incestuous parricide might have avoided his fate if someone had told him he was adopted. Heroes and heroines discovering their true identity in the last chapter, the last act, feature in book after book, play after play, from Shakespeare to Dickens and still on into the present day. It is a theme that haunts writers, because it contains so much about us all. It really does matter to most of us to know who we are.

So, backed up by some professional opinion, I found I could not accept these adopted children's straight denial. In fact, the very ardour of their denial would have been enough to make anyone pause and wonder what lay beneath it.

Many of the other adopted people not seeking out their roots gave more believable reasons for their apparent lack of curiosity. Some were rightly afraid of what they might find, or had been told enough to put them off looking. Some felt they couldn't cope with seeking for but failing to find their mother – the fate of many who set out on the search. Others were too afraid of their mother's rejection. Many said they didn't want to risk hurting their natural mothers, who may have kept the fact of the birth secret from their husband and subsequent children. But the one reason that dominated all the others was that they were deeply worried that they would offend their much-loved adoptive parents. It seemed to them disloyal, or at least they were sure that was how their adopted parents would view it. From my interviews with adoptive parents, their assessment is probably right. Most of them would feel greatly threatened if they knew their adopted children had gone looking for their birth parents. The children did not want to seem ungrateful or unloving.

Most of the children said they thought often of their real mothers during their childhood, but rarely had a chance to talk to anyone about their thoughts and feelings. Rightly or wrongly, they felt the whole subject was taboo. Although they had been told at a young age the bare fact that they were adopted, they sensed the subject was painful, and that their adoptive parents preferred not to speak of it, even, perhaps, to pretend it was not an important fact.

One interesting point is confirmed by all the agencies and social services departments I spoke to. Far more women than men go in search of their mothers. I spoke to several men, but they are greatly under-represented here. On the whole, those who have been in search are less good at talking about their feelings on the subject, so I haven't selected so many of their stories. But in any case, the men are thin on the ground. The vast majority of people in search of their roots are women between the ages of twenty and thirty, most usually around the time of the birth of their first child. Their own experience of motherhood seems to cast their thoughts yet more strongly onto their own mothers. As they go through pregnancy and childbirth, they understand all their mothers went through in bearing them. They find it even harder to understand how their mothers could have given them up for adoption, as they realize how close and how instant the bond is between a mother and her new born infant.

Often they claim that the birth of their own child has sent them in search of their mothers to check on any possible hereditary problems or genetic disorders. They are outraged to find how little information about their medical history is available. In pregnancy doctors ask them if there is a history of heart problems or epilepsy, or a number of other conditions, and they can only answer, embarrassed, that they do not know. I suspect this ostensibly practical reason for seeking out their mothers is only a kind of smoke-screen for far stronger emotions. If the genetic consideration was really the dominant thought, then wouldn't they be just as anxious to trace their fathers?

Another reason why so many more women than men seek out their origins, I tentatively suggest, is the different approach adopted by women and men towards their emotional life. Men have been brought up to deny feeling, to tuck it away, and hide it from the world. It is 'cissy' to want your Mummy when you are a grown man. It is often difficult for grown men to know in any case what their relationship with their mother is supposed to be, without going in search of an extra mother. But women have a good working model for a friendly and easy relationship with their mothers, who are there to help them through the bringing up of their small children. It is easier for them to acknowledge the lack they feel. It is in any case easier for them to show that they suffer, that they feel a sense of loss, that they feel the need of a relationship they have never had. A man is supposed to shrug off the fetters of his family, his mother's apron-strings, and stand alone. At least so says the macho myth that binds so many men into silent angry suffering, and relegates to women all the public feelings and weeping and emotional side of life.

Apart from those adopted people who denied so vigorously that adoption had made any difference to them whatever, the rest acknowledged that they felt their lives would have been transformed if their adoptive parents had in fact been their real parents. They felt in their bones that it was not the same, though of course, like the rest of us, they had nothing with which to compare their upbringing. Most of them were curious about their birth parents, but the dangers of seeking them out were too great. They wouldn't risk the pain to themselves and others. But they thrashed around in an attempt to describe their feelings. They were 'different' from their adoptive families – but they did not seem to realize how many ordinary children of natural parents feel 'different' in much the same way. It had been easy for them to ascribe all kinds of ordinary feelings about family life to the fact of their adoption. They were not good at comparing themselves to other children. Perhaps all children are convinced of the uniqueness of their own feelings.

The other group I talked to in the course of writing this book were adopters. In the stories in the following chapters, most of the adopters were either dead, or refused to talk to me, or their children had not told them of their search. I found it interesting that they were by far the most reluctant group of people, fearful, anxious, unwilling to explore or describe their feelings. To try to redress the balance in the book, I did talk to a number of adopters, though they were not the parents of those adopted people I had interviewed.

I must admit that I did not find talking to them easy. They felt that any deep discussion of adoption was likely to undermine their role. Many tried to deny that there was any difference whatever between adoption and natural parenthood. Perhaps all good adopters have to persuade themselves that this is so. Already the reaction I have had to writing this book has been ferocious from adopters. I have had letters from adopters far and wide asking why I am being so destructive. Why am I sowing seeds of doubt where there is none? What is my motive in trying to destroy very happy families with this talk of the importance of natural parents? I can only reply to them that I have no wish whatever to undermine them, or belittle them. But it is important to listen to the experiences of those adopted children who feel that blood ties matter, even though they have had happy adoptive families.

Many adopters do feel threatened, and become belligerent in defence of their role. As for the natural mothers I spoke to, I have yet to find one who does not harbour secret enmity against the couple who took her child from her. In these stories, time and again, the natural mother pays a meagre lip service to all she says the adopters have done in bringing up her child for her – but yet, thinly veiled, they relish every fault they can imagine or devise in the couple who were lucky enough to be in a position to bring up their child.

Healthy white babies are in short supply – with some 20,000 people each year inquiring after some 2000 children available for adoption under the age of a year. Many more are thought to want to adopt, but know they would not qualify, either because of age, marital status, or some other problem. Many would-be adopters become quite desperate in their pursuit of a child, as we have seen in the recent attempts by some to hire women to bear children for them, and by others to buy children from third-world countries. Those of us who are lucky enough to have children of our own know little of their sad plight, of how devastating childlessness can be. Even when they finally acquire a child, this may not resolve all their problems. By admitting that their child is adopted, they are telling the world of the shame of their infertility. To them it can seem like a fundamental and humiliating failure, and perhaps it contributes to their unwillingness to talk about adoption, with their children, or with others.

At least, however, they should be certain of the value of their role. For these days children placed for adoption usually have no chance of any kind of decent life with their natural mothers, and certainly an institution would be far worse. The social pressures that made mothers sometimes needlessly abandon their children are largely a thing of the past, and those who do so now usually have good reason. But perhaps in the light of what these adopted children say, we should be questioning the way in which adoption is currently practised. Should an adoption order completely sever a child from its natural mother?

Above all, in the light of the findings of the Warnock Committee, I hope that this book will make people question seriously whether we should be bringing human beings into the world specifically for the purpose of having them adopted. Although so far *in vitro* fertilization techniques have brought a great deal of happiness to previously infertile couples, there is the danger that in future the genetic origins of children may become confused, with the donating of embryos to alien mothers. Clearly a child of a donated embryo belongs more completely to a mother who had nourished it in her womb and given birth to it in the normal way – but would the same doubts about its identity still haunt it later in life? Would it feel the same need to know about its genetic origins? Perhaps less so, but after talking to these adopted people, I have come to believe that we tamper with our sense of identity at our peril. It is one thing to do the best we can for unwanted children already born, but quite another deliberately to create children who will start life with a confused identity. No doubt AID (Artificial Insemination by Donor) creates many of the same dilemmas, though it has been in use for many years. Possibly those children, having at least a whole and genetic mother, are less likely to feel the rootlessness of the adopted child, but in America there is now a fierce lobby of AID children demanding the right to information about their genetic fathers.

I talked to some adopters who were more open about their feelings, and could discuss some of the problems they had encountered. 'He didn't look at all like us. He was so huge, with red hair, and everyone commented on it. Do you tell total strangers, or do you let it pass?' Or, more important an observation, 'He didn't do very well at school. We didn't like to put pressure on him. After all, we felt we didn't really know what he was capable of, so we let him go at his own pace. Now I wonder if he were our own if we wouldn't have made him try harder?' Or 'She was a very wild and difficult teenager. I know a lot of girls are, but we kept thinking her adoption had something to do with it. Or at least, we wished we'd insisted on knowing a bit more about her mother and her background. It could have been that coming out in her, couldn't it? And not our fault at all.'

With a child of your own, for better or worse, it is of your own making, your own flesh and blood. You may choose to foist its less desirable features onto your spouse's family, or onto its own inborn bloodymindedness, but there is nowhere else to look for the cause of its bad behaviour or dislikeable traits but yourselves. But the adopted child has unknown blood, unknown genes. If in adolescence it seems to turn for a while, like children can, into some alien monster, then adoptive parents can choose to think they have been saddled with a cuckoo in their nest, a Rosemary's Baby, a Heathcliff. The glue that binds them to their child may be in greater danger of coming unstuck.

Adoptive parents have had a poor look-in in this book. They have been described here in these stories entirely from the point of view of their children – and in particular those adopted children who have gone to the lengths of seeking out their natural mothers. These children often feel that they were not given enough by their adoptive parents, but that may be quite unfair, both in the particular cases, and as a general perception. It may have far more to do with the adoptees' own unrealistic vision of what 'real' family life should be like than with any unusual shortcomings in their own upbringing. I do not know how the complaints of adopted children about their parents match up to the complaints of ordinary children, but in the literature of the world, there is no doubt that parents in general tend to get a pretty poor press from their children.

In this book I wanted to explore the deep and tangled emotions that adoption brings to light, because I think those very feelings reveal how we all established our sense of identity. Time and again adopted children said to me, 'You just take it all for granted. You don't know how important it is to have not just parents, but relatives, places, houses, old photos, cousins, ancestors.' They saw ordinary people often rejecting and neglecting their families, scarcely bothering to keep in touch, discarding them like outgrown skins. They saw their friends casting away things they themselves had never had, and valued highly. These adopted children felt they had been dropped on earth from another planet, delivered by the stork or come sailing down the river like Moses in a basket. So many of them said it didn't matter what their background was, good or bad, rich or poor, likeable, or awful. What mattered to them was having a background at all, being able to place themselves somewhere.

Since working on this book, I have examined myself, with my relations and with my children, and noted how often and in how many ways we constantly reassure one another about the security of our origins, with stories about relatives, comments on similarities, family myth and saga. How often the children ask the same questions about grandparents and other relations, placing themselves in the order of things, counting their cousins, establishing who does and who does not 'belong' to them.

I have never had any interest in genealogy, and I can probably identify my family only as much as most people – I can name five out of my eight great-grandparents, which is probably above average. Yet I realize now that this information which I have valued lightly, told as stories handed down, gives me a sense of continuity that I have taken too much for granted. After listening to the sad and rootless longings of those who do not have these firm anchors, I have come to value it more.

But that is only a part of what these adopted children lack. That is only the outward, easily identified missing part of their lives. Just as they talk so often about their appearance – 'Who do I look like?' 'Where do I get my hands and feet from, or my asthma, or my blond hair?' When they find their families, most imagine that they have found people who look just like them, though usually I can see scant similarity. It seemed to me that their insistence on the importance of appearance and physical characteristics stood for something else, a coded expression of some invisible but more essential bond they were searching for. It was an impossible ideal, a mother's love they felt they had never had, a dream of a perfect parent. They were looking for the mother of myth and fairy tale, the mother of all religions, Our Lady, Mother Earth, every unfulfilled wish.

2

Dorothy and Caroline

Dorothy Peyton is quite adamant that she had no wish whatever to see the daughter she had put up for adoption years ago. She did not want news of her, nor her address. She was, she says, horrified at the very idea of ever coming face to face with her.

Dorothy is a small, lively, grey-haired woman in her mid-fifties. She is a vigorous talker who makes careful and honest observations of herself and her feelings. She gesticulates as she talks and chain smokes at the same time. She seizes on the salient point each time she tells a part of her life story, and she twists and turns her thoughts, examining them from various angles as if solving some problem that was not entirely her own. It is easy to believe that she made an excellent inspired school teacher before she retired. She sits in her neat, bare old-fashioned sitting room in her flat, surrounded by mementos of her father's trips to China, ancient knick-knacks brought back from the Far East between the wars – a carved Chinese dragon bearing a faded lantern, a nodding mandarin.

Dorothy was the only child of elderly parents, Irish Catholics who lived in Liverpool. Her mother was a teacher, her father a merchant navy petty officer, and later a design draughtsman in an engineering works. Her mother was in her mid-forties when Dorothy was born in 1928 and her father died while she was young.

Her parents were delighted when Dorothy won a place at

London University, which she could only afford to attend through a special Ministry of Education grant, which obliged her to do a minimum of two years' teaching after leaving university. She lived in a tightly knit, closed Catholic world, staying in a Catholic girls' hostel during her university years, and then teaching in a convent school, where she also lived in. 'I had been there six years. I was twenty-seven, and I felt I had seen very little of the world. It would be so easy to settle in to that school and stay there for ever. I forced myself to leave, and took a contract for one year to teach in Malta.'

In Malta she shared a flat with two friends. They found themselves the centre of attention there, with so many British boats passing through, and a succession of dances and dinners on board ship, and in the local barracks. 'We were just about the only English girls – apart from the WRENs who were looked down on by the officers. They had a predatory view of us. Every ship that stopped just had one idea – to get a girl into bed.' Her friend warned her of all the dangers. 'But I said I was twenty-eight, I hadn't slept with a man yet, and I had no intention of doing so. I didn't want to get married, and I certainly didn't want to have children. I wanted to lead my own life.'

The festival of St Paul is a great feast day in Malta, with singing and dancing in the streets. She had been taken out once or twice before by Martin, a tall young Scottish naval officer. One of her flatmates heard through a friend of hers that this man had been boasting in the mess that he would sleep with Dorothy. Dorothy laughed at her and dismissed the thought. 'I haven't yet, and I don't intend to. I can look after myself well enough,' she remembers saying. That night they all went out together to the carnival in the streets. Martin succeeded in getting her extremely drunk, so drunk that he and her friends had to carry her home. 'It was the only time in my life that I ever got drunk. I am still deeply ashamed of myself. Others may do it often, but for me, with my upbringing, and my view of the world, it takes away all human dignity.' She was, she says, entirely unconscious. Martin suggested to her flatmates that he would look after her, and see she was all right, so they went off to bed. 'My friends blame themselves to this day. They say they don't know how they could have been so naive, leaving me unconscious on my bed in the company of that man.'

When she woke up next morning, he was there, in bed with her, and she remembered nothing at all of the night before. 'Out!' I shouted. 'Get out of here at once!' And he went. I was horrified. I had no idea what, if anything, had happened to me, but of course I could guess. I managed to put it out of my mind. As I couldn't remember anything, and I didn't seem to have any physical effects, it made no impact on me really. I was very angry, as he'd threatened and boasted he'd get me, and he did. But of course I never should have got drunk. I'm sure he did get me drunk, but I can't remember how. I went to confession, filled with remorse. The priest talked to me about the avoidance of occasions of sin, a very Catholic concept. I had to take the blame as I had put myself into that position, an occasion of sin.'

The priest told her, after her confession, to try to put the incident out of her mind. But a month later she realized she was pregnant. She sought out Martin and told him. 'He laughed. Honestly, he just laughed. He said, "Oh, you can get yourself out of it easily enough." He left Malta a week or two later, typical of the navy. There was hardly a man in the navy who didn't think of Malta, Cyprus and such places as just an opportunity to have it off. The more highly educated the women concerned the more fun the conquest. Then they would clear off and leave the disasters behind them.'

She suffered badly from pernicious vomiting, so there was no hiding her condition from her flatmates. 'The problem then was how to hide it from the nuns at the school. I had to finish my contract without them finding out. That meant I had to stay until July, when I was five months pregnant, and very sick, without them guessing. I would never have been allowed to work again in a Catholic school, or probably any school, if it was ever known I had an illegitimate child. It's easy to forget how different things were in those days. Any hint of immorality in a teacher, and you didn't work again. I had to support not only myself, but my widowed mother back in Liverpool.'

She remembers little about Martin, except his appearance. 'He was a most unremarkable, ordinary naval officer,' she said, with evident contempt. 'He meant nothing to me and I would hardly call it a relationship at all. He was very tall, fair, with pretty hair, soft and curly. He had big grey eyes and a long face, a good skin, and a strong Scots accent. That's all I know, and to tell the truth, it's all I care. I never saw or heard from him again.'

Her two friends looked after her and helped her in every way they could. They sent her to the head of the Nursing Association in Malta, a sympathetic woman. 'She gave me a bit of a ticking off, but she was very kind. She sent me to the King George V Hospital, where of course the pregnancy was confirmed. Then she said, "Right, now we've got to help you get through your teaching contract." She gave me a diet sheet to help keep my weight down, to make the bulge as unnoticeable as possible. I was very small and slight, which made it easier to hide, being only five foot tall, and six stone in weight. She wanted me to tell my parents, hoping they would care for me. But my father was dead, and Mother was nearly seventy. She'd have died of disgrace.'

Dorothy made it through to July without the nuns suspecting, and she hurried back to England. The nurse who had befriended her had written ahead to book her into a Catholic mother and baby home in London. But she could not go there until six weeks before the baby was due. 'All the Catholic hostels for homeless single women were run by nuns, and they wouldn't take me in until I could go to the mother and baby home. They said they didn't want a fallen woman corrupting the others.' Finally, she found herself a place in a non-Catholic hostel for female down and outs in Soho. Her stay there, despite its unsuitableness, was, she says, the only time in the whole pregnancy that was not miserable.

'I felt very bitter about the Catholic Church, and their cruel treatment of me all through this time. It turned me away from the Church, but not from my Catholic beliefs. That Soho hostel was like being back in boarding school, but it was clean, reasonably comfortable, and the people were so very kind and welcoming. There was no disapproval, only warmth and comforting people. I am eternally grateful to them.'

Since she had been back in England, she had been seeing an old friend, James, who several years previously she had converted to Catholicism. He had been in no sense a boyfriend, but when he found her pregnant and helpless, he offered to marry her. 'He stood by me, through all this. But I still knew that I wanted the baby adopted. I never for one moment doubted that. For one thing, I never wanted a baby. I didn't like babies at all, or young children. I taught older children, and nothing on earth would have persuaded me to teach primary-school-age children. But there was another more important reason. I knew James well, and I knew that he would never really accept the baby. It would be there for ever, the sign of my wickedness, and he'd take it out on the child. It would never work, because he was just not that kind of man.' As things turned out, her assessment was absolutely right.

The time came when she had to transfer from the down-and-out hostel, to the mother and baby home, as the date of the birth of her baby grew nearer. James collected her, with her suitcase and her trunk, and took her to the home. 'It was the most appalling experience. It was obvious, the moment I walked in, that this was a place of punishment. The matron was a bitch – no that's not strong enough. She was a violent sadist, a terrible woman. She had been a nun once, but had to leave the convent for some reason. She thought all pregnant women were evil, and made them feel it in every way she could.'

She was taken up to the dormitory in silence, and no one spoke. The bed was cold, hard, and very damp. 'It was the most cold and unloving place I ever saw. It was like a prison. I asked the girl in the next bed where the washroom was. She said, "Find out for yourself!" You see everyone there became like that, they were so unhappy. In the washroom there was only cold water. At breakfast next morning no one spoke. All meals were held in silence. There they were, all these women of all ages, some pregnant, some new mothers, being treated like convicts. We had to file out of the dining room in pairs, and grace lasted ten minutes. That morning, when a plate of porridge was dumped in front of me, I just burst into tears. I hardly ever cry, I'm just not the sort. But I did then. The matron said, "So you think yourself too good for our food do you Peyton?" We were all called by our surnames.'

They were assigned their work for the day. 'I had to clean three large rooms, completely. There was no vacuum cleaner, only a brush and pan. I liked cleaning and housework, so I didn't think this would be any great hardship, and it was a chance to be alone. But the matron's own room was large, and filled with every kind of ornament, and nine rugs on the floor. It was very hard work, and it gave me bad pains. I went up and sat on my bed to recover. I remember a girl coming in, weeping floods of tears and letting fly about the cruelty and unkindness, the misery of that place. Someone was sent up to fetch me to drink my cocoa, but I just couldn't make myself move. I was too exhausted and depressed. Then the matron came marching up to the room. I have never seen a human face express so much disgust. The way she looked at me, and how revolted she was! How she hated us all. She just shouted at me, "Pack up your bags, and get out of here. We don't want you here one minute longer!" It wasn't entirely clear why, partly because her room was not cleaned well enough, and partly for insubordination at refusing to come down for cocoa, I think.'

There she was, about to give birth in a matter of weeks, with absolutely nowhere to go, turned out of the place that was meant to help her. 'I sat on the local station platform for three hours with my suitcase, wondering what I should do next. Eventually, I got a train back to Soho, and the kind hostel for women down and outs. They took me in that night.'

Next morning she was sent to another Catholic agency. 'I went there with James. It was funny, because the woman there, who was very kind, sent James out of the room, before she would talk to me. She explained that was because he was only a recent convert and she didn't want to say anything against a Catholic organization in front of him. Once he'd gone, she said they'd had twenty-nine girls run away or been thrown out of that home. The matron was unbalanced. She had a hatred of sex, and particularly of fallen women.'

A place was found for Dorothy in a non-Catholic WVS mother and baby home. 'The moment I went in, the atmosphere was quite different. The other girls were friendly and chatty and even the matron was kind. She looked at my notes and said, "I see you don't like housework." I explained that in fact I did like housework, I've always enjoyed it, and I told her the story. Later she became a close personal friend of mine for many years, until she died. She was a wonderful person. She'd been the first nurse into Belsen, and she knew all about human suffering.'

In this home she took all the housework jobs, but would have nothing to do with the babies. The other women vied for work in the nursery, but her dislike of babies was intense. 'Horrible things, that awful smell of milk. I had no feeling at all about my baby. It was just a bulge to be got rid of. I never for a moment thought of not having it adopted. In any case, it would have been impossible for so many reasons, the first being that even then, I was sending most of my maternity allowance to my mother. I was supporting her, and she came first.'

Her mother was deeply offended that she did not hurry home to Liverpool as soon as she came back to England. 'I had to invent a story. I said I had no money, and was having to earn my living as a waitress in Lyon's. I promised that I would have enough money to come and see her for Christmas. I knew I would have had the baby and I was promised that it would be adopted in time for Christmas, so I could go and see her, without her ever guessing what had happened to me.'

Then came the birth of her child. It was a hard labour, lasting fifty-four hours. How did she feel? 'When the doctor first held up my baby I thought she was hideous. She had a thick mass of black hair, with a reddish tinge, and these thick eyebrows. She had a very definite nose. She hissed at me like a cat when I first held her, and I said, "Take her away! She's horrible." But the doctor said, "She's a beautiful baby." Perhaps if they had taken her away right then, I wouldn't have given much more thought to her. When they know a baby is going to be adopted, they should never give it to the mother to hold, let alone to look after for weeks. Something happens.'

After the labour ward, Dorothy was left for an hour and a half in a solarium in the hospital, holding her baby, waiting for a bed in the ward to be prepared. 'If they hadn't done that, I'd never have cared. I'm quite sure of that. A bond developed between me and her in that short time. As I held her, I could feel this peculiar reaction starting up in me, however hard I tried to suppress it.'

In the ten days that followed Dorothy tried to detach herself as much as possible. She took every opportunity she could to stay away from the baby. She would persuade other mothers and expectant mothers to feed her child at feeding times. 'But I thought the world of her. I thought she was marvellous and I found everything she did so fascinating. She was a peculiar baby, everyone there said so. She acted like a four-month-old from the day she was born. She always wanted to stand up, even in her bath. She had a fierce temper, like mine. I've had to battle with my temper all my life, and it didn't surprise me that she had the same problem. The matron said it was just as well we weren't going to stay together, as she thought we'd end up fighting like cats.'

James came to see her in the home. 'But he would never once even glance at the baby. He said, "Get rid of the brat quickly, and we'll start a new life of our own." He hated her, the very thought of her. He was full of jealousy and anger. I should have been warned about him then, but marrying him seemed a way out of my problems – a new name, a new life, a place to live. "I don't want to look after that brat of yours," he'd say at visiting times and I knew that he would never ever accept her.' Dorothy hardly wavered in her decision to have the little girl adopted.

The day came for the adoption. Dorothy was told a little about the family her child would go to. She had named her Theresa Patricia, after two of her best friends, but these names would be changed. She was told the family were Catholic. (In practice most children had to be adopted into their mother's faith.) She was told they were wealthy, and that the husband was a successful lawyer. They had two older sons, and wanted a daughter to complete their family. One curious fact about them she was not told – that these parents were already in their fifties, an extremely unusual age at which to be allowed to adopt.

That morning she knew they would come to take Theresa away. The matron sent Dorothy out shopping, to supervise some expectant mothers, so that she would not be there to see the family. She was not allowed to catch a glimpse of them, or anything that might give her a clue as to where her child had been taken. 'I stayed away for two hours. When I came back, she was gone. That was it. That was all there was to it. It was just as if she had never existed – empty cot, no baby. I left the home that day. It was a week before Christmas, just as I had planned, and I had to hurry away up to Liverpool to see my mother.'

She felt ill and desperate, but her mother noticed nothing. A row developed between them almost at once, when she told her mother she was going to marry James. 'Although he was a Catholic, he was a divorced man – and that was a sin she could not forgive. Little did she know about the other sin. We tried to get an annulment from his first marriage, which had not been in a Catholic church, but as the priest could not prove that his first wife was unbaptized, we got nowhere. Annulments were much harder to get then.'

She was married in a registry office straight after Christmas. 'I didn't mind where we married. I was so bitter and angry with the Catholic Church that I couldn't have cared, except for my mother.' She was still in a state of shock. 'It lasted for two years. I felt ghastly. I can hardly describe it. I suffered these appalling pains as if my innards had been ripped out. Of course I went to doctors, but there was nothing wrong with me. I knew perfectly well that it was all psychosomatic. Because my baby had been taken away, I felt it physically, as if she'd been ripped out of me. I never expected to feel so badly about it, or for the feeling to last so long.'

After they were married, they lived in another part of London, and Dorothy went straight back to teaching, in a non-Catholic state school. 'I had to. I had to go on supporting my mother, although she was so angry about my marriage. James said he wasn't going to give a penny of his money to her. He kept his money, we shared the rent and I paid most of the household bills as well.'

The marriage went badly from the very beginning. 'I didn't love him, and I shouldn't have married him. I was in such a shaky emotional state I didn't really know what I was doing. He was angry all the time, and he became increasingly jealous. I never ever mentioned the baby, or my pains, not once. But he kept accusing me. "You think of its father all the time, don't you?"' She resented other teachers at the school who were pregnant or who had new babies. She stared at babies in prams in the street, and suffered terribly. In three months, she signed the final adoption papers, 'But I had no hesitation about that. There was no going back, and it was just something that had to be done.'

She discovered her husband was acutely paranoiac, and he got worse as the months wore on. 'He became so jealous that he accused me every day of sleeping with other men. He became quite terrifying, going on and on every evening when he came home from work. I was thinking of the baby, thinking of its father, he'd say. I couldn't argue with him. I was not allowed out to see my friends. He became obsessed with the idea that my friends were panders providing men for me to sleep with. Absurd, mad. I couldn't bring my friends home, as he said he wasn't wasting his bloody money on them. I had an hour at home before he got home every day, and I had to shop, cook and clean in that time, and have his meal waiting on the table. Then he'd start, "And which member of staff did you sleep with today?" It never stopped.'

Things came to a head when her mother came down to stay six months after they were married. 'That was the end for me. Quite cold bloodedly, he told my mother about the baby. He said, "Your daughter is quite avid about men, I'm afraid. She's very promiscuous, and she gets drunk." Of course it was nonsense, but my mother was stunned. She said, "How could you do such a thing to me? How will I ever face the scandal if it comes out in Liverpool? I can never rest now in case anyone gets to know." She only thought about herself and not about what I had gone through. She didn't stop to think about me, although I had struggled to keep her all these years. All she worried about was what the neighbours would think. I couldn't forgive her for that. But then we were never really close. She was so old and rigidly

Catholic, from a very Victorian background.'

She left James straight after that. But he came back to her and wept, begged her forgiveness, promised to change, and to put a stop to the jealousy. 'I was soft. I should have known he was incapable of change. He was the sort of paranoiac who thought the whole world was wrong and he was the only one who was right. I did go back, three months later, but at once things were worse than ever. He started to beat me. I had to go to the school in dark glasses to hide black eyes, and long sleeves to hide the bruises on my arms. He wouldn't let me go to bed at night. He'd stand there accusing me, and preventing me from leaving the room. His accusations were crazy, like a gramophone with the needle stuck, speaking in this deadly monotone.'

Finally she told a friend at school, who told her to go to a doctor and solicitor. They said it was clear he was dangerous and in need of a psychiatrist, and she should leave at once. The solicitor sent him a letter warning him not to molest her, and that if he did, he would have to be removed from their flat. Dorothy was there collecting her things when he came home and read the letter. He attacked her again, but she just managed to escape, with nothing but her handbag and coat. 'He took a bottle of gin, drank two tumblers straight off, and threw the bottle at me. I was lucky to get out alive. He was white, I remember that, completely white with fury.'

She made a new life for herself, settling into her own flat. She still had many friends from the days before her marriage. 'Of course I never married again,' she says with a laugh. 'I never would have done in the first place except for the state I was in at the time. I never wanted to have children. I never wanted to be married. I was absolutely right, wasn't I?'

She looks back on these appalling two years with a wry detachment now, wondering at her own vulnerability. She is a strong independent person, a successful history teacher who loved her work, and treasures her friends, and her independence. She has taken early retirement and fills her life with reading, particularly history and theology. Apart from those two years, she has lived the life she always meant to lead. Looking back, it seems quite extraordinary now that one drunken evening should have led to such a catalogue of catastrophe. And yet like many wise people, she cannot in all honesty say that she regrets any part of her past.

'Does it sound odd that I can say I am very glad I had a baby, because I feel in some way fulfilled? It is an experience every woman wants to have. If I had my time over again I would do it again. I know now what having children is all about, and I wouldn't have known at all otherwise. And even though I knew absolutely nothing about my daughter, I had this deep sense that I had succeeded in keeping my family going, keeping the bloodline alive. I think I'd have been an absolute failure as a mother. I was a strict disciplinarian as a teacher, because I was brought up that way. I always wanted instant obedience, and I could never have imposed that on my child. I had the wonderful experience of giving birth, but I've no illusions about what sort of life I might have given my daughter.'

After the final break-up of her marriage, she took time to recover. 'It's shocking perhaps but all things pass in life. I felt less and less about the baby. The pain ebbed away. It was like getting over a death, I suppose, and people do, eventually. I remembered her every birthday, and wondered a little about her. I wondered if she looked like me or if she had inherited any of her father's characteristics – but it became a distant thought, and I got on with my life.'

She was badly shaken when the 1975 Act was passed. 'I was in a turmoil, absolutely terrified that she might turn up on my doorstep one day – and I did not want that. I did not want ever to see her again. A few of my friends knew about her, about four of them, but I couldn't imagine explaining her to the other people. I was ashamed. I am still ashamed. It may seem a small peccadillo to you, but I felt I had lost my dignity as a human being that night she was conceived. Lost every shred of decency and dignity. I came of a strict background, and you just cannot shrug off those feelings. I did not want to have to answer questions she might ask. How could I tell a young girl the true facts about her conception? If it had been the result of some grand passion, then perhaps I might have felt differently. But how could I tell her that she came into the world through an act of such squalor and unimportance? How could I tell her the sort of man her father was? I didn't want her to know, and I didn't want her to know me.'

She reassured herself that it would be almost impossible for her daughter to find her. She had changed her name since the adoption, by marrying, and she had moved ten or eleven times since then. Even so, her fear worried her.

And yet, despite all her protestations to the contrary, it was her own action that led to an encounter with her daughter. She insists she never meant it to happen, never wanted it to happen, that her daughter was far from her thoughts. But something about her explanations might lead an outside observer to suspect that tugging away at her underneath, there must have been some desire to make contact. 'A psychiatrist might say that,' she says briskly, 'But I say it's utter rubbish. I know my own mind.'

Not long ago she began to think about making a will. She wanted to leave all her money and possessions to her long-time flat mate and great friend. 'But my friend is older than I, she has plenty of money anyway, and I thought I should make my daughter residual legatee. My friend Sarah can decide whether to pass on the things and the money, or to wait until she dies when they will pass on automatically.'

But why did she want to leave it to this daughter she had never met? 'I have so many family heirlooms, especially my Chinese treasures, that my father brought back from his stay in China. I should like to feel those would stay in the family. I should like to give her something. Of course, if she wants to sell the lot, that's all right with me. It's up to her. I'll be pushing up the daisies, but at least she will have had them, from her grandfather. And with my early retirement money, and a little I've saved, I have some money, and she might as well have it. I have no one else. My mother is very old, and I have no brothers and sisters, so nephews and nieces.'

For some people, the disposition of their possessions takes on a special significance, not easily understood by others. 'It's not exactly that I think possessions matter.' She hesitated here. 'But family is family. Blood is blood. I was really not very curious about her by this time. I did not want to see her. I simply wanted my solicitor to know where to find her after my death.' She thought that when she died her estate might add up to as much as £20,000. 'I doubt if she needs money, with the family she was adopted into. But there it is. That's the way I feel about it.'

She went to her solicitor and asked him to trace her. He explained that he could not do much, beyond writing to the adoption agency, which he did. The agency, once known as the Catholic Rescue Society, had changed its name and amalgamated. 'Just as well, I hated the name "Rescue", as if my baby were being rescued from the clutches of an evil fallen woman,' Dorothy says. She gave her baby's name and date of birth. Adoption societies are obliged to keep their records for seventy-five years, so information would still be available.

Dorothy sat down and wrote to the adoption agency. She explained firmly and clearly her reasons for wishing to contact her daughter. She explained she did not wish to know her whereabouts herself, but that her solicitor should be kept informed, so that her child could be reached if Dorothy died. She laid out certain conditions. The adoptive parents were to be told of the will, and it was to be up to them whether they chose to tell the child. No one was to have any sense of obligation about contacting her. She enclosed a list of reasons on a separate sheet of paper, in case they wished to show those reasons to the child. On this piece of paper, she explained that she had no family, and she would prefer her daughter, and not the state, to inherit such valuables as she possessed. 'I thought that would be the end of the matter,' Dorothy says. But perhaps this was an elaborate fishing expedition.

When Mr Brook at the adoption agency received this letter, he acted in what is probably a most unorthodox way. The law makes it clear that parents have no right to contact their children, or to receive any information about them once the final adoption order has been made. Yet he decided to go ahead and contact Mrs Barnes, the woman who had adopted Dorothy's baby. He appears to have suggested in his letter that in fact Dorothy did wish to contact her daughter, or at least to have hinted at the possibility of a meeting.

Mrs Barnes must be an exceptional woman. She took the arrival of this letter from the adoption society agency, twenty-five years after the adoption with absolute calm. She told her adopted daughter Caroline (once Theresa) about it. She showed some trepidation, and anxiety, but asked Caroline what she wanted to do. Without hesitation the girl said she would like to meet her real mother. Indeed, recently she had been pressing Mrs Barnes for more information, and had toyed with the idea of setting out in search of her real mother. Mrs Barnes wrote back to the agency – yes, her daughter would like a meeting arranged.

Mr Brook from the agency contacted Dorothy. In his letter he told her that the adoptive mother had told Theresa (he referred to her always as Theresa to Dorothy, and as Caroline to Mrs Barnes). He said that Theresa wanted to arrange a meeting. Dorothy was appalled when she got this letter.

'I was so shocked, I didn't know what to think. I prayed that nothing would come of it. I picked up the phone and called Mr Brook. I said that I absolutely would not see

Theresa. I had only wanted my solicitor to be put in touch with her family, and I had never, absolutely never wanted to see her. Mr Brook said he wanted to come and see me, but I told him it would be a waste of time. He wouldn't change my mind.'

He came to see me shortly afterwards. He said he had interviewed Theresa, and she certainly wanted to meet her real mother. He showed Dorothy some photographs of the girl. 'I kept saying, "No, I'm adamant. I won't see her." He wanted reasons so I gave them, pretty good reasons I thought. I couldn't face telling her the truth about her conception. What would be the point of meeting? If we did get on, where could it lead. She's got her life, and I've got mine. What if we don't get on? She might dislike me. She might be ashamed of me, and my humble life. After all, I know she comes from a wealthy family.'

Mr Brook let Dorothy talk on all evening. It was a long night. 'Then he started to demolish my arguments. It was just as he had given up and was about to leave when he turned at the door and said the one thing that persuaded me. He said to me, very quietly, "I don't think she has felt rejected in the past, but if you refuse to see her now, she may feel that having rejected her once, you are doing it again." Then I had to agree. I was forced to. I said yes, but I bitterly regretted it after he had gone.'

She looked at the photographs of Theresa. 'My God, she was beautiful.' She went to see an old friend, one of her flatmates from Malta. Her friend warned her against seeing her daughter, but when she repeated what Mr Brook had said about rejection, she changed her mind too, and that clinched it for Dorothy. 'Take a chance,' her friend said. So she came home and arranged the day on which Theresa was to visit her.

Those days passed in slow agony for Dorothy. She feared the harm she might do the girl. She dreaded having to tell her story. She felt the shame of her past. 'How could I tell the poor girl she had a drunken mother and a raping father? What would it do to the image she might have of herself? I didn't want the whole thing dragged up again, sins of my youth hardly anyone knew about. But most of all, I feared she would despise me.'

What had become of the baby she had given away all those years ago to some unknown couple to bring up?

That morning when the Barneses came to collect their newly adopted baby from the WVS mother and baby home, they drove away with their new acquisition and Dorothy came back to an empty cot. The Barneses renamed their new baby from Theresa to Caroline, and she joined the family as the third child after two much older boys. Mrs Barnes had been unable to have more children and had longed for a daughter to complete her family. Apart from their age, they were in every other way the perfect couple for adopting – upper middle class, professional, religious, stable, and living in comfort in a salubrious suburb.

Caroline, now in her mid-twenties, looks back on her childhood: 'I was told I was adopted right from the beginning. It was never a secret. My mother used to go out of her way to say that I was something special, even more wanted than my brothers. They were able to choose me, they used to say. It sounds a bit soppy, but I used to believe it.'

Caroline is a beautiful girl with thick black hair and dark colouring. She is remarkably composed and self-aware, perhaps because in recent years she has put herself through a great deal of self-analysis, in a prolonged effort to overcome some severe problems. She is, she says early on in the conversation, an alcoholic, and she must never ever touch a drop to drink again. Drink very nearly destroyed her, and step by step she has pulled herself back from the brink. The horror of her life since early adolescence has given her now an air of wisdom beyond her years.

Alcoholics Anonymous rescued her, and for the last four years has been the mainstay of her life. Her view of the world and herself is heavily shaped by the teaching of AA, a narrow view that may be highly constructive in helping addicts to regain control over their lives, but may not provide much genuine insight into human motivations. She insists that her drinking problem was hers alone. It was her fault, and for her to pull herself out of it. It had nothing to do with the fact that she was adopted, nothing to do with the family that adopted her, nothing to do with the academic brilliance of her older brothers compared to her relative failure. An outsider looking in might wonder, but Caroline insists that she alone bears the blame, and there is no need to look deeper for any underlying causes there may have been.

She was, she says, the perfect and much loved little girl, a pet and a delight to the whole family. She talks of her adoptive mother with the greatest warmth and affection. 'She's lovely, kind, gentle, active, has lots of friends. She is independent, doesn't lean on her children. She's seventy-five, but you'd think she was still in her forties. She never moans or complains about anything. She always puts us first. Even when my father died, she hid her own grief and worried about us. But she doesn't like to talk about emotions or anything personal. She's very ostrich-like, buries her head at the first sign of emotional problems. I used to ask her questions about my adoption and it would make her very embarrassed. She would drop her voice an octave, and say, "Darling, we don't really know anything about your mother." I'd ask what my real name was, and she said she didn't know, though of course it must have been on the adoption papers.'

They lived in great affluence in a suburb of Manchester, where Mr Barnes was a successful lawyer. 'I used to have terrible rows with my mother. I was very rude, and manipulative. I would use the fact of my adoption quite unscrupulously. "I bet my real mother would buy me a dog, or a bike or a horse," or whatever I wanted at the time, I'd say. It usually worked. I took advantage of her whenever I could. By thirteen I had stopped being the perfect little pet, and had become quite difficult, I think. The boys, away at boarding school, were amazed at the rude way I talked to our mother. I was sent off to boarding school too, and it was about this time when I started drinking. I was thirteen. Others drank with me, but for them it was fun, while for me in no time at all it became need, and I knew it. I didn't see drink as a bad thing. It made me more sociable, I thought. It took away my self-hatred. I used to go down into our cellar which was always filled with bottles of spirits, given by grateful clients at Christmas, and I would fill-up my guitar case and take it back to school, packed with drink.'

She was expelled from that school, not surprisingly. 'My mother really didn't recognize the problem, although by then I was drunk all the time, morning, noon and night. I was drunk when my father was dying, when I was seventeen, and I didn't behave well. His death had very little effect on me at the time, because all I was thinking about was myself, and drink. My mother kept saying, "It's so awful for you," but I was incapable of really feeling it. My mother kept saying it was just an "adolescent stage", ostrich-like as usual. I knew it wasn't.'

When she was eighteen her mother sent her to a psychiatrist. He sent her to a private nursing home for people with psychiatric problems. 'I arrived there with two bottles of gin. They took them away and locked them in the nurses' cupboard. I used to bribe the night nurse to give me drinks at night. They did nothing at all for me, they had no idea how to treat me. I thought I drank so much because I had so many problems. I was miserably unhappy. I couldn't see any way of getting on in the world. I couldn't communicate with anyone. I had no interests, no ambitions, and no friends, because I was so horrible. I was really impossible, and there was no happy drinking for me by then.

The only thing I hung onto was being pretty. I judged everything and everyone by appearances, because that was all I had going for me.'

At the time, she thought she had many emotional problems, but now, with her Alcoholics Anonymous consciousness, she says she thinks the only problem she had was drink. She was a desperate addict.

At the nursing home she ran out of drink, so decided to pretend she was better. She was given her clothes back and allowed to go for a walk. 'I went to the first pub I could find and drank eight Drambuies. Then I bought a bottle of gin and drank half of that. I came back to the nursing home blind drunk, and finished the other half of the bottle. I blacked out and started having fits. When I came round the doctor was shouting and yelling at me, telling me I was spoilt, and that was my problem. Then he threw me out. If that's their idea of psychiatry, I didn't think much of it. They had no idea how to treat alcoholism.'

Her mother pretended not to know what her problem was. Only recently Caroline has got an admission out of her that the doctors did say something vaguely at the time that her problem might possibly be drink. But she shied away from the thought. Caroline lived from time to time at home, and in a succession of flats. 'Basically, I went to bed for three years, and never got up. I could do nothing without a drink. I couldn't open the door, speak on the telephone, or talk to anyone without a drink first. I was sacked from twenty-six jobs in a year and a half. People used to pity me. My mother pitied me. I was "Poor Caroline who has such a sad problem". But she always welcomed me home, whatever state I was in. She never turned her back on me, however badly I behaved. She was always there, and that was important. She is a marvellous person. If it was me, I'd have thrown myself out.'

She was living in a flat with several friends when things came to a head. 'It was four in the morning, I was blind drunk, and crying again. I was always crying, most of the time. One of my friends suggested I phone AA, so I did. There was an answering machine the other end and I talked into it until the tape ran out. The next morning I got a call from them. "Do you have a drink problem?" the voice asked. I said "Yes". "Do you want to stop drinking?" said the voice. Again, I said, "Yes". I was very frightened by then of what I had become. They said they would send someone round that very evening to take me to a meeting. Of course I had to get completely drunk to face it, but I went to the meeting. I couldn't understand anything that was going on, as I was so drunk, but the people seemed nice and friendly, and they didn't look like alcoholics at all.'

She stayed sober, and a keen AA member for six months, had a bad lapse, went back to AA again, and has now not had a single drink for four years. 'AA has taken up my whole life. All my friends now are AA people. I have three sponsees who I look after. We all ring each other several times a day.'

As she looks back on all this, she is inclined to believe that she has a strong physical and chemical susceptibility to drink. 'It has such an extraordinarily powerful effect on me. One sip now and I can feel it at once in my whole body. For me, it is lethally dangerous. Now I know that, and I'm happy not to be drinking.' Why did it ever begin? 'Because I had this chemical thing. It's no use saying it's because I had these deep problems. If I said that, then I could blame it all on others, or fate, and I'd never have got myself into the right state of mind to take control over my own life and my own drinking habits.'

I wanted to talk to Mrs Barnes. Caroline had mentioned to her that she was to be interviewed for this book, and Mrs Barnes had strongly advised her against. 'She never likes to talk about personal and emotional things,' Caroline explained. She tried to persuade her mother to talk to me, and she called her on the telephone while I was there. She handed the receiver over to me. 'I really have nothing at all to say,' said Mrs Barnes' elderly, precise voice down the phone. 'We are a very happy family. Caroline is the most loved, perhaps especially loved child. We wanted her particularly and I don't think there is any point in discussing any of this any further.' I explained I didn't want to ask her questions she didn't like to answer, but to talk about adoption. 'No, I don't think so,' she answered firmly, and nothing Caroline could say could make her change her mind.

Caroline remembers her own fantasies: 'They went on a long time. You have to remember that I was emotionally entirely immature. People say you stop all emotional growth once you take to the bottle. Well, I was thirteen when I started drinking, and I think I stayed at about thirteen emotionally until I stopped.' When she was a young child she used to fantasize that one day she would go out and find her real mother, especially after arguments and rows. 'Before my father died I did ask him about my mother. "What was her name? Where was I born?" He told me where I was born, but not her name, nor my original name.'

How did she imagine her real mother might be? 'I had two distinct fantasies, each utterly different. In one, I thought she was an ultra-glamorous Joan Collins type. Beautiful, glittery. As I said, appearance was very important to me, and I thought my looks must come from some beautiful woman.'

In another vision, she saw her real mother as a poor little Irish waif, over-burdened with dozens of children, too poor to cope with another child. 'They were both nice dramatic pictures. I liked drama. I felt I knew that my real mother must be something exotically special.' Did she ever feel any resentment towards her for giving her away? 'Oh no. I knew my real mother was a loser, like me. A very nice person, but someone who just couldn't cope. I didn't blame her at all. I identified with her.'

She saw herself as the black sheep of her adoptive family, and imagined her mother was too. She saw her two elder brothers shine at school and grow up into successful lawyers like their father, while she failed exams, went from bad to worse at school, and felt stupid. She blamed it on her blood, her genes. Although no one said so, she felt everyone thought her brain less good because her genes were different to theirs. To meet her today, she seems such a particularly intelligent, thoughtful and perceptive girl. It is quite impossible to believe that she is stupid – but she still thinks she is. 'I know I am. I did a maths test the other day and I was hopeless.' She is the victim of being the youngest child, starting school once her brothers had already set an example that seemed too daunting to follow. Her adoption must have underlined all this in a painful way. It gave her and her parents an easy excuse for her failure.

Fantasies about her real mother drew on all these feelings, and she invented images to suit her needs, reflections of herself. 'Sometimes I thought I was superior in many ways to all those around me, and to my family. I thought I was very attractive, and if I couldn't do well academically it didn't matter because I would lead an exciting life instead, and have wonderful love affairs. I thought I was more honest, more open, more fun than all of them. I thought they were conservative, and boring. I believed I had wild Italian blood. I was sure about that. I was emotional and sensitive and demonstrative. A lot of that was the drink, of course. Open and honest, and awfully drunk. The Italian fantasy was blown up out of all proportion. But that was the Joan Collins inside. I needed a beautiful glamorous mother to prove all these things about myself. Ridiculous!'

What did the waif image represent? 'She was sweet and good, and helpless. A hopeless loser like me, but charming with it. I so wanted to find her in great poverty, with all these brothers and sisters of mine, a great big warm Irish family. My real mother had to be very rich or very poor. My thirteen-year-old crude view of the world demanded drama, above all else. The whole idea of a real, secret mother is dramatic, but I had to make it more so.'

Caroline had been sober for nearly a year, and was well on the way to recovery when the letter from the adoption agency arrived at Mrs Barnes' house. When she visited her mother that weekend Mrs Barnes, with some nervousness, showed her the letter.

'What did I feel? I suppose strong curiosity to start with. I knew nothing at all about my real mother, and here she was, saying she wanted to leave me money in her will. Mr Brook from the agency was asking if I wished a meeting to be arranged. It wasn't clear from his letter if my real mother wanted a meeting or not. There was only mention of the will. The letter was clearly a great shock to my adoptive mother. She never lets on about how she feels, so she said very little, but she did show her concern. She was dubious and worried. I genuinely think she was not jealous. She is just not that sort of woman, and I don't think an ounce of jealousy or selfishness came into it. She was worried for me, though. I was getting better, and we were getting on so well now I had stopped drinking. She didn't want anything to upset me now. At the same time she said, "I do feel so sorry for the poor woman. Of course she wants to know you. It's entirely up to you, darling."'

Caroline wrote back to Mr Brook to say that she did want to meet her real mother. 'Then my fantasies really went wild. I longed to know everything, particularly I longed to meet her other children, my new brothers and sisters. Was she going to be pleased with me? What clothes should I wear? How should I seem to her? I thought about that a lot. As I said, I'm afraid appearances meant everything to me then.'

Mr Brook came to see her after he had already seen Dorothy, to prepare the way for a meeting. 'I asked him all the questions I could. I wanted to know everything.' She was deeply disappointed to hear her mother had no family, no other children, and lived alone.

'What does she look like?' she asked him. 'What was she wearing when you saw her?' He said she had short grey hair, and an ordinary middle-aged woman's kind of dress. 'That was a shock. Middle-aged? To me she had always been young and pretty. Grey hair didn't fit in at all. God, I was so superficial, wasn't I?' She wanted to know answers to all the questions that related most closely to herself. She wanted to know which of her own characteristics she had inherited from her mother and plied him with a host of seemingly trivial questions but which had great significance for her in her search for her own identity.

Did she like cats? 'I adore them you see.' Yes, she did have cats. Did she drink? That was crucial. Mr Brook paused and said he hadn't thought about it in terms of a drink problem, but now she came to mention it, yes, she did have a few. She offered him one, but it was the wrong time of day. That seemed significant to Caroline, searching for reasons for her own alcoholism. Did she have a husband? No, he said, she was divorced. 'That cheered me up a lot. That was interesting, exciting. No one anywhere near our family had ever been divorced. I had a strict Catholic upbringing, and divorce seemed very wicked, so I liked the sound of that.'

Mr Brook arranged a day for mother and child to meet. Caroline prepared herself carefully. She decided on a casual appearance, 'Relaxed clothes, but very, very good ones. I wanted to be well-dressed, but informal. I put on tons of make-up. I really went to town. I wanted her to be proud of me.'

The day came. Mrs Barnes drove Caroline all the way to the door, another act of generosity. Not many other adoptive mothers behave as openly and calmly as Mrs Barnes in the face of the threat of the unknown mother.

'We turned into the road, a small suburban street. Of course, I was disappointed. It was a perfectly nice street, but nothing special. Nothing dramatic. Not rich, not poor. It was mediocre, and that was the one thing I didn't want. I'd have been happy with abject poverty. I'd have been happy with wealth, or at least eccentricity. But this place had no special significance, no resonance about it.' The car stopped outside the door in the quiet terraced street. A small gate led up a short garden path to the front door. 'I had a cigarette. I talked to my mother about silly things, trivia. I was so nervous. I didn't want her to go. I kept saying to her "Are you *sure* this is the right road?"' Her mother, sensing the nerves and anxiety, fearing for Caroline's state of mind, and her unrealistic expectations, turned to her and said quietly, 'Darling, do remember that she is probably a very ordinary middle-aged woman.'

Inside the house this 'very ordinary middle-aged woman' was looking out of the window at them. She has a habit of leaping to the door within a second of the bell being rung, as if she has been watching and waiting for visitors behind the net curtains.

Who should tell the story of their meeting? On the one hand, there is the version from this fanciful and disturbed young girl, in search of a romantic dream that was fast disintegrating with every step she took nearer to her real mother. On the other hand, there as an anxious woman, realistic in many ways, who claims she never sought this encounter. She was afraid that the shocking story of her past would upset a girl she imagined to be the perfect product of a perfect background, the tennis club star, the academic success, and the rich and happy child of a rich and happy family. If their fantasies had been fulfilled it might have been a meeting between Joan Collins and Princess Diana. In the event, a middle-aged school teacher living on a pension with a guilty secret in her past met an unstable girl who had dragged herself through far worse degradations and disasters than her mother ever dreamed of in her guiltiest memories.

'I knocked on the door and this woman answered it at once. I didn't realize it was *her*. I thought it was someone else. I didn't know what to say, so I just said nothing, thinking she'd introduce me to her. She said, "Hello. You're

Caroline? Do come in," and I knew then that this really was my mother. I was astonished. Astonished at her ordinariness. I had been prepared for anything, but not that. I suppose I hadn't taken in anything that had been said about her. I still expected something extraordinary. Here was reality, staring me in the face. Here was no wild Italian blood, no Joan Collins. I felt – diminished – like a punctured balloon. All those dashing images of myself disappeared with one glance at my mother. I had to face that I was just who I was, and no one else.'

Dorothy looked out at the girl standing on her doorstep. 'I thought she was lovely. Quite beautiful. Of course I would have had no idea at all that she was my child. I wasn't expecting any great rush of maternal recognition, and quite honestly there wasn't any.'

She showed Caroline into the front room of her ground-floor flat, where a fire was burning brightly, and a choice of coffee and tea stood ready for her. 'I was embarrassed at first,' Caroline says. 'I commented on the nice, cosy room. She asked if I had any trouble finding my way. It was she who started asking questions first. She asked about my life. How had it all been? I told her the truth, the whole truth. I used to enjoy that, I liked making a good drama of myself in those days. She was astounded, utterly amazed. She kept saying that there was absolutely no history of alcoholism in her background that she knew of. I did notice she drank a lot of Camparis that night. I'm sure she never gets drunk, but she was drinking quite a lot, and that made me wonder. When I went out to her outside toilet, I noticed a box of bottles in the back yard. I can tell you, alcoholics are unnaturally attuned to these things.'

Dorothy talked about her life. Caroline claims Dorothy told her that she drank a whole bottle of spirits a day when she was pregnant. 'That rang a strong bell. Did it predispose me towards alcoholism? I think it did. Babies born to drug addicts can be born addicted, and perhaps I was born addicted to alcohol. She chain smokes too, like me, and she did through her pregnancy.' I have no way of knowing whether Dorothy did tell Caroline she drank so much, but it throws some light on Caroline's outlook. She would like to find a hereditary explanation for her own alcoholism, and Dorothy may drink very little, except on a remarkably tense occasion, like her first meeting with her daughter.

As the evening wore on, mother and daughter began to inspect one another. 'She is the same shape as me, small and curvy,' Caroline noted. 'Our hands are the same, small and round, and we both have identical feet, very beautiful feet. I've always been proud of them. We have the same long faces. When she showed me a photograph album of her family, I could see they all have very long faces.'

Dorothy remembers that early on in the conversation Caroline had said defensively, 'I hope you're not expecting me to be intellectual. I'm as thick as two posts and I can't pass an exam to save my life.' Having spent her life teaching, Dorothy was quick to say that Caroline must have been to bad schools and been badly taught. She was clearly intelligent, but her teachers had failed her. She also thought to herself that Caroline's lack of academic talent must have come from her father.

Caroline felt during this, and subsequent meetings, that Dorothy believed her daughter would never have become an alcoholic if she had brought her up herself. Indeed, Dorothy cannot resist jibes at Mrs Barnes. Although she goes out of her way to say, 'I know Caroline had a very happy, very secure background,' small criticisms still creep in. 'Mrs Barnes is not an intellectual woman. Like so many of the Irish, she does well at keeping up with her husband's social status despite her own background.' And, 'She's only really interested in coffee mornings, cocktail parties, golf and that sort of thing.' The jealousy and the resentment are not far beneath the surface. She says Mrs Barnes is a snob, and that of course she despises her daughter's real mother, and her humble life-style.

After Caroline had told her own, disastrous life story, it was far easier for Dorothy to tell her the circumstances of her birth. 'When it came to the point, it was so easy,' Dorothy says. 'It was clear to me by then that Caroline was not the sort of girl to be upset by a thing like that, so I told her the truth.' Or very nearly the truth. She softened the edges for Caroline's sake, so that she should not think too badly of her father, and therefore of her own origins. At first she told Caroline that Martin, her father, had offered to marry her when he heard Dorothy was pregnant, but Dorothy had refused. She did not tell Caroline straight away that he had in fact laughed in her face and told her to get rid of the baby.

Caroline liked Dorothy, enjoyed her exuberance and her energetic self-mocking account of her life. 'She waves her hands around when she talks, just like I do. She's funny, and direct. I loved her story about the whole pregnancy. It was so terrible, and so dramatic. That at least fulfilled my need for drama.'

Dorothy describes their meeting: 'I liked her, thank goodness. But I didn't feel she was my daughter in any way. She's a person, someone I know, a friend who has crossed my path. She calls me Dorothy, not Mother. I was very careful that there should be no question of pretending to set up any kind of mother-daughter relationship, because it wouldn't work.'

Dorothy goes out of her way to seem calm and rational, unemotional in her approach to all this. And yet things have a habit of slipping out. In her case, a kind of wish-fulfilment is at work. 'Caroline said to me, "I feel you are my real mother." Of course I said, "Stop that at once. I don't feel like your mother. You owe everything to your adoptive mother, Mrs Barnes."' Caroline remembers nothing of this conversation, and denies she said it. Indeed it seems most unlikely. Dorothy also says, 'I think both Mrs Barnes and Caroline realize that Mrs Barnes is very old, and that when she goes poor Caroline will have no one. So it's a good thing that I shall be around if ever Caroline needs me.' Again that doesn't quite ring true.

She talks of her present relationship with Caroline: 'It's the easiest relationship I have ever had. Marvellous. By tacit agreement we keep out of each other's life. Caroline comes round here if she wants to see me, and neither of us introduces each other to our friends. It suits us both that way. Damn it all, how could I go about introducing her as my illegitimate daughter at this stage in my life? No, we go our own sweet ways.' And yet underneath, it is clear she would like to see her more often, and Caroline hasn't telephoned in six months now.

She gave Caroline a beautiful Chinese jade and gold bracelet, a family heirloom. Otherwise there was no more talk of wills, Caroline says. Once Caroline's curiosity was satisfied, once she had drained every last piece of information from her mother, she found there was not very much more to talk about. They had no shared past to bind them together, and little in common in terms of their past experiences or present interests.

Thinking of her makes Caroline feel slightly guilty. 'I think she may be rather lonely. Occasionally she rings me, on some pretext or other. Once she lent me a book, and sent a note two months later asking me to bring it back, because she had read it was going out of print. Another time she rang to say that if I was thinking of going to visit her the next weekend it wouldn't be convenient, as she had friends coming to see her. I hadn't seen her in months and had no plans to visit.'

Looking back now Caroline says, 'I am very glad indeed I found her. It helped me to sort myself out. It stopped a lot of the absurd fantasies. But in doing that, I have to admit it was a sad anticlimax. She's a nice woman, and I admire a lot in her. But I so hoped for a whole family. I wanted brothers and sisters, a whole new world. Instead there is just one middle-aged woman living alone. I ought to see her more often, I know, but, well, it's difficult.'

For Dorothy, meeting Caroline has resolved something in her life that she had tucked well away. Instead of a painful, shameful secret baby lurking in the back of her thoughts, there is a beautiful, likeable girl – a girl who has suffered a great deal, but who has lived to survive it all.

And yet, I suspect there is another loss too. While she never knew her daughter, she put her out of her mind. She decided she never wanted to see or know her. But now she does, and her daughter is only a brief telephone call away. And yet so far, she is not her daughter at all. She is a kind of mirage, a simulation of a child she once had. There is nothing on which to build a relationship now, beyond a card at Christmas and birthdays. It has been a little like losing her child all over again.

3

Cherry

Cherry's first memory was of herself, aged five, standing in an oak panelled court, with her twin brother Garry. It was their adoption hearing, and she understood just enough of what was going on for it to leave a powerful impression.

The twins were the eighth and ninth in a family of ten children. They had been in and out of care all their lives. They stayed in hospital for three months when they were tiny babies, one for bronchitis, the other for 'teething'. She thinks now they must have been taken in for social not medical reasons. After that, their mother used to take them home occasionally for two weeks at a time. She is not sure where they were the rest of the time, has no clear memories, but finally they were fostered out with the Smithsons – the family that later adopted them when they were five.

The Smithsons were quite old, in their early fifties, when they adopted Cherry and Garry. They had four children of their own, all grown up. They had already adopted two older girls when they took on the twins, making up a second family of four children. For years they had fostered children for the council, and continued to do so all through Cherry's childhood. Odd children would come and go unpredictably.

It did not work out well for Cherry. She was fond of Mr Smithson, who was kind to her, but he died when she was eight. She never liked Mrs Smithson, who later, in one of their frequent rows, told her she had never wanted to adopt her. She wanted Garry, whom she loved, and was forced to take on Cherry to avoid separating the twins. Mr Smithson was an engineer, and the family was reasonably well off. Looking back, they were almost rich compared with the poverty of the background she came from originally. The Smithsons' own four children had done well, got scholarships, gone to university. 'Everything was right for them. Piano lessons, ballet lessons, girl guides, and all that.' Things didn't go so smoothly for the adopted four.

Mrs Smithson died some years ago, after Cherry left home. Now at twenty-five, Cherry looks back on her with bitterness. 'I don't know why she took in all these children. I think in a way she got trapped into it. She took one or two just to foster and then the council put pressure on her to take more, saying they had nowhere else to put them. She was a woman completely unsuited to fostering and adoption. She had no warmth, and everything she did was for show. She was a snob, wouldn't let us play with children from the council houses. When she got angry, she said we came from a family of guttersnipes. She never let us bring friends home. I never had birthday parties, not one. She smacked us all a lot, and thought children should have no opinions of their own. Seen and not heard, was her motto. Children had to conform to exactly what she wanted, no individuality allowed. She kept warning us that if we didn't watch it, we'd end up peanut shovelling in Woolworth's. You know, in those days they had hot peanut counters, and as far as she was concerned that was the lowest of the low.'

Although the authorities had taken such care to see that the twins were not separated, it was little comfort to Cherry, or at least, not a comfort she recognized. 'He was a horror. I hated him, despised him. He couldn't do a thing wrong as far as Mrs Smithson was concerned. He would beat me up, I'd cry, and she'd come in and wallop me for telling lies when I said he'd hit me. He just sat and smirked. She bought him everything he wanted, stereos, bikes, new clothes, even a motor bike. I got nothing, horrible clothes. If I said I wanted something, she'd go out of her way to buy me the opposite. Kids really mind what they wear, having what the other kids have got. But I never had anything much.'

She refused to believe Mr Smithson had died. For years she went on thinking he would come back, and she missed him. After his death, she had only one ally in the family, her elder adopted sister Jacky. Jacky was deeply rebellious, the 'bad' one, impossible to handle. Although she was eight years older than Cherry, Cherry spend most of her time with Jacky, in her bedroom. Jacky encouraged her to play truant from school with her. The two have stayed very close.

'When I first went to secondary school, I was bullied. I was small, and bigger girls picked on me, and beat me up. I'd tell Jacky every day, and she'd wait for me outside the school. I'd point out who did it and she'd beat them up, scare the living daylights out of them. Then one day, I went crying to her after school, expecting her to do it again for me. But she started hitting me instead, bashing me about. I howled and yelled, I couldn't think why she was suddenly doing this to *me*, instead of to the bullies. She said, "I'm going to beat hell out of you every day you come home crying."

'She pointed out the biggest bully in the playground and said to me, "You go and hit her as hard as you can. Beat hell out of her." So I put down my satchel and ran to her and hit her really hard. She was so surprised, she couldn't believe it. I was a hero after that, and I always had millions of friends. "That's the way life is," Jacky said. And she's right. I learned a lot from that.'

It was Jacky who told Cherry that she was adopted. She had managed to forget everything about her early life, but when Jacky told her, she knew at once it was true. The courtroom scene fell into place. She could dimly remember her mother, but all she could recall was a woman with bright platinum blond hair. Jacky knew quite a lot about Cherry's family. She had listened at keyholes and hung around at the time of Cherry and Garry's adoption. 'If I was ever going to have illusions about who my real family were, then Jacky stopped me. She said they were like gypos, guttersnipes. "If your Mum had wanted you, she'd have kept you," she used to say. It kept me from getting carried away by any romantic ideas. She used to warn me to keep away from them. She knew exactly where they lived, what their name was, and everything. That's how I knew my real name was Cherry Garfield, not Cherry Smithson.' But she always knew she would want to go out and look for her mother one day. 'When Jacky told me Mrs Smithson wasn't my real mother, I acted tough. I just said "I don't like her anyway. I don't care."' Cherry asked Mrs Smithson if it was true, and she didn't deny it. After that, in rows, the subject always came up.

On her birthday every year she used to say to herself that her real mother must be thinking of her. She thought to herself that one day she would meet her, and she would explain why she had had to give her twins away. Once her sister Jacky said she'd take Cherry to look at her real family. She knew where they were, and it wasn't far. But she lost her nerve. 'Jacky realized that if she was caught doing that she could be in real deep trouble. The laws on adoption and secrecy were strict, and she knew that, because she was adopted too. Sometimes I did used to think that if my real mother knew what life was like for me with the Smithsons, she'd come and take me away. But Jacky kept me straight on that, and said, "They're just a load of yobbos."

'Mrs Smithson was very strict with us. We were never allowed out after nine o'clock. "Only nasty, bad girls hang around at night," she'd say. But as I got older I learned to use my tongue. I could belittle her and intimidate her. I spoke good French. I was good at school, and I used to swear and shout at her in French. I could run rings round her verbally, seize her up in a small ball, just with words. Sometimes I'd ignore her for days on end. Sometimes she threatened to put me in care. She took me to Child Guidance once or twice.

But they told her she should look to herself to find the cause of the problem. There was nothing wrong with me, they said, so she stopped taking me there. She wouldn't give me any money, not even my dinner money, as she said I spent it on the wrong things.'

But Cherry did well at school. She got nine good O levels, and ran for South West London in the school athletics. Her reports were glowing, and she could and should have stayed on to take her A levels. But she was desperate to leave home. She took a job working for a solicitor for £10 a week, and shared a flat with a friend. 'We starved. We hadn't enough to eat. The rent was £10 a week. Mrs Smithson wouldn't give me a penny. She was glad to see the back of me, wanted me out of the house. She just said, "You'll get nothing from me. You came to me with nothing, and you'll leave with nothing." I was too proud to ask anyway. I never let her know that I wasn't fine. I wouldn't give her the satisfaction.'

After she left home, she stayed for a year in the solicitor's office. She and her friend earned more money by working several evenings a week in a night club. There followed a long succession of jobs in shops, offices, hotels, and the summer season in seaside resorts. She didn't like work with too much discipline, and left the bank where she had a job briefly after cheeking the manager and calling his staff 'nothing but a load of muppets'. She went to work in a hotel in a Home Counties town, where the prospects were good, and she rapidly rose to become assistant manager, with heavy responsibilities, since the manager was an alcoholic.

It was here that she met her husband Sam. 'He was tanned and wonderful looking,' she says, smiling. 'He'd just come back from working a contract in the Middle East.' He was then working for a firm of builders, but now has his own small builder's contracting firm. He used to come back to the hotel every weekend and finally he asked her to come and live with him, near his work, 'I said if I was good enough to live with, then I was good enough to marry – so we got married.' She laughs at her own boldness.

Cherry is now twenty-five, a small energetic girl, with piercing eyes and a strong chin. She laughs as she talks – a tough caustic wit, keenly critical of others, alarmingly direct in all her dealings with people. She takes no nonsense, has a powerful sense of the absurd, and a sharp eye for the slightest hint of hypocrisy. She has a clear view of the world as a place that is hard to survive in, where only the hard survive. Her childhood has taught her that.

Underneath a certain surface ruthlessness, one can sense in Cherry a real sense of loss. There had been nothing gentle or loving in her life until she married. The one person she loved was Jacky who gave affection back, and taught her harsh lessons in life. She almost seems to know what is missing, but is right to be proud of all her achievements.

Here she is now, when all the odds seemed to be stacked against her, happily married with two children, living in her own three-bedroomed modern house. It is an immaculately clean and tidy place, with a minimum of decoration and a great sense of order. She runs her own life and her children's to a pattern. She gives her mornings to running her own now very successful contract cleaning business, built up from nothing without a penny of capital or a pound borrowed. Soon, she says, she will sell it for a handsome profit, and start something else.

Although she denounces the strictness of her own upbringing with Mrs Smithson, she is firm with her two little daughters, extracting Pleases and Thankyous from them, restricting their television and their pocket money with care for their future sense of values. She loves them deeply and says often, 'My main aim in life is to see that nothing ever happens to my children. I never want them to go through any of the things I went through.' She never smacks them. 'Violence breeds violence, and I had too much of that when I was a child.'

Talking about her work, and the success of her small

company, it is clear she is equally firm with clients and employees. One of her workers telephoned, to ask for an advance in his wages, as he was having trouble. 'No way,' she said. 'Once you start that, where does it end?' She refuses to take on clients she doesn't like the look of. 'I can afford to pick and choose,' she says briskly.

Cherry is a strong, determined character and she must have been a forceful little girl, right from the day of her adoption. The disasters and disruptions, the sheer unhappiness of her childhood have left her with a firm conviction that she has to survive on her own, or not at all. She has the same attitude to the rest of the world – a strong belief that people should all stand on their own two feet and look after themselves. She has no time for 'whiners' and 'moaners', and tells her own story with anger towards those who hurt her, but not a hint of self-pity.

She has a quick tongue, as if in permanent self-defence, where she finds it difficult to talk about her feelings. Even now, secure and content, with children of her own, and Mrs Smithson dead, she is unrelenting. Cherry must have been a difficult child to bring up, fierce and wary, by her own description of herself. Had she thought again, and wondered how hard life must have been for Mrs Smithson, bringing up four adopted children, alone, after her husband died so unexpectedly? What of her trials and tribulations? What of her motivations? Must she not have had some good in her to wish to take on so many unwanted children? Cherry is unbending.

'When Mrs Smithson was dying, I went to see her. She tried to say to me that she was sorry. She hadn't loved me much. She wanted to make deathbed amends. But it was too late then, wasn't it? Much too late. She never said a kind thing to me in the days when it would have counted.'

It is easy to imagine that people are somewhat in awe of Cherry. Her wit and her funny turns of phrase are a delight, her sheer exuberance a pleasure. She talks about life as if she had seized it by the neck and forced it into submission, modelled it into her neatly ordered present existence. There she sits in her spotless sitting room, not a mark on the carpet, not a thing out of place, never doubting for a moment that she can handle whatever else life throws at her. And yet, the bitterness and the anger are there too, a sense of outrage at all she has lost and can now never find.

Into this organized and well-ordered life, she was now about to invite a new and gigantic chaotic element. She would survive the shock of it, but she had little idea of what she was about to let herself in for. A weaker character than Cherry might have crumpled.

Cherry had always kept in close contact with Jacky, the only really affectionate family tie she has. 'Jacky is the one person who I would turn to if I needed help. I could ring her now and say I needed her, and I know she'd drop everything and be here in two hours flat. And I'd do the same for her. I help her out with her kid, as they haven't much money, and we talk on the phone all the time. I asked her whether I should try to contact my real family. She said, "Don't. They're trouble. Keep out of their way." She always made jokes about my real family. I remember once we had a load of gypsies camped down the road from us, hordes of scruffy kids, the women with that bright dyed platinum hair. I said to her, "Jacky, I bet that's my real family." She said, "You don't know how near the mark you are, kid." You see, I never had any illusions about them, which was lucky as things turned out. But I always knew, whatever Jacky said, whatever warnings she gave me, I always knew that one day I was going to go out and find them.'

She talked about it to Sam. 'I kept saying to Sam, "Shall I do it? I know I won't be disappointed with what I find. I'm not at risk, because I already know so much about them."' He agreed that if that was what she really wanted to do, then she should go ahead and try to find her family.

She contacted all the local social services, whose duty it is to guide and counsel adopted children before they seek out their parents. She sent in her birth certificate to the social services locally, the certificate of her adoption, which gave her name as Cherry Smithson.

She was summoned for an interview with a social worker. 'He had some papers on the desk. Before he said anything, I said, "I already know my real name. It's Cherry Garfield, isn't it?" You could have knocked him down with a feather. "You're not supposed to know that!" he said, really shocked. He was amazed and horrified that I had always known so much about my real family.' The social worker asked her if she was sure she really wanted to pursue her family. Cherry says, 'By the time you've gone that far, it's really just a formality. I don't think anyone who has gone as far as getting their papers and their true birth certificate would want to leave it at that. He had to sign a document to say he had interviewed me, and that I was of sound mind.'

The social worker offered to help her in any he could. In fact she could tell him more about her family than the official papers revealed. 'The social worker wasn't much good at tracing, didn't know where to begin. I made all the running, and suggested to him ways of going about it. The birth certificate had the family's original address, in Kilburn. I knew from Jacky, that although they had moved, they had stayed in the same area. I suggested to the social worker that he contact the local Kilburn social services, to see if they had any contact with them. After all, if the children had been in and out of care, the family must be known to the social services.'

However, that line of inquiry drew a blank. The social services in that area had heard nothing of the Garfield family for at least five years and they had moved since then. 'Quite an achievement, to have kept out of their hands all that time, I thought,' Cherry says, with a laugh. 'But of course the children had gown up, so they wouldn't have been the concern of the social services any more.'

She found all the birth certificates of all the Garfield children. As she had known, there were many children. But one fact came as a great shock to her. Her mother had another younger son, born after Cherry and Garry. He would have been three at the time of the twins' adoption. 'That was a terrible slap in the face to me. Why had she given us away, but not little Andy? What was wrong with us? I could understand it if she had reached a stage where for some reason she just couldn't cope with any more children. But she had another, and she hadn't allowed him to be given away for adoption. Why had she done that to us?'

Cherry was sure that they still lived in the same area. 'The social worker thought this was the end of the line, but I was determined. I suggested that we went through the electoral register, to see if we could find them that way. "Good idea," he said, as he'd never thought of it. We went through all the lists, but of course, they'd never registered to vote and they often moved, so they weren't on it. That was a big disappointment.' She tried the telephone directory inquiries but they were now ex-directory. 'I later learned that was because they had kept changing their number, and they were always hiding from someone or other.'

If she hadn't been heavily pregnant, with another small child to care for, she would have gone down to Kilburn and spent several days making her own door to door enquiries at the addresses where the family had been known. 'I know I would have found them easily that way. They were well known in the district, being so many of them. But it just wasn't possible at the time.'

She did find out one further fact about the family. Her father Mr Garfield, had died a few years ago. 'I was very sad about that. I would so liked to have met him, at least to have seen him once. Later I learned that he had been against us being adopted but he hadn't been able to prevent it happening.'

Next, she decided to put an advertisement in the personal

column of the local Kilburn paper. She asked for anyone knowing the whereabouts of Maureen Hazel Garfield, (maiden name Hinchcliff) to telephone her number. She said nothing about the reason for her search, nor did she give her name. She put the advertisement in the paper just after her second child was born.

'There was nothing the first day, and I thought that would be the end of the matter. I was very disappointed. But then, the next day, I was sitting at home in the morning, feeding the baby, when the phone rang. I knew at once, I just knew instinctively at that very moment that at last, it was them.'

She lifted the receiver, and heard a woman's voice at the other end of the line. 'I'm calling concerning an ad in the paper,' the voice said. Cherry says she almost recognized the voice, and she knew at once it was a sister of hers. Cherry was cautious and she just said, 'Yes?' The voice said, 'I think I know who you are.' Cherry, still careful, said, 'It's a personal matter.' The voice said, 'Why are you looking for Maureen Garfield?' Cherry stalled again, 'It's very personal. I wanted to contact her.' The voice said straight away. 'I'm sure I do know who you are, and why you are looking for her.' 'You tell me,' said Cherry. The voice said, 'It's Cherry, isn't it? That's why you want to find her?'

It was Carol, two years older than the twins, the sister later that Cherry was to like best of her whole new family. 'I was so glad that they all knew of our existence. It hadn't been a secret. Of course, some of the older ones remembered us, and knew what had happened to us. Carol said her mother always remembered us on our birthday, and mentioned our names.'

Carol said, 'How are you?' Cherry laughed as she remembered the conversation. 'How was I? After all those years? It was a funny question to ask. I just said "fine". We talked politely for a while, exchanging information about our marriages, and our children. Where do you live? What are your kids called? It turned out that I'd called my kids names that my sisters had chosen for theirs if they had girls, but they all had boys. A small coincidence.'

Eventually Carol mentioned their mother. She was in hospital having had a minor stroke. Cherry said firmly that she didn't want her mother to be told, in case the shock would give her a second stroke. She asked Carol repeatedly whether her arrival on the family scene would cause upset and unhappiness. But Carol assured her that everyone would want to see her.

Carol asked about Garry, but Cherry gave an evasive answer. It had been made very clear to her that the new law allowed children to seek their parents, but not the other way round. If he didn't want to see them, then it wasn't fair for them to contact him. She just told Carol that he was fine, but wouldn't give an address or telephone number for him. She hadn't told him yet that she was searching for their family. She thought him more vulnerable than herself, and in any case, he had never shown much interest. She had kept in touch with him over the years, and liked him better after their adoptive mother, Mrs Smithson, had died. She was never close to him, but she didn't dislike him any more, and felt some responsibility for him. Mrs Smithson had made him her favourite, so after her death, that bone of contention between them was removed – 'And he is my own flesh and blood,' she says, a fact that stays important to her in all her dealings with her real family.

Dazed, she put down the receiver at the end of her talk with Carol. Almost at once, the telephone rang again. It was Pat, another sister. Then it rang again, and it was Sally. After that her brother John telephoned. He said they were all going up to the hospital that very afternoon to tell their mother that Cherry had been found. Cherry begged them not to, fearing that it might be the death of her, but they insisted.

'I went back to feeding the baby, just feeling numb. It was extraordinary. I wished I could have talked to my husband, but he was at work. Everything was happening so fast, so many of them telephoning one after another. They sounded very nice, very friendly, really delighted that I had been found. They had often wondered about Garry and me.' She noted, though, that none of them had asked her much about her childhood. No one asked if she had been happy, or what life at the Smithson's had been like. 'None of them ever asked me later either? Anyway, I'm not a moaner, so I wouldn't tell.'

It was early in the afternoon that the next call came. 'There was this harsh rasping voice. I have to admit, it was a pretty horrible voice. I knew it was her at once, the mother. She said she wanted to see me, right away. Was I all right? How was Garry? She said all the others, all of them were at her bedside and they all wanted me to come down to London right away, that very day. I said I couldn't possibly. I had the kids to look after, but more than that, I needed time. I was so stunned by it all, that I didn't want to go right away.' She promised to go at the weekend.

But when Sam came home from work, and she told him what had happened, he suggested they all go down the very next day. 'You'll only sit and brood about it all week otherwise,' he said. 'Let's go tomorrow.' They set out the next day taking the children with them. 'We were laughing all the time on the train, making jokes about what we would find. We tried to imagine the very worst, to protect ourselves. I remember Sam saying they'd probably come and collect us in a pick-up truck.'

When they arrived at the station, Carol and John were there to collect them. 'I thought I wouldn't recognize them, and we'd have trouble finding them. But there was no denying it. She was my sister all right. We look so alike, it was obvious. She looks just like me. She was very nicely dressed, and I liked her straight away.'

Cherry imagined that they would be taken first to Carol's flat, to meet the others. She was taken aback when John drove them all straight to the hospital where their mother was. Hospital visits can be difficult and tense encounters at the best of times, and it didn't seem to Cherry that this one was going to be easy.

'We walked towards a ward with three women in it, where the mother was lying. As we came in, it was obvious the others had told the whole story to the nurses, which really embarrassed me. It was private family business, and I didn't like everyone knowing. But they can be like that, no sense of shame. I thought the story was shameful, and they had no right letting everyone know. The nurses were very helpful, but very knowing too.'

Cherry, Sam and the children came into the ward behind Carol and John. 'I took one look round and I knew at once who she was. Not because she looks like me. She doesn't, not at all, but because of all that I already knew about her. It was obvious, painfully obvious. Even in a hospital bed she looked scruffy and dirty, a horrible old nightdress and dirty dressing gown. Sam whispered to me, "Ugh, give me the baby, I don't want her going near her." He took the baby from me.'

Her mother just said 'Hello' and Cherry sat down by her bedside. 'I've never kissed her yet, and I certainly didn't then. I started to laugh. I don't know why, nerves I expect. All the others were standing round staring at me. Sam handed me the baby and the mother said how nice she was. "Well, babies are," I said. Almost right away one of my sisters said, "I hope you don't think we've got any money, because we ain't." Then the mother said, "Got any fags?"' Her mother was only slightly paralysed down one side, and the doctors assured them she would recover fully, which she did shortly afterwards.

'The mother didn't ask me anything about myself. She didn't seem interested. She did ask after Garry, and where he was. I had to be vague, though she kept saying she wanted to see him too. It was such a strange meeting. It seemed like hours. I was aching to go, aching to get out of there. She never mentioned the Smithsons, didn't ask about how life had been for me, though she wanted to know about our life now, what sort of house we had, our jobs, and so on.'

They were taken after the hospital visit to stay at Carol's house. 'It was lovely and clean and respectable. They'd made everything ready for us, with nice places for the children to sleep, somewhere to change the baby and everything. I thought then that I had quite the wrong impression of the family, and I had been unfair to them. I really liked them all, especially Carol.' The men took Sam down to the pub, while Cherry put the children to bed.

'That night I felt really at home, really at ease with them, though I was still feeling overwhelmed by them all ... so many of them, and all this coming on me so suddenly. They asked me the basic outlines of my life, but nothing more. I didn't go to them with a sob story, that's not what I'm like, and what'd be the point? I think they looked at me and thought I had done well in the world, compared to them. They thought I'd been born with a canteen of cutlery in my mouth, and I was the lucky one. I wasn't going to tell them it wasn't so. I wasn't going to tell them how it really was and how I'd worked for everything I'd got. I think all the trouble later came from their feelings that I had been plucked out of a poor struggling family, and put down in a well-off home.'

It took a little while, counting up all her brothers and sisters, for Cherry to realize one was missing. 'Where's Susan?' she asked. They told her she was dead. She was a drug addict and had died very young. She had been the apple of her father's eye. He had loved her best of them all, and was heart-broken when she died. His own death followed six months later. He had never recovered from the shock, and died, they said, of a broken heart.

Cherry asked for no explanations that night about why she and Garry had been adopted, and none were offered. It was a subject they all kept away from. She thought she would learn later from her mother, and, overawed by this huge family, she was not keen to plunge straight into her painful past, and the reasons for it. The weekend went well for them all. They went on a shopping expedition together, and enjoyed each other's company. 'Looking back, I think it was all so good then partly because the mother was out of the way. All the trouble in the family seems to start and end with her. She incites them, she stirs it. She can't live without trouble.'

She was glad to get away back to her own home, at the end of the weekend. 'I did like them very much. I was very glad I had found them. But even then, in the back of my mind, I had a nagging feeling that this was all going to lead to trouble. I felt I had to be wary of them.' She telephoned Garry, to tell him what she had done. 'But he wasn't interested, and he didn't ask me any questions about them, so I didn't mention it to him any more.'

Her mother came out of hospital soon afterwards, and would telephone frequently, as did other brothers and sisters. Finally her mother invited Cherry and the children to come and stay, now that she was fully recovered.

She arrived with the baby and her three-year-old at her mother's address, which was a flat at the top of a shabby high-rise block. 'To say it was filthy wouldn't begin to describe it,' Cherry says. 'It was honking, stinking, from the moment the door opened. You stuck to the carpet, it was so dirty. They didn't use ash trays, so there were fag ends and ash everywhere. We couldn't use the toilet, it smelled so terrible. The cooker was solid grease. You put your hand in the utensil drawer in the kitchen and everything was greasy. She never really washed up, just ran things under cold water with no washing up liquid. The fridge was black, all through. It had gone past mould, and was just caked. Springs came through the mattress, and the sheets were dirty. Under the beds were piles of dog-ends. I never even had a cup of tea the whole time we were there. I took the kids out to the Wimpy and fish and chips for food. You couldn't eat from anything in that flat. There wasn't a place clean enough to put the baby down to change her. It stank to high heaven.'

She thinks her sisters, Carol in particular, have made efforts from time to time to clean the place, but since it reverts to its usual squalor as soon as they turn their backs, they have given up. Now only Andy, the son who was younger than the twins, still lived at home, and all the others had left. But they all stayed close by. Through ferocious fights and rows, they clung close to one another, saw and telephoned each other frequently.

Right away, Cherry said, her mother started to ask for money. She needed a TV licence, or the milkman paying. One way or another in the early months she paid over about £200, which she could ill afford at the time, with her new baby. 'I took pity on her. She used to whine and wheedle – "I've had a hard life," she'd say. "I've suffered. I've got no money, only a small pension."'

Cherry had hoped that this weekend would be an opportunity to talk more to her mother, to get to know her better, and most of all to find out the true story of her adoption, and the reasons for it. But she never for a moment saw her mother on her own. Andy or one of the others was always there. 'Looking back now, I see that in all the last three years, since I first met her, I have never ever been alone with her for a moment. Isn't that odd? Maybe she protects herself. She likes a lot of people around. Maybe she's wary of me and what I might say.'

Her mother, she says, has a butterfly mind. She talks and talks, but never keeps to one subject. She jumps from topic to topic so it is hard to get her to follow a train of thought or answer a question. She remembers the very few occasions when the subject was even touched on by her mother. 'Once she said she hadn't wanted us to be adopted, but the authorities had made her do it. I said how come her signature was on the papers? No one forced her to sign. You don't have to have children adopted. But she went off on another subject. She did say my father hadn't wanted it to happen. Another time she claimed she had tried to look for us through the Sally Ally, but I'm sure she didn't. Anyhow, you can't look for your adopted children. Once she did say, "You know, you should resent me, you should hate me," but before I could say anything, she was off again on some quite different subject, and I missed the chance. I don't know what I would have said, but at least we might have talked. Then, just one other time, it was on that weekend, she leaned over to me and said, "Cherry, I want to have a heart-to-heart with you." Then she was off again. I wondered if the heart-to-heart was going to materialize, but of course it never did. If I ever started on that conversation, she'd talk about something else.'

Cherry would like to know something about her mother's background. But again, that seems to be a subject that makes her mother uneasy. At least she hasn't managed to get her to talk about it, as she slides away from so many questions. From the little the others know, Cherry has gained the strong impression that her mother may have come from a well-heeled family. She is a woman who has come down in the world, and perhaps that is why she can't bear to talk about it. But Cherry knows no more than that.

She contemplates her mother with sad regret. 'Things could have been so very different. She could so easily have made me feel better about her. I wouldn't mind the dirt. I'm not a snob, although I know they all think I am. I wouldn't mind what she'd done, and maybe I'd sympathize a bit more with her hard, rotten life. It wouldn't have taken much on her part to satisfy me. But I can see now nothing ever will be different.' She paused and shook her head. 'You know, sometimes I'm tempted to go right round to her, on the spur of the moment, and try to see once and for all if I can have it out with her. But what's the point? It wouldn't work. I'm realistic and I can see that.'

From talking to her many brothers and sisters, she has pieced together various facts and stories about the life of the Garfields. Odd fragments, sometimes, like the fact that her mother kept a monkey at home when they were young. And then there was the family story about the night the coalman came for his money. Their mother had hidden in the coal-shed and sent Carol to the door to tell him she was out. 'Never mind,' the coalman said, 'I'll leave a couple of bags for her all the same, and she can pay me next time.' He tipped two full bags of coal down the coal hole, right on top of their mother.

Then there were tales she didn't like. Once her mother boasted that when the twins were little, it was handy sending them into care for a couple of weeks. She'd send them in with no clothes, no knickers, and back they'd come a fortnight later with a suitcase full of good new clothes, which she would distribute amongst all her children.

Cherry learned one reason why the family had been so poor. Although he had a good job when they were young, Mr Garfield was an alcoholic and he drank all his money. He was violent too, when drunk. Cherry says firmly, 'I can never understand why women put up with such things. I certainly never would. No man would beat me up and walk back in through the front door ever again. No man would drink all my housekeeping money for my kids.' Cherry is a woman who can fend for herself and considerably better than her mother. She has little patience with weakness in others, having had to make herself so unnaturally strong. She sees her mother as a natural victim, but also as a woman who needs trouble and violence around her.

What could have made all this different for Cherry? She had a quick answer. She knew exactly what she wanted. 'If she gave me some reason, any reason. If she said to me, "I did it because I thought it was right for you both at the time." Or just "I'm sorry about what I did to you, and I regret it." Or "I couldn't cope at the time, but I was so sorry later." Or maybe if she'd even sit down and ask me if I had been happy, and how things were at the Smithsons.'

She gets angry with her mother sometimes, but rarely shows it. She recalls with bitterness. 'We were sitting watching TV one day, and there was something on about children in need. She said, right out loud, "When I see sad things about children on TV, tears come to my eyes." I couldn't believe it. She didn't give a toss about us, did she? But I said nothing.'

In so many small ways, as she talks, despite herself, there is the old longing for her real mother, hopelessly unfulfilled, and unfulfillable. She resents the fact that her mother has never ever given the children anything. 'It wouldn't take much. A 10p piece for pocket money would be a treat to them. A tiny gift, wrapped up nicely. It's not the money, it's the gesture. She's all take and no give. We're not rich, but we're a lot better off than her. It doesn't mean my kids wouldn't appreciate a gift from her, a token. They're little and they don't know what things cost. She's only ever once, in all her life given me anything, and that was one birthday card, the year after we first met. It had written inside "I didn't forget", as if she was trying to squeeze the last bit of guilt and duty out of me.' Her mother has given her nothing, and it nags – a symbol of all else her mother failed to give. Cherry always refers to her mother as 'the mother', never 'my mother'. 'That's how I see her, the mother of that family.'

Not long after her trip to London her mother came to stay with her, bringing four of her brothers and sisters with her, with assorted husbands and wives. Cherry's house is small, a modern three-bedroomed house, so it was a tight squeeze. 'If you ask me, all they came for was a free nosh-up,' she says, and laughs at herself as she remembers it all. 'They ate me out of house and home. They drank all our drink. My mum even fingered the sitting room curtains, and asked me if I wanted them. I'd only just washed up lunch and they'd start saying it was getting near tea time. The kept saying they were beginning to get hungry again. I was just their slave. Not one of them offered to help. They'd send Sam out for a bottle of whisky when we ran out of what we had. They used the phone all day long. They sent Sam out for the Sunday papers and ordered half the newsagent shop. They said, "Let's put the heating up, it's chilly," and "Let's rent a couple of videos tonight." I was too busy ever to get the chance to talk to any of them, scrubbing pots and pans. They wanted to go to the Wimpy, and ordered everything in sight. They hadn't any money to pay for a thing. Finally the mother asked for the money for her train fare. I gave it to her as she didn't have any.'

Her mother, she says, looked so terrible, that she was embarrassed taking her to the shops and round the streets where she lived. 'She smelled terrible, hadn't had a bath in twenty years I'd think. She had great holes in her tights, her hair hadn't been touched, and she wore baggy acrylic sweaters, coughing and spluttering over her fags. When we met people, I didn't know how to introduce her, and she used to butt in and say, "I'm her Mum". I got some funny looks.'

Shortly after that exhausting expensive visit, Garry came to stay with Cherry, which he does from time to time. Suddenly he was interested in his real family after all. He wanted to know everything about them, wanted their address, and telephone numbers. Cherry was anxious, and wondered whether Garry had the emotional strength to stand up to all this. She warned him that he should keep his distance, if he did go and see them. "Stay wary," I said to him. "You don't know what you might get yourself into."' It was good advice, but little heeded.

Garry went straight down to London, and called on his mother. 'As soon as he met them, he thought they were all wonderful. He just dived in there, and loved his lost family. I couldn't believe it, but within two hours of first meeting them all, he decided to move right in with the mother. Of course she was delighted, really thrilled. She thought he was the most wonderful thing on earth. Maybe, since he'd always had Mrs Smithson, and she'd died, he had a real need to find himself a new mother, which I didn't have. If he hadn't been a bit vulnerable, I think he'd have been more careful and gone in there with his eyes open. But he didn't want to see any problems. He was just looking for the good, and the good was all he saw. Come to think about it, I just don't know how he *could* have moved into that filthy stinking hole of a flat. He was really looking for something, poor Garry.'

Ever since she came to know her real family, Cherry began to get calls from her mother, or various brothers and sisters informing her of the family rows in progress. She became a kind of arbiter, or at least a friendly ear. Pat would call to complain about what Sally had said about her to her mother. Her mother would grumble about what John had said about Carol. It was hard ever to get to the bottom of the rows, but they were persistent and fierce.

'I could never find out who started it, but there was always some kind of fighting going on. They seemed to live on fights and rows, just as a normal part of their daily life. They were trying to rope me in on it. If I gave any sympathy to one, she'd repeat it to another who would ring me up and shout at me. It was a bit of time before I realized that I'd got to keep absolutely out of all these arguments, or I'd go mad.'

Garry did not last long in that household. After a succession of small arguments, a huge row blew one night. 'The mother rang me, crying and sobbing. She said there was the most terrible argument going on involving Garry and would I please, please come down to London right now and help sort it all out. She sounded so upset that of course I said I would. It wasn't easy, but I felt I should. Well, when I got there I walked right into a battlefield – a great big barney, with all of them. A huge How's-Your-Father. First, they wanted me to take them all in the car round to Christine's house. Then it all began again. I couldn't get to the bottom of it. Garry was there, in the middle of it. Two of them turned on me and nearly clobbered me, at which point the mother weighed in, both fists flying, saying no one was to lay a finger on me. "I'm going to sort you all out!" she yelled, and laid into the lot of them in all directions.'

Cherry tried to find out what it was all about, but by this time the dispute had escalated into several separate rows between different members of the family. Eventually she pieced together the fact that Pat was accused of telling Garry lies about their father, which Pat hotly denied. Garry was being attacked for repeating the lies. Then he told them that it was Cherry who had told him the stories about his father. What story? The fact that Mr Garfield had gone to prison for stealing and embezzling from his job, and it hadn't been his first offence either.

'Then Christine came up to me and poked me hard, saying, "Don't you ever tell stories about our father." I poked her right back, quite hard, and I let rip, I really did. That was it, getting me all the way down to London, just to bring me in on their stupid family rows. "You little slut," I said. "Don't you dare ever lay a dirty finger on me again. You can't afford to touch me." I said. "You get back in the gutter where you come from."' Cherry smiled wryly at the memory of it all. 'The violence was getting really bad. They'd had the police round for rows before and I thought they would turn up any minute. There were three separate fights going on round the room. The mother was belting Christine, Garry was being belted, Pat was in a fight with Sally. I got out of there as quick as I could, and went off home.'

The next day the telephone rang. 'It was Christine. She warned me I ought to be careful of the others, a funny lot. I pointed out to her that she was the one that poked me in the first place. I gave her pretty short shift, I'm afraid.' A few of the others rang sheepishly that day, all blaming each other, and trying to rope her in on their side, though by now it was impossible to identify 'sides', just angry people, locked in combat, for no purpose.

It was shortly after this episode that another worse scene erupted. The family called her to ask where Garry was. Following the last row Garry had left his mother's house and disappeared. 'He's a disgrace to his family, he is!' Cherry's mother had complained down the line to Cherry. Cherry laughed. 'Talk about the kettle calling the pot black!' she says. She wouldn't be specific, but a number of things, she said, had got a bit hot for Garry in London, and he'd taken off. Now the family wanted to trace him again. Cherry knew where he was, but she wasn't going to tell them.

They complained to Cherry that Garry had rented a video when he was staying at his mother's, and he had never taken it back. Now the video rental company wanted it back, or their money, or both, and they all refused to pay. 'They put a lot of pressure on me to tell them where Garry was, but I wouldn't. They kept ringing me, one after another. I eventually said, "You're all mad!" and put the phone down on them. Because of my business, I've got an answering machine, so I didn't have to speak to them if I didn't want to.'

This made them even angrier with Cherry. The whole family turned against her, as if they wanted to get their revenge on her for some unspecified crime – perhaps sheer envy at the quality of her life compared with theirs.

'Of course that wasn't the end of the matter,' she said. 'It got worse.' One evening a man telephoned and asked to speak to Sam. The voice said, 'Mr Hendry, do you know that your wife has filed a divorce suit against you?' Luckily Sam didn't believe it for a moment and just said, 'Oh yes? I'll ask her,' and put down the receiver. Shortly afterwards, the same man called again, 'Mr Hendry, I thought you'd like to know a few things about your wife. Did you know, for instance, that she has a criminal record, and I can prove it to you?' Again, Sam put the receiver down on the man, and laughed it off. Later, Cherry found out that it was Christine's boyfriend who had been put up to make the calls.

Then at two o'clock in the morning, came a knock on the

door, a loud authoritative rapping. 'I thought we'd be chopped up in bags and dumped on the M1,' Cherry said and reached for the phone, to call the police, but to her relief, when she looked out the window, she saw it was the police at the door. She and Sam let them in. 'We've had a complaint from a Kilburn police station,' said the policeman. 'Some people walked in there a short time ago and lodged a complaint against you for making persistent abusive phone calls, and harassing them.'

Cherry was outraged, and she tried to explain the situation to the police. Luckily she hadn't used the phone at all that day, so she urged the police to check her outgoing calls with the operator. The police said the operator was able to confirm that there had been no outgoing calls from that number, and they were satisfied with her story. 'Do you want to press charges against them?' the police asked, and suggested that she should, in order to stop it happening again. 'But I couldn't,' Cherry said. 'They *are* my family, and when it comes down to it, I just couldn't cause them that much trouble. In any case I wouldn't stoop so low. I'd be as low as them if I started getting into that kind of fight with them.'

The police in Kilburn clearly gave the family a bad fright, and leaned on them heavily for wasting police time, malicious accusations and the like. 'They kept thinking I might press charges. They didn't dare phone me, not one of them, for eight months. They were frightened that one call might bring the police down on them. Maybe they thought the police were checking my line to see they didn't call any more. It was a blessed relief. I had called their bluff, and still to this day they wonder whether I mightn't press charges if they do anything like that again. I wouldn't, but they don't know that. They are very careful of me these days.'

Eventually, eight quiet months later, Mrs Garfield did call. Her youngest son, Andy, was in trouble. He'd been caught defrauding the company he worked for with dud cheques. They had a friendly talk, and her mother promised to call again next week.

'Next week! She didn't call me for three months after that, and again it was because she wanted something. I said to her, "You were going to call me next week. It's three months later. What happened?" The mother had the nerve to say, "I forgot." Forgot! I ask you! She forgot us once before, didn't she? We seem very easy for her to forget.' Cherry never rings any of them now. She waits for them to call her. 'They only call now when there's a row on and they want to rope me in on it. I'm their Samaritan, their social worker – and, if I'm not careful, their Flexible Friend.'

Does she regret ever contacting them? 'No,' she says, without a second thought. 'It was important. And it was an experience.' She laughed as she thought about it. Does she feel bitter about having been given away for adoption? 'Yes, because my mother has never given me a reason why, or talked about it, or faced up to it.' Would she rather she had been left with her original family? She thought for a while before answering.

'I'd say that you shouldn't mess around with children. It's not a good thing. And the family I was put into was not properly examined beforehand by the authorities. The Smithsons should never have been allowed to foster and adopt the way they did. They were quite unsuitable.' How would her life have been if she had stayed with her own family? 'I can see that very clearly. I think I'd have been very like Carol. I like her, and I think probably we are alike as people, as well as looking alike. But she's never really been able to escape and get away from them all. The mother depends on her for everything, and she feels she has to be loyal to her.'

She paused again, and thought hard. 'If Carol had had some chances, if the mother wasn't so dependent on her, then maybe she could have made more of her life. But she hasn't been able to. I owe nothing to anyone, there was nothing and no one holding me back. I think I was better off being adopted, in spite of everything. When the family look at me jealously, and think I'm the lucky one, they're probably right.' After all, if Cherry has suffered from having little love and no mothering in her childhood she doubts if she would have had much anyway. Her own mother, she thinks, was not a particularly loving, giving mother to the children who stayed with her. 'Though she does hold tremendous power over them. They're all still there, around her. She manipulates them. She stirs it, and sets one against another, to maximize her power.' She wonders whether after the mothers' death, she might find she gets on with the rest of them reasonably well.

Does she think it a good thing, then, to remove all children from severely disadvantaged, unloving homes? 'But what that child has to live with, all her life, is the feeling that her mother has given her away. She wasn't wanted. That's a terrible feeling to grow up with.'

Was the new law allowing children to seek their parents a good idea? 'I don't think people realize all the dangers. If I'd been eighteen, and not married, without a firm life and family of my own, I could have been destroyed by it. Luckily I was that bit older, and absolutely secure in myself. The social worker should stay with you and follow the work through for the first year, beçause there can be so many problems.'

But she does feel, somewhere underneath, a strong tie to her family. She says she knows telepathically if her mother or sister is going to ring her on a particular day, even if she hasn't spoken to them for weeks. 'Sam tells me I'm better off without them. They're nothing but trouble. Why do I see them? Because they are my flesh and blood. Do I need them, I ask myself? If so, I'm in bad trouble. Do they need me? Perhaps. Do I need them to need me? Perhaps.' It is not only duty that keeps her in touch with her own family.

4

Judy and Joanne

Judy is a cheerful and kindly young woman, unassertive to such a degree that she never answers back to anyone. She is open and affectionate, trusting, perhaps too much so. She has spent a lot of her life being careful not to hurt others – her natural mother, her adoptive mother, or anyone else. She is not one to seize initiative or to take risks, but in an almost resigned way, has sat back to wait and see what would happen next – even over something she has cared more about than almost anything else in her life – the search for her missing family. Like many adopted children, though she longed to look for her mother, she held back, afraid of the harm it might do her, or the offence it might cause her adoptive mother.

Twenty-seven years ago Judy's mother walked out of the maternity hospital in a daze, leaving her baby behind in her cot. A nurse noticed her go and shouted after her, 'Come back! Mrs Morris, come back here this minute! Your baby needs feeding!' But she kept on walking, and she never saw her baby again. She was going through a severe nervous breakdown, but she had two fourteen-month-old twin girls back home waiting for her, and three much older boys. Her lover was dead – Judy was a posthumous baby – she had no money, and she returned home to a life of utter poverty and hardship.

Judy, the baby she left behind, was taken to Dr Barnado's. When she was eight months old, and her mother still hadn't said she'd take her home, she was put up for adoption. Her mother was firmly presented with the papers to sign – and she did as she was told. She had no option. She had three low-paid jobs already, and couldn't make ends meet. Another baby was out of the question. But that decision cast a cloud over the rest of her life, and she never recovered from the shock of giving away her child.

But Judy knew nothing of this when she was growing up. She was adopted by the family of a successful civil servant who already had one adopted child, a little boy a few years older whom they had taken on when he was already three, and difficult. Two years after they adopted Judy, as so often happens, to their astonishment they had a child themselves, another girl. In some ways, when this happens it is often difficult for the adopted children, as they can feel the difference straight away, real or imagined, between the natural child, and themselves.

The Allens, her adoptive parents, were open and honest about Judy's origins. They told her as soon as she could understand, and they encouraged conversation about it. When she asked questions, they told her all they knew, which was not very much. They had in fact met her natural mother once, just before the signing of the papers. Judy's natural mother had insisted she wanted to see the couple taking her child, to check they were well off and would give her a good home, and to be sure they were Christians who would bring her up to be religious. All Mrs Allen could remember of the meeting to tell Judy later was that her mother was a very small woman, and that she was wearing navy blue. She seemed poor, and tired. They always stressed to Judy that her mother never wanted to give her up, but had been forced to as she couldn't manage a baby.

'Navy blue was always my favourite colour after I heard about that meeting,' Judy says. 'I used to look at every small woman in navy blue on the bus or in the street, and wonder if she might be my mother.' Her adoptive mother made a point of never trying to pretend Judy was her child. She always used to say at birthdays and Christmas, 'Remember who else will be thinking about you today.' Judy says, 'I felt very loved at home, but I always felt different. It was a bit of a problem that I was much less clever and intelligent than my younger sister, their real daughter. I knew I came from somewhere else. I didn't look or feel like them. I was someone else, and I didn't know who.'

She regretted telling friends at school she was adopted. It came out when the class was issued with Sunshine Books from Dr Barnado's. They featured pictures of Barnado's children, and babies. Judy pointed at them proudly, and said she was one of those once. 'After that I was always called Banana, and they teased me rotten. I hated it, and wished I'd never told.'

When she was twelve she began to grow increasingly anxious about her real mother. It became an obsession. She dreamed up all kinds of fantasies about who she really was, and why she had been given away. 'I had several versions. I kept a photo of my adopted mother's brother, and I wrote on the back, "My Dad". Of course I knew it wasn't. I had an Auntie Hetty, who had no children, and I used to think perhaps I was hers. Again, I knew really that I wasn't. When my mother found out about these fantasies, she used to say, "Look Judy, I promise you that if I knew anything at all about who your real parents were, I wouldn't hide it from you." I knew that was true, but I still went on dreaming.' At about that time she read about Princess Margaret's much publicized affair with Captain Peter Townsend. 'Well, of course, that explained everything. I knew I was her child, and his, and they'd had to keep me secret, so they'd dumped me quietly in Dr Barnado's. One day she'd drive up in her Rolls-Royce and collect me.'

This longing to know didn't come out of any unhappiness at home. Her father was overworked and distant, but she was very close to her adoptive mother. Although she felt that her younger sister was the 'real' child and she wasn't, she says her mother never showed overt favouritism. 'But people would just say to my sister, "Oh, you're like Auntie so and so," or "You're like Uncle such and such." And they wouldn't say anything to me because I wasn't like anyone known to them.'

She felt at school and with other friends and relations, that adopted children are looked on as oddities, treated cautiously. 'It was as if we were not to be trusted. I felt it about myself in a way. Was my mother a prostitute, and did that mean I'd be one? I was probably illegitimate, and I suppose everyone knew that about me and my mother. People tend to say, "It's always in the blood," and that makes me mad. It's so unfair. It hurts.'

Once, when the family were moving house, the children were sent to stay with strange distant cousins for a week. 'While we were there, someone let drop to this cousin that I was adopted. She was so shocked and horrified, she wouldn't speak to me again. Her attitude was "How could they dump this strange child on me? I thought I knew who she was, but she could be anyone's." She was furious with me, disgusted, and I felt dirty. I couldn't understand her attitude. I often had the feeling at that time that there was something wrong with adopted people. They came from mothers with low morals or low intelligence or both.'

She became so obsessed and depressed at about this time, that her mother worried about her, and thought perhaps it would help if more could be found out about her real parents. She contacted the woman who had arranged the adoption from Dr Barnado's, whom she had kept in close touch with over the years, sometimes sending her photographs of Judy. This social worker agreed to see Judy, and to tell her as much as she knew, to see if it would put her mind at rest.

'I was taken to her house one day, and left there. She sat me down and promised to tell all she knew, which wasn't very much. She said my mother was forty-six when she had me. She already had two boys, of sixteen and nineteen. They were so shocked and horrified by an illegitimate baby, that they refused to let their mother bring me home. She didn't tell me I had twin sisters just fourteen months older. I'm sure now that she was protecting me. If I had known that, it would have made things worse. I would have desperately wanted to meet and know them. It wouldn't have dampened my curiosity, but it would have made it worse. After all, I was only twelve, and the law hadn't yet been changed. As far as she knew, I would never ever see my real family again.'

That interview, although it told her so little, seems to have helped. 'I didn't dream any more about my real family. I did have a few fantasies about these older brothers of mine. I didn't hate them for making my mother give me up, but I did want to know them. I used to imagine that any male teachers of about the right age could be my brothers. Also, once I knew I was born in Lincoln that place took on a very special fascination. I used to want to know all about it. Anything, any mention of Lincoln was interesting to me. But in fact in the next few years, I thought a lot less about my real mother and family. I calmed down and I felt much better. I don't know why it all came to a head when I was twelve – something to do with growing up.'

The difference between herself and her younger sister was often painful. Her sister went to grammar school, while she went to the local secondary. She wanted to become a children's nurse, and take a Nursery Training course. The reason for that, was that she wanted to go and work in Dr Barnado's, where she came from. To her great disappointment, she had to give up the course before the end, as she had problems with her feet, having been born with hammer toes. Nursery nursing meant being on her feet all day, and the pain made the work impossible, so she became a GPO telephonist instead.

She had had several boyfriends, none of them serious,

when she met her present husband. He is twenty-six years older – an age gap that looks enormous when you see the two of them together. It was hardly surprising that her parents disapproved strongly. At the time they met, Bill was a scrap metal merchant, but now he works as an animal keeper at a research laboratory. They have a small flat, and a three-year-old daughter, Emma. Why did she choose someone so much older? 'I liked his dominance and the security he gave me. Also, I always felt that if you marry someone your own age, they might leave you. Better to marry someone older who won't. I need security and certainty.' She dismisses absolutely the rather obvious suggestion that she was in fact looking for a father figure. 'No, not at all,' she says. She insists that the age factor made little difference. 'It was just fate. We are perfect for each other, and it's just unlucky that I happened to be born twenty-six years too late.' Looking at them, that seems unlikely; the age difference is a dominant part of their relationship. He makes the decisions, he is in control.

When she was eighteen, shortly after she first met Bill, the adoption law changed. 'I thought very hard about going in search of my mother. I knew I could go to Somerset House, or wherever, and look in the books to find out more, but I didn't really know how to set about doing that. I did talk to my Mum about it, and she encouraged me, saying I could if I wanted to. She never made me feel I'd be being disloyal to her if I did. I thought long and hard. I knew my real mother was a divorcee, and it seemed likely she would have married again. What if she hadn't told her new husband about me? I might ruin her life if I contacted her. My adoptive mother always told me that my real mother never wanted to give me up, but she had done what she thought was best for me. That made me think I had a duty to do the best for her, and not risk hurting her and damaging her life.'

But the change in the law did make her think a great deal more about her real family. 'I used to go to church and puzzle things out. I expected God to send a bolt out of the blue, telling me who my mother was and where I would find her. I was always very interested in older women, and liked talking to them, maybe because they could have been my mother. She was forty-six when she had me and would be sixty-four when I was eighteen. I kept reading about people who found their real families. I was very tempted. But if I started looking, then I'd never stop, and I would certainly contact my mother if I ever came to know her address, so I left it on one side.'

When she was pregnant she began to become obsessively worried about the possibility of genetic disorder, or inherited disease. 'They ask all these questions about your family history, and I had to say I didn't know. Nothing, absolutely nothing. I was terrified of giving birth because I thought there would be something very wrong. Haemophilia maybe. I was so anxious that they gave me a special scan to show me that as far as they could tell, the baby was normal.' Her daughter was indeed quite healthy. 'But then I didn't know if she should be given whooping cough vaccine or not, because if there is any family history of fits, they don't do it. Well, they should have medical records. That's the very least they could give adopted children. It would have helped me a great deal.

'I don't think ordinary people understand what it means not to have a single person in the whole world connected to you by blood. Then, when you have your own child, there is this person all your own flesh and blood, and it feels wonderful. At this time I thought a lot about contacting my mother. I thought of going to Lincoln, but I knew if I went I'd have to go through the records, go to the hospital, and I would find her. And what if she rejected me then? What if she wouldn't see me? It would have broken me completely.'

A year later a letter was sent to her adoptive parents. It was a miracle the letter ever reached them. Had it been written two days later, they would never have received it. It came from a social worker at Dr Barnado's, and was sent to an old address. The occupiers of that house, who had bought the house from them many years ago, were about to move out in two days' time, and the next owners would never have known where to forward the letter.

It was a brief letter, asking if they would agree to a meeting. It said so little, that it was not clear what the meeting was to be about, nor whether it concerned Judy or her elder brother, also adopted from Dr Barnado's. They telephoned the social worker and agreed at once to a meeting. They told Judy about it straight away.

'I was so excited, my heart thumped. I hoped and prayed it was about me, and not my brother. I knew, I just knew it was my mother, at last, coming to find me. I couldn't sleep or concentrate at work all week. When the day of the meeting came, I stayed in all day beside the telephone. It was a Monday night, and Bill hadn't come in from work yet, when the phone rang. Mum just said, "We had a very interesting meeting. I think it would be to your advantage to come over straight away. Don't drive yourself. Just give Bill his dinner and ask him to drive you." I could hardly wait. It must be something so dramatic if I wasn't allowed to drive.'

Bill came in from work tired. She asked him if he would drive her over to her mother's flat, as soon as he had eaten his dinner. 'He just said, "What on earth for?" and he wouldn't. I'd been waiting for this all week, and now I couldn't go and find out. I burst into tears. Eventually he realized how important it was, and after he'd had a bath, he did drive me over there.' As Judy recounted this part of the story she went to the window to check that Bill was not about to come back.

When she got to her mother's flat, she was given coffee before they would tell her what had happened. 'This lady, your natural mother, well, she is looking for you,' her mother said. Judy says, 'I remember my mother looking at me hard to see what my reaction would be. I was just stunned. I don't know how I reacted.' Judy was told that her mother and her family had been looking for her for years. They had made constant inquiries with the social services. Letters had been left in the records, in case Judy should ever herself seek her mother out. All these years that she had been scrupulously trying to protect her mother by not making inquiries, her mother had been desperately looking for her. The letters, many of them, were being held for her, if she wanted them. Would she like to be sent them? Judy immediately said she would.

It was later that she learned of the lengths her mother had gone to to find her. Once, she had spent two days in London, sleeping in a railway station, tramping the streets of the city staring at every young girl, convinced she would recognize her own, even eighteen years after she had given her away. Not having been to London before she had no idea how difficult it would be, and she returned exhausted two days later, in deep despair.

Judy's father made her wait for two days before she finally decided whether to ask for the letters that were waiting for her. He warned her of all the problems that might arise. 'I never for a moment doubted. I wanted those letters more than anything. But I waited the two days, and when they were over I telephoned him to say that I did want them. He gave me the number of the social worker and I called her. She promised to send them to me right away. The next few days were hell, just waiting. I cried a lot. I was useless at work, but luckily my boss understood what I was going through. I'd thought about my real family almost every day for all these years, and at last I was going to find them.'

The letters did not arrive for a week. In desperation she went to the post office, and found they were waiting there, since the postman for her road had been away sick, and no one had delivered them. 'I'd been through such a bad time waiting, I couldn't believe this could happen. I never heard of letters not being delivered because a postman was off sick. It was just bad luck.'

Inside the big brown envelope were six letters, some from her mother, one each from her twin sisters. The letters were cautious and tentative. 'It was as if they were very nervous about intruding on my life,' Judy says. The first letter from her mother laid out the bare outlines, with the names and ages of the family members.

The letters were addressed to 'Joanne'. Judy had no idea that her christian name had been changed. Her mother signed her letters oddly, 'Mrs Hayes' – because she couldn't quite bring herself to write either 'Mum' or her christian name. She gave a brief account of her family. She had three grown-up sons by her first marriage. Then much later, there had been the twins, rapidly followed by Judy. Their father had died. She was now remarried to a Mr Hayes, and the twins were both married, with children of their own, and lived close by in Lincoln. The first letter ended: 'Please excuse the writing and spelling. Permit me just to say that you have never been out of my mind. May God Bless You and Keep You Healthy and Happy, Yours, Mrs Hayes.'

'All her letters were full of how much she had always loved me, and how long she had been looking for me,' Judy says. 'She said if I didn't want to see her, then it was enough for her to know I was happy and well. The letters from my sisters were just as warm and enthusiastic. The amazing coincidence was that we all had a baby within a week of each other, so we all now had three-year-olds.'

Large chunks of her mother's letters were deeply religious. She explained how God had helped her, and faith had pulled her through. Some of these sections were disjointed and a little odd, Judy thought. Her mother described how many organizations she had written to for help in tracing her child. The twins had grown up always knowing they had a younger sister somewhere. They all remembered her on her birthday and longed to see her. One of the twins had called her first daughter Joanne, after her.

There were photographs enclosed with these letters.

Almost every adopted child I have met has fallen upon the looks of their long-lost family, and claimed to find remarkable resemblances. Usually I can't see it at all. I politely agree because it matters to them so much, but I find little likeness. But Judy really does look very like her twin sisters, (they are not identical twins) and a little like her mother when she was young.

She carried the letters with her all the time. 'I was in a daze. I could hardly believe it. To find a mother, and then two sisters so close in age, it was wonderful, wonderful.' Judy had been told firmly by the social worker that she was not to contact her new-found family directly for the first time, but should act through her as intermediary. So she called the social worker. Despite the fact that the unorthodox approach had been made by the mother not the child, clearly the social worker felt some shred of the legal requirements should be adhered to. She said Judy should wait until she could interview and counsel her first before contacting her mother, but the interview couldn't be for several weeks, as she was so over-worked. 'I was so upset. I knew I couldn't wait that long, not after those letters, and I didn't see the point. So when Bill came in he said we could get the phone numbers for ourselves easily from the directory inquiries. He got them for me, and there they were. It was happening too quickly. After all these years, my family were just on the end of a telephone line.'

Judy was told in the letters from her sisters that her mother was now in her early seventies and not well, suffering from angina. This was one reason why the Hertfordshire Social Services had been willing to try to help her look for her daughter. 'I thought if I telephoned my mother out of the blue, I could give her a bad shock, and maybe a heart attack, so I decided to phone one of my sisters first. I wasn't going to bother to wait for the social worker to do it for me. I was too impatient. I felt I had to talk to them right away.'

She picked up the receiver and dialled Marjorie's number.

'It rang and rang, but then suddenly there was a voice at the other end. I said, "Hello, is that Marjorie? You don't know me, but you wrote me a letter, which I have only just been sent. My name used to be Joanne." I didn't know what else to say. There was just silence at the other end, and then there was this sobbing. She cried and cried, but she didn't say anything. I said, "Hello, are you there?" I couldn't believe I was really talking to this person, this person who was my own flesh and blood, very nearly myself. We talked a bit, and she asked a few questions, but she was too upset to say much, except how all her life she'd wanted to find her little sister. She said her twin Denise would just break up when she heard my voice. She promised that she would ring our mum to break the news gently. I told her to say that I would call her at exactly seven o'clock, so she could be sitting by the phone ready and not be taken by surprise.'

Next she called Denise, but she was out and her husband answered the telephone. Judy just left a message with him to say her sister called. Of course he assumed it was Marjorie, though he may have wondered at her southern accent, lacking any familiar Lincoln burr. Later she called again, but Denise had come in and gone out in that time. 'Is that Marjorie again?' her husband asked doubtfully. Judy said, 'No, it's not her sister Marjorie, it's her other sister, Joanne.' He was so astounded to hear this that he sent Joanne's namesake, little Joanne, running down the road to the bingo hall to find her mother, and tell her the astonishing news. After all these years, her sister had at last been found.

Seven o'clock came, and Judy called her mother. 'Hello Mum?' she said. 'It's me, Joanne.' Her mother, though she was sitting waiting for the call, found herself struck dumb. She could hardly speak a word Judy remembers. 'She just sighed, and kept sighing. Then we did talk a little. What did we say? So hard to remember the words, though I remember the feelings so well. She said she recognized my voice, even without having met me. I don't know how, since I don't talk like them, but I knew what she meant. I said how I'd love to come up there, right away, but we had no car on the road and not much money. We'd have to wait until bank holiday, ten weeks ahead. Ten weeks seemed such a long, long time. I wanted to jump on a train and go there at once. But it couldn't be done.'

That night she was in a state of wild excitement. 'I smoked dozens of cigarettes. My heart was pounding. I've never taken drugs but I imagine that's what it feels like – out of my mind. But that night Emma had a terrible asthma attack. She'd had asthma before but nothing like this. We had to rush her to the hospital. It was the only time she ever had a bad attack, poor mite. I think perhaps it was to do with my own state of over-excitement.

'I cried all night, and I didn't know if I was crying for Emma, or crying for my new family. It was all too much for me, and perhaps too much for Emma, who couldn't really understand why I was in such a peculiar state of mind.'

After that, telephone calls flew between Lincoln and London. 'Our bill that quarter was terrible. We had so much to say to each other. We took it in turns to phone. I think they thought I was very posh. I don't think I've got a posh accent, but I suppose their Lincolnshire accent is very strong. I think they thought I was rolling in it, even though I hadn't the money to put together to get up to Lincoln. But they were happy to wait the ten weeks. They lead slow lives, where everything is ordered and planned, and nothing happens suddenly. I found I was talking to my sisters as if I'd always known them, and I was just away from home on a holiday. We laughed a lot on the phone, and I think we felt we were all very much alike.'

The twins had discovered about Judy's existence when they were nine. 'It seems someone let it slip. Denise took it very badly indeed. She became obsessed with the idea of her lost little sister. She stole a photo of me from Mum. I was amazed to find Mum had photos of me as a child. Certainly my adoptive parents had no idea of this. My adoptive mum sent some to the woman from Dr Barnado's, the person I met when I was twelve, but she certainly didn't know this woman was passing them on to my natural mum. One of them showed me on holiday in Pegwell Bay, standing by a Viking ship. After that my mum took her holiday at Pegwell Bay, hoping that we went there every year and she might be able to find me. But we only went there one year.'

Judy remembered the photograph well. 'Of course I had a lot of pictures taken of me as a child, but for some reason that particular one always stuck in my mind. It jumped out of the book at me, though there was nothing at all special about it. Now I think it was some kind of telepathy. My mother and Denise were poring over it, and thinking of me so much, that somehow, maybe, it communicated itself to me. When Denise stole it, she slept with it under her pillow every night. They knew from the picture that I looked very like them.'

The weeks passed. They saved enough money to hire a car for two days to drive up to Lincoln. 'I kept telling Emma she was going to meet her new Nanny. We got lost on the way, and I still had my hair in heated curlers when we got there, late. I was pulling them out of my head when Bill and Emma got out, and there she was, standing at her front gate. Emma went straight up to her and said "Nanny" and gave her a kiss. My mum just burst out crying and they went into the house. I came in just after, and there written on the mirror in the front room, was a big sign saying, "Welcome Home Judy!" Everyone was there, and they were all crying their eyes out. My sister Denise was leaning over the sink, bawling. Mum still had Emma in her arms, and she was crying and crying. Poor Bill was standing there bewildered. Then Denise turned round to face me, her eyes all red, and we gave each other a big cuddle. Mum looked older and iller than in the photos she had sent. She just said, "Let's have a cup of tea," and started putting on the kettle. I usually cry at anything,

I'm dead soppy. But I didn't cry at all, not a drop. I don't know why. I was just sitting there, accepting things as they happened. I went outside a minute and a neighbour passed by and called out to me, "Hello Marjorie," because that's who she thought I was, I looked so like them.'

They sat down to a huge meal and Judy surveyed the family. The sisters had warned her that Mum's husband, Ernest, was a scruffy old man but Judy noted how clean he looked in her honour. It had, her mother later explained, been a marriage of convenience. She was grindingly poor, bringing up the girls alone. He was lonely and had an increasingly infirm old mother to care for. She took care of his mother and they married. 'But it was purely for comfort and economy, she always says. Everyone's life looked up after they married. They weren't nearly so poor. But Mum keeps saying there was never any more to it than that.'

Judy found in her mother everything she had hoped for. 'She was my mum, just my mum and that's all there was to it. I felt I'd been away from her a few weeks, not twenty-seven years. We just knew everything about each other, how each other was feeling. She always said she'd know me anywhere, if she saw me walking down a street, even if I hadn't looked like them. She said she'd always know her own child, just by instinct. You could say there was an instant bond between us. It felt natural to cuddle up to her. I'd had a mum all my life, a good mum, but now I'd found a mum who looks like me, feels like me and understands everything important about me.'

Judy met her three elder brothers too. Two of them had moved away, become distant to the family, but one was close to his mother still. They were in their forties and fifties. She had been well prepared for the family's circumstances, since her mother had frequently referred in letters to 'only living in a council house' as if she expected Judy to despise her for it, or indeed to be in much better circumstances herself, which she isn't. The sisters seemed to expect Judy to be rather grand and aloof. They imagined smart private schools and foreign holidays.

Certainly her experience of the world was a bit wider, for the twins had scarcely been outside the Lincoln area. There had been little money for holidays, and they had never travelled to London. 'I did find them full of bitterness about their childhood. They felt they had had a very hard time indeed. Mum was working at three hard jobs, and had only time for the bare essentials – no time for games or stories or fun. They had nothing, only hand-me-down clothes, and there was no furniture in the house. Even their shoes had holes. I felt bad about that. I felt there had been no happiness at all in their childhood. They made it clear that there really wouldn't have been enough money to bring me up too. Also, something terrible happened when they were eleven. They were both raped, by a vicar who offered to take them on holiday to his caravan, and made them scrub and slave for him and his children.'

Her mother's religion is the only part of her that Judy doesn't really understand. From time to time her mother talks vehemently about God, though she doesn't try to convert Judy and the other girls pay no attention to it. She is a strong Pentecostalist, and was in the Salvation Army for years. 'Finding me again has made it worse, if anything,' Judy says. 'She promised God all kinds of things if He found me for her. She says she never doubted for a moment that He would find me, and now He has.'

She is mystified still about her father and never really believed her mother's version of the story which doesn't hold together. She asked her nicest brother if he could remember anything much about him. 'All he could remember was that he was a good-looking, tall, strong man. He loved mother a lot and it was the only love in her life. Her first husband, my brothers' dad, was a wicked man, and she did right to divorce him for cruelty. But what happened to our dad? The story doesn't sound quite right to me. I haven't been able to get my mum to talk about him. I feel there's something hidden there. The funny thing is that my sisters aren't in the least interested. I think perhaps they know the story we've been told isn't quite right, and they don't want to know any more. But I do. I think they suspect if we found out, it would turn out our father wasn't this good, loving man after all, but maybe he did abandon our mum and all of us.'

The story is that he left her at home with the two girls, pregnant with Judy, to go to London to look for work. When he found a job and a house, he'd call for them and bring them with him. But she never heard from him again. No letter, nothing. He was married with a wife and child living just a few streets away from Judy's mother. The only way Judy's mother discovered he was dead was when she heard that his two daughters by his wife had taken the day off school to go to his funeral in Oxford, some three months later. But what was he doing in Oxford? Judy wants to go through the records and see if she can find out. She wonders if he is in fact dead at all?

Judy came away from that first meeting with her family in a state of euphoria. It was infectious, and Bill too was delighted with these new in-laws. 'We wanted to get a job and a house in Lincoln and move right up there. It's a lovely place and we could be so happy there. But then, when we calmed down, we could see all the problems. The worst is that my adoptive mum and dad would be very upset and might think they'd lost us, and I would hate to do anything disloyal, or anything they might misunderstand. At the moment, living in London, we are exactly half way between my real mum in Lincoln and my adopted mum in the West Country, so it seems fairer to stay here, stuck between the two.'

Judy's adoptive mother has been calm and supportive. Judy said to her at the beginning, 'Get one thing straight, you are still my mother and I think the world of you.' Her mother smiled and said, 'If I thought this or anything could have come between us, then I don't think I'd have helped arrange the meeting in the first place. I know you can't do away with twenty-seven years of love.' And there has been no problem since.

Judy has been back to Lincoln several times now, and speaks to them every week on the telephone. 'I have met so many aunties and uncles and cousins, I can't keep count. One thing they all say is "Thank God you've turned up! She never stopped going on about you. She always said she'd find you, but we didn't think she would." I definitely got the feeling that she'd been very insistent and boring about me!'

Rosie Hayes, Judy's mother, lives in a council house on a large but pleasant estate in Lincoln. Roses grow round the door, hanging baskets and flowers fill the garden at the back, where her husband Ernest spends most of his days, summer and winter.

Now in her mid-seventies, she is a small, roundish woman with a prominent nose and bright blue clear eyes. 'I can only say that my prayers have been answered. This great weight of pain and guilt has been lifted from me at last. After twenty-seven years of waiting and searching and regretting, I have my daughter back, the one I should never have given away.' She shook her head, and her eyes were moist. 'It's not that I feel sorry for myself. I don't. There's a lot of people in the world who have never done anything wrong who have suffered terribly, having children die and so on. But all the same, I think I have had a very hard life. Now, these last months have been some of the best in my life, in retirement, not so very poor as we used to be, and my Joanne – oh that's Judy to you, but she still feels like Joanne to me – my Joanne back again, and her not blaming me for what I did.'

On the wall behind her was a wooden poker-work sign – 'God Cares. He is able to do exceeding abundantly above all we ask or think.' She glanced up at it, as if to acknowledge the truth of it in her own life, eventually. 'I don't know that I really did so much wrong in my life to suffer like I have – but then perhaps I did.' What did she mean? What wrong?

'Certainly not leaving my first husband. That was the right thing to do, leaving my three boys' father. We were married very young, and he was a jealous and violent man. He hit me, and tormented me. There was no doubt it was the right thing to do. But then when I took up with William, I did take him from his wife and daughters. They lived up the road, not far from here. I still see her sometimes, getting on or off the bus. We've never spoken though. William and I worked together in an army canteen, and we fell in love. I felt I just couldn't live without him, the only love in all my life. I'd had precious little affection. But I suppose you could say it was wrong and I had no real right to have him. Of course my three boys didn't like him moving in, because we weren't married and they were embarrassed. And he didn't have enough money to keep all of us and his own family down the road too. Then the twins were born, and times were hard indeed. They were only five months old when I got pregnant again. I walked back from the doctor's in a daze, after they told me I was pregnant. I was really shocked. I told William and he just laughed. "What's all the fuss about?" was all he said. "Women are made for having babies. What did you expect?" Well, that was the last straw. He had no sympathy for me at all, or for how we were to feed six children – and his own family. I got angry and told him to go off back to his wife. I'd had enough. Well, he did try to go back to his wife, but she wouldn't have him, so he went off to London instead to look for work. But we'd fallen out by then.'

She never heard from him again, but then she had hardly expected or wanted to. She only knew he had died because her sister's daughter went to school with one of William's daughters by his first marriage. The little girl had taken the day off school to go to Oxford for her father's funeral, and that was how Rosie came to hear of it.

'I told the girls I was heart-broken over it, and that if he hadn't died, he'd have sent for us to go down to London with him. It was a nice story, and they liked to think I was heart-broken over their father. I did check that he was really dead, when I saw the National Assistance man. He went and checked for me, and found his death certificate. I used to have at least half a dozen photos of him, but I've none now. I think the girls took them and kept them, a memory of a father they never knew. And of course Joanne – Judy to you – was born after he was dead.'

When she went into hospital to have Joanne, the twins were taken into foster care, as there was no one else to care for them. 'My family were never very kind or helpful to me in those days when I really needed them. I see a lot of them now, but I can't get it out of my mind that they are only fair weather friends, and I was desperate then. They accepted the twins, more or less, but when I was pregnant again, they didn't want to know.'

She still finds it painful now, looking back on the time of that birth. 'I went temporarily funny. I was out of my mind, with the worry of it all. I always had a horror of mice. It was made worse when I was a child when my father put one in my hand for a joke, though he knew I hated them. When I was in the hospital bed after Joanne was born I had this feeling the whole bed was running full of mice. I feared mice, and I feared this terrible decision I had to make, and I suppose I put the two together. The man from the Church of England Adoption Society was a kind man. He came to see me at home before I went into hospital when I was at my wits' ends about what to do. He said, "Don't worry. Just don't look at the baby when it's born, don't even take a glance at the child, and we'll take it away right then." He seemed to understand how it felt. But of course the nurses in the hospital didn't, or else they didn't care. They knew this baby was going for adoption, yet they gave her to me to hold right away, and they made me feed and care for her. That did it, of course. I said to the adoption man when he came that I couldn't go through with it after all. He was understanding and said they'd take her in temporarily, while I made up my mind. I had to pay eight shillings a week towards her upkeep at Dr Barnado's, but I couldn't make up my mind to let her go for ever.'

She walked out of the hospital in a daze, the nurse calling after her to come back and care for her baby. She can't remember how she got home. The baby was taken away to Barnado's. As soon as she got home, that very day the foster parents brought back her eighteen-month-old twins. Dazed, half crazed and profoundly depressed, she had to care for them alone with no help and almost no money.

'I was so tired in those days that sometimes I used to lie down on the sitting room floor and just leave them crawling about all over me, because I couldn't keep my eyes open any longer. I knew there was no way I could manage a baby as well, and yet I couldn't bear to make that final decision. I was full of nerves, and all run down.'

Finally, when the baby was eight months old, Barnado's asked her to come to London for the day to talk over the child's future. A woman, the one who years later was to counsel Judy when she was so distressed at twelve, came to meet Rosie at the station. 'On the way to the home she explained that there were these people who had fallen in love with Joanne and wanted to adopt her. I could meet them if I wanted. Well, I did meet them, and I wasn't very taken with them. The lady seemed snobbish and stuffy. But of course,' she adds politely, 'I must say she has been good and kind to Joanne, all the same.' She paused and thought about it. It always seems a struggle for natural mothers to find nice things to say about the adoptive parents they have come to see as interlopers at best, predators at worst. She sighed, 'I did ask them if they would keep the name Joanne. They said it was a very nice name, so I thought they would, but of course they didn't, did they? It's only a small thing, but it seems to mean wiping me out altogether, as if she had never had a real mother who gave her a christian name.'

She went home to think about it. She did find a couple in

Lincoln, through friends of friends, who wanted to adopt a child, and her spirits rose at the thought that she would at least be nearby, that she would at least know where she was, and maybe, if she was lucky, would catch a glimpse of her from time to time. 'I wouldn't have interfered. And of course they might have moved away, but just a very little contact, just to know how she was would have made all the difference to me.' But the man from the C of E Adoption Society was stern and firm. These people, he said, were not on any approved waiting list of adopters. In any case, such arrangements were frowned on, even before they were made more or less illegal. Mothers must realize that they are not the mothers any longer – or not according to the law. They have no rights, nothing. This was something Rosie never felt or believed or really understood – not because she is unintelligent – far from it, she is a highly intelligent woman – but because it went against every fibre of her being, every belief she had in God and natural law, and the rightness of things. Mothers are ordained mothers by God, and nothing on earth changes that fact. 'I've had too many children, you might say. I hated my first husband and should never have had three children of his. And then another three. But there they are, all healthy grown-up people with lives to live. Something tells me they had to be born, had to have a life. It's all such a puzzle to me. Where would they be if I hadn't given them life? I think about that often, but I don't have the answers.'

When she finally signed the papers and consented to the couple she had met adopting the child, she says she asked Barnado's if she could write from time to time to find out how her little girl was getting on. 'Barnado's promised me that they would keep me informed. They said the family had promised to send reports to them, and they would let me know. That was important to me.'

The kindly social worker whom she had always dealt with at the orphanage did keep her in touch, for a while. She was sent a photograph when Joanne was toddling, and another one when she was about six, and on that holiday in Pegwell Bay, standing in front of a big mock Viking ship. 'But then things changed. I think that lady left Barnado's, and their attitude changed. The next time I wrote, I was told they had lost touch with the family, who had moved, and they had no further information to give. I thought at the time it was a lie, and I didn't like the tone of the letter, which seemed to be saying I had no right to ask. I wrote again, but I always got an answer from the same matron. This time she said, "You don't seem to have understood what adoption means, Mrs Hayes." She said there was no point in my writing, and I had no right to information or contact of any kind. That was it. They denied they'd ever promised to keep me in touch. But they did at the time. I'd signed the papers, she always said, and that was final.'

But Rosie was never able to accept that final deed. She felt she had been cheated by Barnado's who had made verbal promises to her. She didn't expect to be allowed to see her child, but news and photos would have helped. Or perhaps they would simply have made it worse, some might say. Those who advocate the clean break might think it better for the natural mother to have as little as possible to dwell on. But even with nothing at all, it seems that these mothers continue to think of their missing child, and to feel its loss.

'When they brought in the new Act I was very excited. People were saying at the time that mothers must be protected against their children coming to find them. Protected? I thought about her all the time, and I waited for her to come knocking on my door. I thought any child of mine, any child of our family would naturally want to know. I thought she'd be born with the same family feeling we all have. My worst fears were that she mightn't want to know us. She'd find we were poor people, only living in a council house, and her perhaps very well off, and she'd not bother to come and see us.'

A now defunct tracing organization called Jigsaw was receiving some publicity at the time, and Rosie sent off her membership subscription straight away, hoping they would find Joanne for her. It was about this time that she took her trip to London, to attend a Jigsaw meeting, but she lost the address, and spent two days wandering the streets, lost. It was this trip that Judy talked about rather differently, describing her mother in a daze, looking for her among the eighteen-year-old girls in shops and in the streets. Perhaps Judy has invented a more romantic version, or perhaps that's what her mother told her.

'I did think of going back to Barnado's at Barkingside, and talking to them again. I wanted to confront them. They had promised to keep in touch with the family that had her. There might have been someone there who would have taken pity on me and given me a clue – but that matron put me off.'

It was then that she happened to read an article about John Stroud of the Hertfordshire Social Services, and he sounded so sympathetic and welcoming that she wrote to him. Because she was so old, and ill with angina, and plainly so desperate to find her child again before she died, he helped her. Because he was on the inside track, he managed to obtain information from Barnado's that they would never have given directly to Rosie – and so he found the last address but one of Judy's adoptive parents.

'We wrote those letters and sent them off to him, hoping against hope that Joanne would get them, and that she would want to know us. They were hard letters to write. What do you say after all those years? How can you say enough? And yet I didn't want to frighten her.'

Months later, due to a variety of delays, came the phone call from Judy. 'I always loved her. I never stopped loving her. I wanted her to know that she hadn't been given away because she wasn't loved. I wanted her to know not a day had gone by without my thinking of her. I wanted her to know how hard I looked for her. The twins missed her so much too. They used to say, when they looked at that photo taken at Pegwell Bay, "She doesn't look happy Mum, our sister. She looks as if she's nearly crying," and that would make them cry to think about when they were little girls.'

Now she has met Judy, indeed seen her several times, and had her to stay for a fortnight. She says, 'In some ways, it's as if the time between has fallen away. But I've missed her growing up. I'd like to have her here with me, and not in London – but she's got a husband.' She stopped and thought about her husband. 'He's a nice man, a good man, but, well, twenty-six years older. I'd say she was looking for a father in him. If I'd brought her up, she'd never had a father then, well, people would have put the blame on me, wouldn't they. They'd have said that was why she married a man so much older . . .'

Finding Judy has made her, if anything, more religious. 'I prayed. I committed the decision to give her up to God in the first place. He knows I didn't do it without a lot of thought and pain. He knew where the child had gone, even if I didn't. I was sure He would bring her back to me one day. Though often I used to pray "How long, Lord, how long?" Some people's lives are mapped out all wrong, and it's hard sometimes to know why. But finding my Joanne has shown me that God has forgiven me for what I did wrong. Joanne has accepted me, she loves me, and that's taken all my guilt away.'

5

Georgina

It was not quite an adoption, not in the formal sense. It was a strange situation, and exactly how it came about will never now be known for certain, either by Georgina or anyone else. The most likely version of the facts is that her father more or less stole her away from her mother, but when it happened, her mother was not devastated and may have felt it was a relief to have the child taken from her.

Her mother was a night club hostess and manageress, living in a flat above the club. Her husband was a man of a very different kind, a chief dental officer from Warrington, Cheshire. They met when he came into her club one night. He was, it turned out, a desperate alcoholic and the marriage did not last long. She had a child already, an older boy who was twelve when Georgina was born. The day of Georgina's birth, her father was drying out in a special clinic. He wrote a brief note to her mother suggesting Georgina be put up for adoption, but it didn't happen. The two children were looked after much of the time by their grandmother, since night club hours hardly fit easily with bringing up children.

Georgina thinks she can remember little scenes here and there of that life. 'My mother was bubbly, bright and smelled delicious. She did love me. I can remember it. I remember her feeding me with a spoon. She laughed and told me not to eat the spoon too.' Although she was only two and a half when her father came back and took her away, she can remember the event. He took her on a bus and a train, saying they were going on holiday. Her new parents collected them in what seemed to her like a huge black limousine. She wondered where her mother was, but she did not ask anyone. In fact she never asked again. Her mother stayed as an unspoken thought, never mentioned by anyone, a memory cherished in secret by a child who sensed that any questions or any indication that she remembered would be profoundly unwelcome in her new home.

Her father took her to the house of friends in Warrington, kindly generous people, the wife a dentist, the husband a vet. They had never had a child of their own, and longed for one. The father and daughter moved in with them, Georgina sleeping on a camp bed in his room for many years. But he was, irretrievably, a drunk. She remembers lying rigid in her bed as her father stumbled in every night, reeling, drunken. She remembers the piles of gin bottles in the bedroom, and to this day shudders at the smell of gin. Drunkenness is terrifying to children, particularly in their parents. A loved and wise figure of authority turns as if by some malevolent spell, into a montser, wild, unpredicatable, smelly, a parody of all they once were.

Early on, the couple tried to adopt Georgina, but her mother refused to allow them. But it does not seem that her mother made any real effort to get her child back. Although Georgina was taken from her mother, she was hardly a tug-of-love child. Her mother loved and wanted her enough to refuse to allow an official legal adoption, but not enough to fight to get her back, or even to ask for her back in a serious way. But then perhaps she knew that such a fight would be lost from the start. What court would award custody of a child to a rackety good-time girl in London in the face of the middle-class security of living with her father under the protection of a vet and a dentist? But perhaps she did not even want her child back. The couple later told Georgina that it was her mother who said she wanted them to adopt, but Georgina's aunt – her mother's sister – swears it was the other way round.

Apart from the fear and the anxiety he caused her, her father played little part in Georgina's life. Why did she sleep in his room? She is not sure but thinks it was her own choice. Some part of her felt safer with her natural parent, even though she remembers little love for him, and much fear. It seems an odd arrangement now. The couple became what Georgina now calls her 'step-parents'. To all intents and purposes, they were her new adoptive parents, and her father was an extra, hard to place but impossible to dismiss. They must have been extremely good people. It is one thing to take in a beautiful and delightful little girl to call your own, and quite another to take on responsibility for her drunken and difficult father. Yet it is likely that the transition from one life to another was much eased by Georgina's father staying with her. She was not dumped on strangers and left. Though she felt she was snatched from her mother, at least some shred of continuity remained. At least she always knew something about who she was, because she had a father, for better or worse.

Georgina was an exceptionally beautiful child. Today, in her thirties, she is a very beautiful woman, though oddly childlike in appearance and demeanour. Her face has been her fortune, and she is still a fashion model, her bony elegant body a long languid shape for hanging new clothes on. She was an enchanting child, a delight to her childless middle-aged adoptive parents.

When she was eight, two important things happened. First, her father died. She was told he died in an accident. Secretly she felt it was a relief. 'He was never, ever coming back again, no more drunken nights. I was glad. I don't think I felt anything more about him than that,' she says.

When she was grown-up she discovered that he had not been in an accident. He had hanged himself with his dressing-gown cord in a hotel in Jersey. He had lost his job as a chief dental officer, through drunkenness. He could not practise as a dentist as he suffered badly from psoriasis, and patients could hardly be expected to want to be touched and probed by scaly hands. He had no money left, not even to pay his hotel bill. 'That was why he killed himself. Over the bill,' Georgina says, shaking her head. But she says again, she was not sad at the time. 'Perhaps he might have been a good man, had it not been for his drink problem.'

She remembers his funeral, the chill and sombre sensations, the people dressed in black. 'As we came back through the door my mother turned to me – I mean of course my step-mother, or that's the name I gave her, though I called her Mummy. She turned and said, "Uncle Peter (her husband) is going to become your new daddy now. So you can call him daddy from now on." Georgina was shocked at the idea. She had a daddy of her own, the one they had just put into the ground in a box. Without thinking about it, but needing some answer to the problem, she just said, 'I'll call him Boom.' And Boom he remained. 'It was a name that came to my lips from nowhere, but I couldn't call him Daddy.'

All these years she had thought often and secretly about her mother. 'I always thought I'd see her one day. But some other part of me thought she had been killed in a car crash, and that is why they said nothing to me. I used to dream about her. I kept having one dream in particular. I was walking along a road holding my mother's hand. There was a man on a roof shooting at her, killing her.' That dream seems too apt to be sheer coincidence. Did the dream come later? Young children hear so much more than adults give them credit for – jumbled phrases, half heard whispers, fragments of adult conversation waft over them, and leave behind some clear impressions.

Perhaps some part of her eight-year-old consciousness knew but couldn't bear to know what had become of her mother. Her mother remained half fact, half fantasy, a blond woman, a loved woman, who might one day come and take her away – or who must really be dead, or why else had she not come for her already? She felt no resentment towards her, only love and some longing – all in secrecy. No one in the house, not her father, nor her adoptive parents, ever mentioned the word 'mother', ever talked of the past, or said a word of the half-brother Georgina clearly remembered from her infancy. No one said she was adopted – no one said why she was there, or where she was from.

She was eight when she went one day to her step-mother's underclothes drawer, a place she should not have been. A child's naturally prurient curiosity led her to look into the drawer, perhaps for no other reason than that it was a place of secrets, a place of unknowns, unmentionables of many kinds. Women keep things in that drawer, secret, hidden, because they think no one, not even a thief, will violate their secret place. Yet every burglar with an ounce of sense makes for that very drawer. He knows that is the place most women go first to hide their secrets, jewels, rings, letters, mysteries, tucked in amongst the bras and pants, the suspender belts, contraceptives and anything else not meant for public gaze. Children know that secret too. What child never looked in its mother's underclothes drawer?

In that drawer, among the underclothes and other things, Georgina found a secret that did not belong to her adoptive mother. She found her own secret, the answer to herself, and why her mother never came to take her away. She found a pile of yellowing newspaper cuttings, with photographs and graphic descriptions.

These cuttings told the story of Ruth Ellis, the last woman to be hanged in Britain, who went to the scaffold when Georgina was three and a half. Georgina's name was Ellis. Her new parents had not taken it away, and changed it for another. In the instant she saw the cuttings, she knew it was her mother. She recognized her dimly, a hazy picture, carefully cherished and embellished, for all those years. But it was her. This Ruth Ellis was her Ruth Ellis, her lost, and longed-for mother.

She sat there reading on the bedroom floor. With her eight-year-old reading ability, and her eight-year-old understanding of the world, she tried to take in what the world had done to her mother. 'When I saw the photographs of her face, I remembered the house where she lived, or part of it.' She felt, she says, just sadness. Poor woman, poor mother. She struggled through the difficult words. Gaol – that word made no sense. Nowadays they spell it jail, so much easier. She thought it had something to do with de Gaulle, a name she plucked out of the air, but she could make no connection. 'Murderess' was there, and 'Hanged'. The outline of the story imprinted itself on her mind. Her mother had taken a gun and shot her lover dead. Now they, the state, the jailers, had taken a rope and hanged her mother. She would never see her again. She had no mother. There was no one in the world for her except her adopted parents.

Something else fell into place, as she read the story, and gazed at the pictures. She recalled a scene when she was four, or nearly four, that was ingrained on her mind because she had been surprised at the sharpness and anxiety in her step-mother's voice at the time. She was going to a party, a small girl standing in her vest, waiting to get into her party dress for a birthday tea. Her hair was bound up tightly in rags, to make it curl. Outside in the street there was a car, or maybe more than one car, and a whole group of men. Some of them had cameras. She went to the window to stare out at this odd scene, and the cameras at once pointed up towards her. Her mother shouted at her to come back at once, stay away from the window, don't let anyone see you! She jumped back, surprised by the passion and vehemence of her mother's voice. Now she knew what it was. At the time she thought vaguely that she was not supposed to show her hair in curlers to the outside world. But now she knew that the photographers wanted a picture of the murderess's daughter. They had tracked her down, at the time of the hanging, and a mournful picture of the lost little girl would add to the human interest of a story already brimming over with human agony.

Did it change the course of Georgina's life? Hard to know, but reasonable to suppose it did. She tosses her long blond hair and shrugs. No, she does not think so. It was sad, but there it was. That was all there was to it. Nothing special. No trauma. She takes the world as it comes, looks after herself, is her own person, owes nothing to anyone, blames nothing on anyone. A free spirit, independent. That's how she says she sees herself and her life.

But if an eight-year-old can discover a monstrous secret like that, and it leaves her unscathed, then why do we bother to protect our children from anything? How much worse a discovery can a child make about her mother, and herself? She told no one for years that she had found out about it. She was too afraid of the trouble she would get into for having looked into that underclothes drawer to dare reveal her knowledge. The sexual taboo of looking in the drawer combined with the knowledge of her mother's crime, and the world's crime against her mother.

Georgina, of all the people I interviewed for this book, is the least willing to investigate her own feelings, or reach into the past and produce a portrait of herself and her feelings as a child. She resolutely insists that people are born the way they are. Their characters are unchanged by childhood experience. Whole personalities spring from the womb spontaneously, each different, each responsible only to itself. No cause and effect. No genes, even. Especially no genes.

All the other adopted and lost children I talked to greatly over-exaggerated the importance they attributed to genetic factors in their own characters. A musical talent from some grandparent, a gift with the hands from some great-uncle.

But not Georgina. She has inherited nothing, owes nothing, traces back nothing. Is that because it hurts too much to inherit from a hanged murderess?

She suffered for much of her childhood after that. She was persistently seriously ill with cystitis, a curious complaint for a child. She was never quite well, and often in excruciating pain. 'It clouded everything, everything I remember of my childhood,' she says. She thinks it possible that her illness might have had some connection with the thoughts and fears in her mind. She shrugs and says illness often comes from the mind – but she does not remember mental torment, only physical.

In her early teens, sent away to boarding school, she finally divulged her secret to her best friend, a dearly loved, entirely trusted friend, who immediately betrayed her. What child would keep a piece of gossip as juicy as that to themselves for long? Or what adult either? The whole school knew at once. 'It changed everything. Their attitude to me altered overnight. I was suddenly interesting, but not quite nice to know. I had always known that would happen. The reason that I never told anyone before was because I knew they would think badly of me. Being a murderess's daughter was no good at all.'

She became a difficult child after that, an impossibly rebellious adolescent. She deeply disappointed the high hopes of her adopted parents. They wanted her to become a doctor, but she wanted nothing more to do with school or education. All she wanted was a good time, money, boyfriends, cars, clothes – hardly the things she had been brought up to put first in life. Her adopted parents were quite old by then, in their late fifties, and their sympathy with this wild and wilful girl plunging headlong into the youth culture of the swinging sixties was stretched to breaking.

She is slow to admit it, but looking back, yes, she thinks the fact that everyone knew whose daughter she was coloured their view of her, made them quick to expect the worst. And perhaps it made her quick to behave worse, and to expect the low and the wicked in herself.

At thirteen or so, in a violent row with her adopted parents it came out. 'I bet my real mother would have let me!' she shouted, flailing around for a weapon with which to assault them, just like so many other adopted children at this age. It caused the required shock. Until then nothing had been said about who she was, or what her precise status was in the house. She loved these parents, is still close and fond of them, despite the bad times she put them through. Yet she lets slip that she never quite felt their house was her house, or perhaps not as other children do. She longed for a home of her own, as if she did not quite belong in the house where she was brought up.

After the subject was brutally broached, from time to time her step-mother would consent to saying a little about her mother. 'But I didn't like the things she said, or the way she said it. She said, "They say she was a prostitute but we don't really think it is true." The way they said it, it was clear what they thought. They never said anything at all good about her. It was always disapproval, and dislike. They gave me a book about her from the library, but it was horrible, making out that she was a terrible person. It was entirely unsympathetic, like them. I knew she was also good, or at least I didn't want or need to hear any of these bad things.'

When she was sixteen she packed her bags and ran away from home with a man. At seventeen she was married to him. She never visited or called home for a whole year, leaving her wretched parents to worry and fret about what had become of her.

With her spectacular looks, a face entirely attuned to the doll-like look of the late sixties, she had high hopes. She still looks like a child, talks like a child, with a light husky voice. She walked straight into a modelling agency and was hired at once. She had affairs with Richard Harris and George Best – both men famous for tempestuous scenes, trouble and problems. If she wasn't driven to act out something of her mother's catastrophic life, then the similarity is odd. 'I always knew what I wanted right from the start. I wanted London, glamour and modelling. I wanted fast cars, film stars, footballers, racing car drivers. I like that life. I knew it was for me, and it was no use my mother and father trying to stop me. I left home to get those things, and I got them.'

Now she is married for the third time. She has four children, ranging from twelve to two and she lives in a twenties semi-detatched house in a Manchester suburb. Her husband is struggling to set up his own small business, and she still does a little modelling in Manchester to make extra money.

Ten years ago a newspaper found her out, and wrote a lurid version of her story and her mother's. 'I was afraid that would do my modelling career harm. I thought that clients wouldn't want their products advertised by a face that was known for being a murderess's daughter.' But it didn't work out that way. In fact the story has brought her a great deal of publicity and interviews over the years since then.

Now she is writing her own life story. In the course of working on it, she is starting to trace her family's origins, and to find out more. Her aunt, her mother's sister, told her most of what she knows. Her grandmother is dead, though she remembers her from her infancy. 'I used to want to write to her sometimes, but my step-mother would try to put me off and say, "I shouldn't" or "I'd leave it for now". So I stopped.' Presumably this was because her adoptive parents feared the story of her mother's hanging would come out in such a correspondence.

She did find her half-brother. Or at least he found her. From her aunt she had heard a little about him. He was a severe depressive who had become addicted to his anti-depressants. She met him just once. 'He was a tramp,' she says with distaste. 'I had nothing whatever in common with him.' They sat and talked a little but said nothing of importance to one another. 'He said I had all Ruth's strength and he had all her weaknesses. But I don't believe any of that.'

Her brother killed himself two years ago. When she surveys her family now it is a bleak prospect. She has a hanged mother, a suicide father and a suicide brother. Also, her mother's youngest sister died shortly after the hanging, it was said, of a broken heart. Yet there stands Georgina, tall, beautiful, tough, determined. No one ever, she says, is going to shape her life. No one is going to control her, like her mother allowed her lover to dominate her life. 'There are a million men out there. No single one of them is going to matter that much to me. I wouldn't kill for love – it isn't that important.' She is the sole survivor of her tragic family and she fights like a survivor.

All that toughness took her through her childhood, and her turbulent adolescence. All that toughness seems to have drained other things out of her. She insists that she is ordinary, and unaffected by it all. It only leaks out in stray words and phrases that there might be other thoughts and feelings there too.

No, she says, she does not think that family matters at all. She surveys her own four children, and she doubts whether she has any impact whatever on their characters or temperaments. They are what they are. Children are not affected by their parents or their upbringing. Basically, she insists, they bring themselves up. 'I know exactly who I am. I don't need to know who my parents are or any of that.' And yet even as she says it, she begins to describe the exhaustive research that is going into her book, including digging out stories of her grandparents, aunts and others. Some of it matters a great deal to her, other parts of the story she has cut away from herself. From long training all those years, she tells herself that it does not matter at all who her mother was. It matters, yet it doesn't matter. It has shaped her life, or it has left her utterly untouched. The one message she gives out again and again is that she does not believe in inherited characteristics. I said how different she was from other adopted children I had talked to. Even when the knowledge about their true parentage was sad, unsatisfactory, inadequate, even when their mothers turned out to be nothing like the romantic pictures they had cherished throughout their childhood, these people still believed that somewhere there, somewhere in the depths and the recesses of their mothers was to be found the secret of their own personality, the answer to the question of their own identity. But not Georgina.

6

Tom O'Mara

Let no one doubt the desperate urgency some adopted and lost children feel in their search for their parents. It can become a grinding obsession, a full-time waking and sleeping need that drives them on beyond the limits of reason. It can leave their families puzzled, worried, and sometimes angry at this single-minded determination, which over-rides everything and everyone else.

Tom O'Mara always intended to set out to look for his mother, but the need did not take hold of him until he was in his forties, and very happily married with two children. Once he decided to embark on his search, then nothing on earth could hold him back. He worked at it in every spare moment, he thought about nothing else night and day. He spent all his spare money on it. Every rebuff, every set-back only spurred him on further. And when the final disaster struck and his mother refused to meet him, even that did not stop his determination to know his family. He laid siege to her. He contacted those around her, and he watched her secretly, unknown, unrecognized. He began to lay siege to his half-brother too, and he turned in search of his father at the same time.

Tom lives with his family in a small house he owns himself in an outer London suburb. He works as a bank clerk, and wishes he had a better education. In his front room he keeps a large pile of books and folders in which he has chronicled every part of his search for his family. He has carefully preserved every scrap of paper, copies of every letter he has written and received, photographs, odds and ends of every sort that bind him to the family he has never met.

He has also kept long rambling diaries. 'I had to write everything down. It helped me to sort out my thoughts, and to come to terms with what was happening to me. I had to keep writing, to get it out of my system. Sometimes I stayed up late at night, writing and writing.' The day I first met him, he was about to set off to the south coast to meet a man who had taught in the same school as his half-brother once, and who might have an old photograph of him, or a story or two to tell. He might even have a lead which would take him to his half-brother himself. It was a long-shot, but then the whole story has been one long succession of chasing hares and disappearing down fox-holes that lead nowhere. He has become quite used to that.

His wife Barbara is tolerant. She supported him wholeheartedly until the time when he finally found his mother, and she refused to see him. 'I thought that should be the end of it. I cannot understand the woman. She must be a terrible person, not a mother at all. I wanted him to give up then. But it went on and on. It is getting a bit better now. He isn't spending quite as much time as he did on it.' All the same, for a trail that has reached a dead end he is still persistently following it – though he knows now it can never bring to him the thing he most wants, his mother.

Tom was born in 1939, son of an Irish girl, Edna O'Mara, living in Folkestone, working as a domestic servant. His father was an Irishman from the same village, working as a farm labourer outside Folkestone and living in a boarding house. The couple had been 'walking out' for four years, when Edna became pregnant. Thomas, her lover, denied paternity, and disappeared rapidly. Edna was referred to a Catholic adoption society which also ran an orphanage. When the baby was born, he was fostered out for his first two years to a Folkestone couple, and Edna did occasionally visit him. The baby's god mother was the society's social worker. After that, as was their practice, the orphanage reclaimed him and took him into their all-boys institution in London.

It is not clear from the letters and records why he was not put up for adoption. Occasionally the society suggested that Edna sign the papers, but they never pressed the point. Indeed they said there was very little chance of boys finding a home. Adopters wanted girls. Edna kept in touch with the society, though not with Tom. She was required to make payments first to the foster mother, and then to the orphanage. He says the files show the letters she wrote begging to be allowed to pay less, or nothing. She fell a year behind with the payments. Even if she had wanted to keep in touch with her child, the society made it difficult, by moving him from place to place, first to Rugby, and a large orphanage there, and then evacuating him to a huge institution in Devon. She was working for the NAAFI in Kettering.

> Dear Father,
>
> I cannot pay. May God protect him and keep him safe, and I am so glad little Tom is safe and happy, and so grateful to the society. But it is impossible for me to pay 5 shillings a week when I am only paid 10 shillings. I am hoping you will find someone to adopt him, and I am looking myself for someone too, a good catholic family of course.

There were many letters in the file in that vein, until one came announcing that she intended to get married, and could no longer pay, because her fiancé knew nothing of the baby's existence. The social worker at the society and the Father wrote back a wise and kindly letter. 'We feel it would be a big mistake not to tell your fiancé about Thomas. Many men do decide to adopt a child when they hear that there is one . . . The weight of the secret can tell as the years go on . . . It may come out in some unfortunate way, and the shock would be worse . . . However, he is a very nice little boy, and I hope that we shall not have too much difficulty in getting him adopted.'

She wrote back, 'I'm sorry, Father, but I am a coward. I could never tell him. I would rather remain single then tell him about Thomas. He is becoming a Catholic now. It would be very hard for me to give him up, for I love him dearly. I will do everything in my power to help your Catholic society.'

The priest agreed to release her from all obligations to pay any more towards Thomas's upkeep, on the condition that she was married in the Catholic Church. After that, she lost touch with the society. She made no further inquiries about her son, and she left no forwarding address. As Tom sees it, 'I was just left there like so much left luggage, and she never bothered to find out what happened to me once she was married.'

Nothing more happened about an adoption. In the files Tom says there is an exchange of letters that suggests a South African couple showed interest, but before they saw him, they saw another little boy, and took him instead. There is no further suggestion that the society made any effort on his behalf, either to have him adopted or fostered, or to keep in touch with his mother. He was simply dropped into their pool of 200 boys of assorted ages and sizes, a great anonymous cluster of orphans, and forgotten about.

The orphanage was run by nuns, and the children were taught on the premises, so they had very little contact with the outside world. 'We were kept clean, fed, and in order. That was about it, the basic minimum, no real care and absolutely no love. I was lucky as I was very small for my age, so I was petted by the bigger boys, and even a bit by the nuns. I was good at making friends. There was a lot of bullying, and the boys were allowed to get on with running things. The nuns didn't want to know about what was going on. But I seem to have been protected because they liked me, and I was so tiny.'

He is still a small, elfin-faced man, thin and boyish, with great charm, almost as if a part of him has never quite grown up. It is easy to imagine him as a vulnerable child whose charm and quick wits saved him from the torment so many of the other children there were put through. Unhappy, lonely, isolated children make the worst bullies, and orphanages like these became tough little *Lord of the Flies* communities, unsupervised by adults, unhumanized by loving parents.

They were all dressed identically, in grey flannel shorts, grey shirts, grey socks and boots made to last with horse shoe studs. In the summer they wore khaki shorts and sandals. They slept in dormitories with thirty beds. 'We had a small locker between each bed where you could keep your "crodge" – that's what we called our few personal belongings.' The building, he remembers, was huge, with great Victorian spires and crenellations. It has long since been demolished. 'We all had to work hard at cleaning jobs around the place. I got the easy job, looking after the sacristy – a very cushy number.'

It was, he says, a regime of fear. The older boys systematically beat the younger and weaker ones with cricket stumps. 'The more you yelled the harder you were hit, and the nuns would pretend to know nothing. I used to get my ears whacked, a bit boy slamming both ears hard, cracking my head in a kind of sandwich. My hearing's not too good now, and I often think it's because of that repeated bashing of the ears.'

At thirteen they were sent out to the local school, for their two last years of education. 'If anything we used to see ourselves as privileged at school. At least, we ran the place, because we stood together in a group against all the others, and we protected each other at school. We thought they were namby-pambies who had been molly-coddled by their parents. Also, it was a very poor area, and we were mostly better dressed and fed than they were.' But they ended up with very little education. 'We could barely read and write when we left school at fifteen. We were no use for anything much. But although I was hopeless, I decided I wanted to work in an office.'

When he was demobbed from the RAF he went back to live with the Reillys, and found himself a job first as a trainee supermarket manager, then as a sales rep for an engineering firm. When he married Barbara, he took a job in the bank where he still works, so as to qualify for a cheap mortgage.

'All this time I always thought of my mother. Often, in the orphanage, when the lads came of age and it was time for them to leave, their mothers would surface and take them home. That made some boys bitter, as they thought their mothers only wanted them now they could earn money. We all thought we'd earn big money once we got out into the world. We didn't realize what low wages we'd be getting. Thinking about it now, I think a lot of mothers came to collect their boys because they literally couldn't support them until they could earn. I doubt if they were after their money at all.' If his mother had turned up to take him away at fifteen, he would have been delighted. He waited and hoped for a message from her, but none came.

'From time to time I would try to get information about my mother from the nuns. But they always fobbed us off. I doubt if they knew anything at all about us as individuals. The society would have had our files, but the nuns would have had nothing to do with that side of things. Maybe the Mother Superior had a little sketchy knowledge about each of us, but if so, she wasn't letting on.' The nuns did not like the children to make inquiries. They had their own answer, firmly handed out, which was supposed to solve each child's problem with his identity. 'You are special children,' they used to say. 'You are especially lucky and blessed as your mother is in heaven. Our Lord's mother takes special care of orphans, and you are to think of Her as your mother.'

Some children assumed from this that their mothers were

dead. Others knew very well where their mothers were, as they had kept in touch. But most were in Tom's position – free to fantasize about their real mother who would one day come and take them away from this desolate orphanage. 'I knew my mother must be alive. To me she was young, beautiful, glamorous and loving.'

When he left the orphanage, he had a final interview with the priest in charge of the society. 'He had a file on his desk full of things I wanted to know, but he was certainly not going to show it to me. It made me angry and bitter. I needed to know all there was to know. All he gave me was a little vague information. He said my mother couldn't keep me and wanted to have me adopted.'

The society operated a fostering system for children setting out in the world. A Catholic family was found who would take him in as a paying guest, and keep an eye on him. 'They were nice people, the Reillys, but they were very intellectual and I wished I fitted in more. I was jealous of their son, who was good at everything, scholarships to Oxford, Oriel College, for instance. The mother said just call out like the rest, but she never told me what to call her – Mum or Auntie, or whatever, so I never called her anything.' He discovered that his tiny wage at the office where he was found work as a messenger boy was not covering the cost of his keep. The society was subsidizing the Reillys. 'That really upset me. I thought I was a grown-up independent person, earning my own living, but I found I wasn't.' It spurred him on to get a better-paid job so he could pay them more.

He grew up deeply ashamed of his origins, of having no roots. 'When other people talked about their mum and dad, I just said mine were dead. I didn't want anyone to know I came from an orphanage. It was shaming, and I didn't want their pity.' He went into the RAF for national service, where he only told one close friend about his background. 'I didn't want to tell him, but he cornered me by pointing out that I'd never said a word about my family. I made him promise not to tell anyone else.' Everyone got letters, except him, and he never received a single one from anybody, a fact he tried to hide. 'I didn't want to be thought different in any way.'

The 1975 Children's Act did not affect Tom in a strictly legal sense. He was not adopted. His name was his own, and his birth certificate had never been changed. He did once, when he was on leave in the RAF, make a half-hearted attempt to find his mother. He went down to Folkestone, to the address his mother had put on his birth certificate. He had her name, but no one at the house had ever heard of her. It was all nearly twenty years ago, and she had long since moved on, leaving not a trace behind. At that time he gave up, but still strongly believed that one day he would find her, and a great reunion would take place, to their mutual joy. 'All my life my mother has never been far from my thoughts.'

It was later in his life that a series of events made him decide to go out on a more serious search for his mother. If it began as a rational decision, it was soon to become a consuming obsession.

'I was transferred to head office, with much easier working hours. I was earning more money. My son had been born five months earlier with coeliac disease – an allergy to wheat and cereals, of which he nearly died. I had just fallen ill, and was diagnosed as having the same illness. It is hereditary, and I wondered if my mother suffered from it too. I had a lucrative evening job, selling replacement windows, so we were feeling quite well off. At about this time I had to go and get myself a copy of my birth certificate from St Catherine's House for something I was applying for. All the family came too, as we all thought we'd look ourselves up, and find our own records, which was great fun.' Here the fun stopped. Gazing down at his birth certificate, the mysterious unknown name of his mother written there, the address where no one knew her, he was seized by a desperate desire to know, at all costs, who he really was.

He had once, at about the time he had gone to that

address, written again to the society to try to prise more information out of them. He had nothing but a brief reply of a vague kind, mentioning her marriage to a soldier and the fact that she was last known to have been working in the NAAFI in Kettering. The tone of the letter was perfunctory and abrupt, implying that it was an impertinence and an intrusion for an abandoned child to attempt to contact the mother who had given him away. That was the general attitude before the passing of the 1975 Act. Children had no right to know and absolutely no right to intrude upon their mothers' privacy. Although Tom was not directly affected by the change in the law, as he was not adopted, in fact he, and many others like him, found a great change in official attitudes towards them, once the Act was passed.

He now began his search in earnest by contacting the society again – and this time the doors and the files were opened at once to him. Not only that, but he was welcomed, helped and encouraged. They kept in touch with his quest, and aided him at every point they could.

He was systematic in his approach, as minutely chronicled in the logs and diaries he kept. He went back to St Catherine's House and searched until he found his mother's marriage certificate. He knew her name, and more or less when she would have married, from the letters in his file at the society. It was a lengthy process, and he snatched half-hours amongst the ledgers in his lunch hour each day. Once he had her husband's name, he went to the War Office records where he found the man, Alfred Carson, had survived the war, and a demob address was given, in Nottingham.

That was thirty years ago, and following their trail was hard. A letter sent to the Nottingham address came back 'unknown'. He went up to Nottingham to look in the electoral register. Then he wrote again to the occupiers of the houses enclosing a £5 note for their trouble, explaining why he was looking urgently for Mr and Mrs Carson, who had lived there in 1949. Would they kindly examine their deeds and see who were the previous owners from whom they had bought the house, and what their subsequent addess was, at the time of the final signing of contracts.

He was lucky, as the address was there, and it was back in Folkestone. The Carsons had returned to the place where he was born, and where his mother had been working as a domestic servant. He checked the electoral register in Folkestone and found they were still there.

First he went for advice to the social worker at the society, who warned him to go carefully, since his mother might not be prepared for the shock.

Although impatient to rush to his mother at once, he decided to take the precaution of doing a certain amount of research. He traced Mr Carson in Folkestone, and discovered he worked as a departmental manager in a big department store. He decided to call on his mother while her husband would be out at work, to make sure there could be no question of embarrassing her.

He decided to go with a friend of his wife's who had a small baby. For some reason he thought the sight of a tiny baby would melt her heart. They parked the car a little way down the road from the bungalow in Folkestone. His friend stepped out and went up to the door, carrying her baby in her arms. Tantalizingly, Tom could not see much from where he sat hidden in the car. When the door opened, he glimpsed no more than his mother's forearm.

'Mrs Carson?' said his friend.

'Yes?' said his mother.

'I'd like to talk to you on a personal matter.'

At this his mother sighed and passed her hand across her face. Where most people might express shock or surprise at such a request from a perfect stranger, Mrs Carson seemed to know already what this was about. It was the knock on the door she had awaited and dreaded for forty years, ever since her marriage. It was the knock on the door that she always thought would come, her heart full of Catholic guilt. Her dark pigeon had come home to roost.

'Oh dear. It's not at all convenient to talk at present,' she said, turning to look furtively over her shoulder.

'That's quite all right. I'll call back later,' said Tom's friend, with some firmness.

'What's it all about?' asked Mrs Carson, too late, for by now it was clear that she knew all too well. Indeed, she proved it by stepping out and half closing the door behind her.

'You have a son called Tom who wants to see you,' she said, shifting the baby on her arm, to emphasize the point.

'I can't! I couldn't possibly. Tell him not to come here! I've a family of my own now, and they don't know. I couldn't possibly tell them. Tell him it would ruin my life!' She scuttled back into the house and shut the door.

Tom's friend returned slowly to the car, wondering how to tell him. 'She thought I would be devastated, but I told her it was all right. I had been half expecting it really, underneath, no matter what I hoped.'

He asked his friend to describe in detail everything she had seen inside the house, from the doorstep. She told of pictures of priests and nuns and saints, lots of them, and one particular priest in white, whom she assumed to be the Pope. This gave him a clue he needed. Perhaps the Church would force her hand and provide him with a way into her life. He asked the priest at the society, now a Monsignor, to act as intermediary on his behalf. But the priest was considerably less moved by the spirit of the new Act than the social worker at the society who had been so helpful. He dragged his heels, reluctant to disturb this woman's peace of mind. Finally he was induced to write a letter to Mrs Carson's parish priest, who was asked to deliver to her a letter in person, at some time when her husband was out. The letter warned that if she absolutely refused to meet her son, there was a serious danger that he might just turn up himself on her doorstep one day, so desperate was his need for a meeting with her. This letter produced nothing. Perhaps the parish priest was timid. Perhaps he just handed it to her and hurried away.

Here the splendid social worker from the society decided to intervene on Tom's behalf. He could see how desperate Tom was, and he knew from previous experience that mothers often need some strong persuasion, but are usually delighted once they have overcome the first shock of the encounter.

Mrs Carson agreed to meet the social worker away from her home on the condition this meant no obligation to see Tom. She chose the house of a friend, her old employer from the days when she was in service and she became pregnant. The interview was painful and difficult, and the social worker had to report sadly to Tom that he felt he had made very little progress.

Tom drained him of every scrap of information, every impression, every shred of a nuance in his mother's words. Each step nearer seemed to draw out of him a greater need to know her.

'As the social worker described her, she was a woman full of self-pity. She talked of the hard life she had had. She had one son. She had actually named him Thomas. Isn't that an extraordinary thing to do? Especially as I was named after my father. She has two sons named Thomas! She thought she could wipe me out of her mind, wipe me out of existence by giving my name to him. She performed a mental abortion on me, and gave everything to my brother – everything, even my name. She said she had made great sacrifices for her Thomas, and he had gone to university and become a teacher, and she was very proud of him. She said I was well cared for, well fed and well brought up in my orphanage, and I was the lucky one, not her. She had been in love with her husband when she married, but he turned out to be a man of intolerant and rigid views, who had made her life a misery. If it hadn't been for her religion, she would have left him long, long ago.'

At this difficult interview, she talked most of the time about herself, trying to explain why it would be quite impossible for her ever to meet Tom. She showed very little curiosity about him, or compassion for him. The social worker told her that he was happily married with two beautiful children, a charming and good man, who only wanted to meet his mother, not to cause her any suffering. He had no thoughts of recrimination, only a wish to know her. 'If he's as good as you say,' she said, 'then tell him not to force this meeting. If he goes ahead, tell him I might be forced to do something silly. I can never, ever see him. I have nothing to offer him. Tell him I'm glad everything worked out so well for him, and I only wish it had for me.' Nothing would move her.

This was the point at which his friends and his family, especially his wife, thought he should give up. Maybe his mother would change her mind one day. Maybe her circumstances would change. But there seemed to them nothing more that could be done. His great search had reached its end – a blank refusal. Barbara had supported him keenly until now. From here on, she became dismayed when she found his passion for more knowledge quite unabated.

First, he wrote to his mother, sending the letter to the social worker for forwarding.

'My Dear Mother,' he began boldly. 'The social worker has told me of your determination not to meet me. But it is a desire I have had over all the conscious years of my life. I am sorry to hear news of all the hard years you had because of me, and I am sorry that your attempt to clutch at a chance of happiness did not work out well. I can well imagine how it was, a girl in the uncertain years of the war, hoping for a better life, withholding from her fiancé the knowledge of her child. I am sorry you do not enjoy the best of health, and I am conscious of the emotion this letter may carry. I have three requests that are most important to me. I would like three photographs, one of you at the time of your marriage, one of your family, and one of you now. I promise to return them, but seeing them is very vital to me.' He outlined his own and his son's medical condition and asked if perhaps she had the same problem, but it might be as yet undiagnosed by the doctors. It is a disease, he said, especially prevalent amongst the Irish. He enclosed photos of his wife and children but not of himself, hoping that curiosity would get the better of her.

He describes this letter to his mother with a wry smile. 'It was a carefully calculated letter, not exactly written from the heart. If she was a self-pitying woman, then perhaps she'd like a letter full of sympathy for her. She would certainly not like a letter that described my own hard childhood, or anything like that.'

His mother did not reply to him directly. 'She has never written to me. She sends me messages via others. I think part of the reason is that she cannot bear to address me, either as Dear Son or as Dear Thomas, since she has another Thomas already.' His mother wrote back to the social worker.

'Thank you for the letter,' she wrote. 'I was glad at our meeting that you did not talk down to me. Tom seems set on meeting me, but he has no consideration at all for my feelings, for my age, or for how upset and strained I feel. He must have a greater consideration for my emotional state. I cannot contact him direct. I thank him for the photos he sent of his children, and I am pleased to hear his son has made a full recovery. About his concern for my health, I can say it is due to all the hard work and the worry I have had over the years. I have a very kind, good, understanding doctor, I thank God.

'I know Tom is aware that forty years ago I was involved with a real rotter, I would not insult Tom with his name. In any case, he is long since dead. I have worked really hard keeping body and soul together since we came here. If Tom feels he has been deprived in life, then so have I.'

She went on to say that with the kind help of a non-Catholic she had acquired the bunaglow where she and her husband live on a meagre pension, since he had taken early retirement due to poor health. She had lost her mother and her father during the war within a year of each other, which had been a great blow to her. She claimed to have few members of her family living, and they were scattered about Ireland, but she did not say where.

'I only hope that Tom will respect my wish not to see him. I cannot understand what he wants from me.' She ended, 'What he does after I depart this life is his business. I hope he will not judge me harshly, but it is only the judgement on the Last Day that counts. If I was younger, perhaps I would cope better. If and when I ever get a chance, then perhaps one day we might meet.' She enclosed a photograph of herself, showing a good-looking woman in her sixties, quite well dressed in a red cardigan, and neatly coiffed hair, sitting in a garden.

Tom was determined to see her. He set off down to Folkestone and lay in wait outside her house on a Sunday morning. He was lucky that Mr and Mrs Carson went to church at different times. He watched as she came out of the house. 'She passed me in the street, she looked at me for a moment. She did not recognize me at all.' He followed her to church. 'I was surprised at how agile she was. She tore along, very sprightly for someone with all the ill health she claimed.' He talks of this first sighting of her with such a curious mixture of emotions that is hard to know quite what he felt.

How did she look to him? 'Not at all attractive. Not as nice as in the photo she had sent. She did look as if she had had a very hard life. She looked quite battered by it. She looked like the stereo-type cleaning woman, in a loose coat, her skinny legs in horrible bootee things. She had a head scarf on like the poor Irish often wear. Only the aristocrats and the poor wear scarves. She had a small face, sunken eyes, and sharp features.' Was all this a disappointment? 'It was a most wonderful feeling. I sat there in the church, only one place away from her. I couldn't take my eyes off her, through the whole service. I gazed at her, and I just couldn't look away for a moment. I was drawn to her. I felt so very close to her. It was a tremendous thrill. My mother! I felt it in every bone of my body. I think I would have known it was her, as I felt such a strong affinity.' He paused and shook his head sadly. 'It's very hard to describe the feeling, but it was very strong indeed.'

He went back six, seven or more times, and waited and watched, often accompanying her secretly to church. He laid siege to her – 'Like a lover,' he says, still perplexed at the intensity of his own feelings, and bewildered as to their mysterious source. 'I know what kind of person she is, and I do not like her. She is selfish, self-centred, weak-willed and unloving. But there it is. She is also my mother. He is like a man caught in some cruel enchantment.

Suddenly one day to his horror, a For Sale board appeared outside the Carsons' house. He hurried to the estate agents to inquire. He found his mother owned the house herself, and it did not belong, as she had claimed, to her old employer. He discovered that her doctor had advised a change and he surmised his own arrival on the scene had a lot to do with it. He happened to be there watching her the day she moved out, and he saw the pantechnicons come and go. She left no forwarding address with anyone, not with the neighbours or with the priest, nor with the estate agents. She had lived there forty-five years, and simply uprooted and vanished. Her friends and neighbours were astonished. Tom was appalled. 'She had promised to let the social worker at the society know if she ever changed her address, but of course she didn't. I think she may have been about to move anyway, but she certainly speeded up her plans once I arrived in her life.' Had she perhaps realized she was being watched by him? Had it terrified her? He is sure she never knew. At least she showed not the slightest recognition of the man loitering around at the margins of her life.

Something someone said led him to think she had returned to Ireland, probably to the area of her birth and childhood. He went all the way over to Dublin himself to seek for her birth certificate there in the Customs House where all Irish records are kept. It was a lengthy process but he found it, eventually, with the village she came from clearly stated in the address. He took a bus out to the village, fifty miles from Dublin, and walked around, looking for a sign of people newly moved in. 'I hadn't very long to look since there was only one bus back a day. I happened to walk in the wrong direction. Just as the bus was coming into sight I stepped into the post office in the village and made inquiries there for the Carsons. Yes, the post mistress said. The Carsons were just moving into a new bunaglow they had built at the other end of the village. Who should she say called? He gave his name as Reilly, and jumped on the bus, hoping his mother would guess he had been there and found her.

He felt some satisfaction in letting her know that she had not evaded him, and she never would. He took a malicious pleasure in knowing how unnerved she would be to find herself followed all the way to Ireland where she thought she was safe. While he was looking in the Dublin records office, he had checked on her family too, and knew all their names and ages, and that they were very much alive and still living in the same village. She would be terrified that she had come so close to having her secret disclosed here, right on her family's doorstep.

He now turned his attention to other members of his family. First, he wanted to know his brother, Thomas. He was keenly jealous. This brother of his, this usurper, had taken his own name, his mother's love, and money and energy. He had had the best education, the best opportunities, a family, everything that he Tom had been denied. And yet, in his mind's eye, he also pictured his brother and himself as the best of friends, long-lost siblings.

The Carsons' parish priest let slip to Tom that his brother Thomas taught in a school near Folkestone, a boys' private school. He telephoned all the private schools in the area, asking if a Thomas Carson taught there. 'I wanted a verbal description of him. I had no idea what he looked like. Then I wanted to see him for myself.' Finally, he reached the right school. Yes, they had a Thomas Carson on the staff. Tom pretended to the school secretary that he was an old university friend trying to trace him. 'Could you tell me what he looks like?' he asked. 'I want to be sure this is the same Thomas Carson that I once knew.' The secretary obliged with a description – tall, dark hair, a receding hair line, wears glasses.

Tom decided to go down to the school and try to get a look at his half-brother. 'It was surprisingly easy to get in. I posed as a prospective parent, and I was given a prospectus for the school. I checked his qualifications by going through the prospectus which lists the staff and their degrees. I found he had an MA from Worcester College, Oxford, in Physics and Chemistry. I went to a reference library and checked the year he got his degree in an Oxford year book. Then I wrote to Worcester and asked for a photograph of him, giving the years he was there. But the college secretary said he was too busy to dig it out, so that got me nowhere.' He discovered the school had a fete in July, and went back there to try to catch a glimpse of his brother. 'I got there but he had left early. I asked someone to point Mr Carson out to me. They said he had just this minute left, so I never saw him.'

He kept tabs on his brother, by telephoning the school in holiday times when he knew he wouldn't be there, to check he was still on the staff. He longed to write to him or to confront him, but he felt duty-bound to honour his mother's wish that he should not tell anyone in his family about his existence. 'She's a very lucky woman that her son is such a decent, honourable man,' Barbara, Tom's wife, points out, and of course she is quite right. Many an adopted child, maddened and enraged by a second rejection, might choose to intrude upon their mother's family, out of sheer revenge. But not Tom. 'There were times when I really wanted to. But since she had begged me not to, I felt I couldn't. I had to keep saying to myself, "What am I doing all this for?" I had to keep my eye on my true goal – and that was to meet and make friends with my mother. Sabotaging her life would not bring that about.'

Then suddenly, his brother's prep school folded and closed down. But just before that happened, a friend of Tom's who could bear the suspense no longer, confronted Tom's brother one day, and told him the story. 'This friend of mine saw that I was morally bound not to contact my brother, but he didn't think himself bound by the same constraints. So on my behalf, he appealed to my brother to meet me. He knew how very much I wanted to meet him.' His brother, not surprisingly, expressed shock and amazement to hear he had an older brother brought up in an orphanage. He said he needed time to think about it. He said he would certainly not discuss it with his parents, and most definitely not with his father. He promised to keep in touch. But then he disappeared, and neither Tom nor his friend ever heard from him.

Tom wrote to his brother care of the ex-headmaster of the defunct prep school, whose new teaching post he had found. The ex-headmaster forwarded the letter to Thomas's mother in Ireland. Tom had cautiously signed the letter Tom Reilly. If anyone read the name O'Mara in that village, his mother's secret would be out. The letter was returned to the ex-headmaster promptly with a brief note saying that Thomas Carson's whereabouts could not be revealed. He was seeking a new teaching post, and no more details would be forthcoming. The scrap of paper containing those few curt words was signed by S. Phillips. But Tom was not fooled. He immediately recognized his mother's handwriting. Of course she had guessed that this Tom Reilly was her son Tom O'Mara, and she would not reveal to him her younger son Thomas's address. Tom continues his search for his half-brother, but cannot think quite how to proceed. He must be teaching somewhere in England. Tom's persistent detective techniques will do doubt discover his brother's whereabouts before long. Though if his brother will not see him, it is not clear quite why it is so important to find him.

Having been rejected by both his mother and his brother, Tom now turned his attentions to his father. The original letters and documents in the file of the society had required Edna O'Mara to reveal the details of the child's father. His name was written down there as Thomas Flanagan. Tom had not bothered before to try to trace his father, as his mother had stated so plainly in her letter that he was dead. Nevertheless, Tom decided he would like to know about his father, even if he was dead. He wanted to know if he had married, in which case perhaps he could find some half-brothers and sisters – a thought that filled him with hope.

He knew his father was Irish, so that meant another trip to the Customs House, Dublin, to look in the records. He found his name and address there. Then he went to an archivist in Folkestone to look for any sign on the electoral register for him. No luck. He went to St Catherine's House to search endlessly for a Thomas Flanagan who had died sometime in the last twenty or so years. It was a long exhausting job, with so many Thomas Flanagans, and no date of death. Eventually he found one that looked right. A Thomas Flanagan who had died recently, had been a farm labourer, and had been single at the time of Tom's birth. He died, though, in Newcastle. He checked back for a marriage certificate. Yes, he had been married, and he had a daughter. Addresses were there on the marriage, birth and death certificates that would surely lead him to his father's family.

He followed through inquiries about his half-sister. He found her marriage certificate, and hence her address. He even found the birth certificates of her children. He decided to approach her. He wrote her a long letter explaining the whole story. He said he was almost certain that his father was also her father, and they were half-brother and sister. To his delight, she telephoned him at once. 'She was the most warm, and helpful person. She was as delighted as I was at finding a new brother. We talked and talked. Of course she said she could not imagine her father doing such a terrible thing as to get a long-standing girl-friend pregnant, and then disappear. Also she said she knew nothing at all about his ever having lived on the south coast. He had only ever talked to them about Ireland and Newcastle.'

The friendship developed rapidly. His half-sister came down to visit them in London, and Tom took his family and hurried up north to see them. He gleaned everything he could about her father, every story, every part of his history and character.

Eventually, his new sister dared to mention the whole thing to her mother. 'Of course her mother was deeply shocked, and very angry at the suggestion. She said she knew for certain her dead husband could not be my father. He was just not that sort of man. Also she was certain he had never been to the south coast. She refused point blank to meet me, and said she never ever would, as she didn't believe I had any place in her family. I wanted to know more about her husband, my father, but she wouldn't see me.'

His investigations into every aspect of his family continued. In the course of yet another visit to the Customs House, Dublin, he came upon another Thomas Flanagan. A Thomas Flanagan who was born in the very same village as his mother, Edna O'Mara, and a Thomas Flanagan who was still very much alive. This gave him a severe jolt. He realized that this must be his real father. It all made considerably more sense. His mother had only told him that his father was dead to put Tom off the trail, or perhaps because she wished him dead. It did seem odd that his mother should have returned to that small village with her husband, knowing that her ex-lover still lived there. The danger of revelation was great – and yet it seemed that she had indeed done so. The draw of returning to the place of her birth had overridden whatever fears she might have had at meeting Thomas Flanagan again.

Now Tom was faced with the great embarrassment of telling the Flanagan family in Newcastle that he had made a serious error. By the time he could contact them again Mrs Flanagan had just died. He fears that his false revelation about her late husband may have hastened her end. However, her daughter was as friendly and forgiving as ever. She was deeply disappointed that Tom was not, after all, her long-lost brother, but they have, despite everything, remained good friends, and she follows the further progress of his investigations with interest. This episode, though, is a sobering example of the dangers to families everywhere from the haphazard searchings of lost children, longing to pin their paternity on anyone who might reasonably fit the bill. He feels great guilt about Mrs Flanagan and the pain and anger he caused her, and promises that in future he will always proceed with more caution.

In a fit of anger at finding his mother had lied to him about his father's death he looked about for someone else to act as an advocate on his behalf with his mother. Or that was his ostensible purpose. Probably there was a desire to let her friends know how badly he felt she had treated him. She had promised not to lose touch. She had even hinted at the end of her last letter that maybe one day they would meet. Then she had flitted away, escaped, hared off without a word to anyone. How dare she do this to him! He who asked for nothing more in the world than a mother. Now his feeling became mixed with anger and resentment. Half of him loved her, the other half longed for revenge.

He wrote to his mother's old friend and employer in Folkestone, Mrs Forbes, to whose house all letters from the society and the priest had been addressed, to avoid her husband finding them. This old friend was probably the only person in his mother's life who had ever known of Tom's birth, since Edna had been in her employ at the time. Tom wrote to Mrs Forbes begging for her intercession on his behalf. But it was an angry letter too.

He wrote at length. He called it 'obscene for a mother to reject her child'. He regretted having been bound not to approach her family, or reveal her secret. 'I have a brother, and I have a right to know him.' He told her the tale of the disastrous encounter with the Newcastle Flanagans. He accused his mother of lying to him, and laid the blame for that misadventure at her door. 'My mother is your friend, and I lost her for forty years. As soon as I found her, she ran away. She is my own flesh and blood. So is my father, who I am determined to meet. I wish to find my roots.'

He intended now to frighten his mother. 'I expect no truth any longer from my mother, after she wrongly told me that my father was dead. I am anxious to know my father, but anxious too not to make the same mistake again. I believe he is living in his old village of Tregarn, and unless I hear from my mother or yourself, I intend to go there and find him.' He knew that the threat of arriving in Tregarn, asking for his father, would cause panic. He did not reveal in the letter that he already knew that his mother was living there too. But they would guess. 'Only the truth about him will prevent me crashing into other people's families. I shall go to Tregarn unless I hear from you shortly.'

This was the angriest letter he had written. He did not like the tone of the letter he received from Mrs Forbes, and it did not answer any of his points. She had not apparently passed his letter on to his mother, and she said nothing much about his father's whereabouts.

'Dear Mr Flanagan,' Mrs Forbes wrote, 'Let me put the

facts to you as they are known to me. Your mother's conception was a great medical rarity. She was virgo intacta at the time of your birth, a very rare and unfortunate event.' Tom does not believe this, nor does the idea of his mother's immaculate conception matter to him at all. 'She was very young and green at the time. She had been courting her boyfriend for a long time. She was under nineteen when you were born. There she was, very young, with no money and no home. She couldn't possibly have gone home to Ireland.

'Your father behaved disgracefully. He ceased seeing her as soon as she told him of her pregnancy. He was no good and irresponsible. On her small salary' – Tom laughs wryly to himself over this, since Mrs Forbes was his mother's employer at the time – 'she could not have kept you. Adoption was the kindest thing. Your mother has high blood pressure and has to take pills for her heart. Her husband is a very difficult man, and if he were to find out about you, it might put the marriage in jeopardy. If you have any respect for her, do not contact her, I beg of you. Be happy and content with your own family, Yours sincerely, Celia Forbes.'

He noticed from this letter that his mother's age was wrong. 'It seems to have fluctuated mightily,' he laughs. 'She was twenty-four when she had me, not nineteen. And twenty-eight when she married, though she lied on her marriage certificate and pretended she was twenty-two, and younger than her husband. Perhaps that's another secret she doesn't want known.'

He wrote back to Mrs Forbes at once. 'My mother has made no concessions to me at all. She has been offered meetings by the society and her parish priest, which would have guaranteed absolute security for her secret. No one need have known. Also, she gave me her word she would let me know where she was, but she disappeared without trace. For just one time in my life, I would like to be able to have a normal conversation with my mother. I just want to be friends. I am grateful for your letter, and I do not plan to correspond with my mother, as I dread any action of mine making her secret known. But I am not prepared to surrender by birth right to know about my family. I will find my brother, and I will find my father, and if he is dead, then I will find his grave.' He asked if she had any photographs of his mother, and especially his brother.

To this letter he received only a curt reply. Clearly Mrs Forbes wished the correspondence to come to a quick conclusion. She said his mother had expressed anger at his having written to her friend at all, and said he was breaking what she thought was an understanding between them. Mrs Forbes added that she herself would be out of the country for a while, so there was no point in his writing again. And that was that.

He was not sure how to find his father, but he was practically certain that he would still be in Tregarn, his old village. Indeed he was right. He had fled straight back to Ireland and home when he escaped from Edna, leaving her alone, pregnant and friendless. Again, as with so many other children looking for their parents, Tom seems to have sought out his father with little thought of revenge or recrimination. Had his father been a decent man, the whole course of Tom's life would have been quite different. And yet Tom's longing for love and the companionship of a real father over-rode any thoughts of the harm his father had done him or his mother in the past.

He contacted the same woman in the village post office who had revealed to him his mother's address. He wrote to her, pretending to be an old man called Thomas Reilly conducting research into his family tree. He said he was looking for a Thomas Flanagan, who had been a friend of his in Folkestone during the war. Could she give him his address, and put him in touch with his old friend? The post mistress replied promptly to say that she had talked to

Thomas Flanagan. He remembered his old friend Thomas Reilly very well indeed, and would very much like to see him again! Clearly Tom had been lucky in his choice of pseudonym, a name he had stolen from those foster-parents of his, when he was fifteen. Thomas Flanagan went even further. He invited his good old friend to come over to Ireland for a holiday to stay with him.

Tom was overjoyed. This was a piece of luck beyond all expectation. He wrote at once to his father, still carefully signing his letter Thomas Reilly, thanking him for his kind invitation and promising to take him upon it almost at once.

There was no reply. Undeterred, Tom wrote again. This time, cautiously, he began to probe and ask pertinent questions. Was he indeed the same Thomas Flanagan who had lived in a boarding house in Folkestone in 1939? Had he known a certain Edna O'Mara? Still there came no reply to this letter either. Then he wrote again, and this time all his letters were returned to him. A note from a neighbour said that Thomas Flanagan was in hospital for a hip operation, so had not received his mail.

Tom contacted the hospital at once, afraid his father would die before he ever got the chance to meet him. In his anxiety, he talked at length to the sister in charge of his ward, a nun – 'And like all nuns, very nosy and interfering. But she loved my story, she really did, and she promised to do everything she could to help me.' The nun spoke at length to Thomas Flanagan, as he lay helpless in bed, and explained everything to him. When Tom telephoned next day, she announced to him that his father was willing to meet him if he would like to pay a visit.

Tom left everything behind and went straight over to Ireland. It was New Year's Day when he arrived in the ward. 'I can't say I felt anything like the same anticipation or the same pleasure at meeting my father as I would at meeting my mother. It was much more a matter of interest, not of deep feeling. I wanted to know everything about him and to be friends with him, but it had not a fraction of the importance to me that meeting my mother would have.'

His father, an old and sick man, studied his son as he came into the ward. Tom sat down at his bedside and gazed back at him, looking for signs. His father started out straight away. 'I wanted to see you at once,' his father said. 'Because it is most important that I set the record straight here and now. I am not your father. I am *absolutely* not your father. Yes, I was going out with Edna O'Mara for four years or so, before she got in the family way. But it was not me. I never would have done any such thing. She was going out with other boys at the time and I am certain it was one of them.' Tom was disappointed at his father's lack of honesty. 'I can see you are a very nice chap,' his father continued. 'But I can see you are no son of mine. I have no son. Look at you, you are much taller than I am, for one thing.' Tom protested that as a child he had always been exceptionally small, and he is certainly not a tall man now. His mother is quite tall, so Tom regards his height as another proof that Thomas Flanagan was his true father. He was also deeply disinclined to believe that his mother had been promiscuous. It was quite unlikely and out of character. It was much more likely that after four years she thought she was going to marry Thomas Flanagan, but then he changed his mind.

'All that day I sat with him in hospital. I don't think he had many friends. He lived alone on his bit of land and he had never married. He spent the entire day maligning my mother and the O'Mara family. I think perhaps over the years he had come to believe his own version of the facts. He needed to believe them, to come to terms with what he had done. I don't think by then he realized he was lying any more. He seemed very shocked by the whole thing, but not shocked enough to confess the truth. He was quite put out when I pointed out that the society records show he never denied paternity at the time. He kept saying, 'I can't be a father now, not at my age. I know you're a nice chap, but I just couldn't be anyone's dad, not now.'

Tom spent all day with him. 'I enjoyed his company. It was a long day, drawing stories out of him about his family, which is also my family. But of course it was not a meeting long enough to last the lifetime I had missed. I completely dismissed his story. Women do know who the father of their child is.'

When he got back to England he wrote at once to his father, enclosing photographs of his wife and children.

'Dead Dad,' he wrote, in the hope that this would elicit the required paternal response. It did indeed sting him enough to reply by return of post. His letter is scrawled, illegible and makes little sense. Words and sentences are disembodied and meaningless. He managed to explain that someone actually did his writing for him, but that person was currently away. 'I am not your father,' he manages to keep writing but he says he will always welcome visits from him as a friend, not a son.

He did enclose a charming photograph though, of himself and Edna in Folkestone, a carefully posed studio portrait for sending home to relatives. 'I was so touched that he had kept that lovely photo all these years. It showed that it was something important to him, even if he did run away in the end,' Tom says, gazing affectionately at the faded brown picture of those two young Irish lovers in their best Sunday clothes, frozen together in a stiff photographer's pose. A formal picture of his parents to show people is a great prize to Tom. Where all his life he had no one to talk of, no one to show, now he has at least got this. 'I no longer feel left out when people start talking about their mum and dad. I can talk about mine too.'

He wrote back to thank his father for the picture, and said he'd be over to see him again. 'Let's have a beer together,' he said. This letter, addressed again to 'Dear Dad,' was returned opened, with the single word 'Deceased' scrawled across it. The letter had been sent all the way to his father's sister in Canada, who must have got a shock when she saw 'Dear Dad,' inside.

The death of his father was a shock, but it did not cause him great grief. 'It was no worse than a tooth being pulled,' he said. 'He never admitted he was my father. He was a nice old man, but I couldn't say we had a great deal in common. I wanted to know how he had died. I telephoned the kind nun at the hospital. She found out for me that he had been killed in a car crash, not far from the village, and that was all there was to it. The end of that trail.'

It looks like the end of the trail altogether. He knows where his mother is, but she won't see him, and he feels duty bound not to write to her. He knows nothing of where his half-brother might be, but he intends to track him down. Since his half-brother already knows of Tom's existence, and took avoiding action, that seems likely to lead nowhere. 'Perhaps he thinks I'm after my share of my mother's money. Of course I'm not, and I could tell him so.' But the search and the research go on. 'He seems possessed by it,' Barbara says. 'Sometime I hope it will stop.'

Has it all been worthwhile? Does Tom wish he had never embarked on this, never suffered a second rejection from his mother? 'I've enjoyed it, oddly enough,' he says with a rueful look. 'I think of it every day. I dream about it. I ponder about her, and think, why? I plan my next move in my campaign. I try to solve the problem, as if there was some vital key that would open all the doors, if only I could find it.' He paused and thought it through again. 'Unless you are an orphan, you don't know how it feels. I can't describe it to you, but you just have to take my word for this. It matters. My mother is a part of me. Maybe she's a horrible part of me. It's like having a sore leg. You don't want to cut it off, because it's sore, do you? My mother may be no-good, selfish, and cruel, but she's still my mother. She's still my leg, and I won't have it chopped off.'

Love and anger combine uncomfortably. The fantasy mother stays there, somewhere hovering uncertainly in his mind. Perhaps he thinks the magic meeting will soften her heart, and reveal the true mother in her, which she is so resolutely hiding from him now. But then there is the hatred too. 'She's made me into the aggressor. But I'm not. Or at least, that isn't what I want to be. I don't want to threaten and hurt her, yet she seems to think I do. It's not my fault she kept me secret. I am not her bad secret. Her secret is her own, and I am myself, and she is my mother. Sometimes I think she's a real pain, not a nice person at all. But then, I didn't choose her. I didn't choose to be born, did I? I didn't choose to be put in an orphanage. And despite all that, she treats me now as if I were to blame for all this. Perhaps in her mind I am my father. I am the bad penny, I am the embodiment of her shame, and therefore a shameful person just by being.' He shakes his head in frustrated uncertainty. 'I have tried and tried to understand this woman, this mother but I fail, of course.'

7

Louise Cameron

Louise Cameron is a tiny spritely woman. At first, she seems misleadingly cheerful and ebullient. But that impression falls away as she talks of her life with bitterness and resentment. If a little happiness or satisfaction was achieved here or there, then she is grateful for that, but she presents her life as one born to tragedy and disappointment. Impossible to tell if she was born with a gloomy and pessimistic outlook, or whether the hardships in her life made her despair. Some people, indeed many that I have interviewed for this book, seem to overcome disasters and retain a remarkably buoyant and hopeful character. Alas, not Louise Cameron.

She was born in Newcastle in 1937. Her mother was the daughter of strictly puritanical parents, horrified at the birth of an illegitimate grandchild. Louise's father was a married man and disappeared from the scene immediately. Louise was placed in a christian children's home in Gateshead, called the Carol Home. The twenty children housed there were known at school and in the neighbourhood as 'The Carols'. 'I have some very happy memories of that place,' Louise says. 'My mother never loved me, never wanted me. I should have been left there, and then my life might have been different. I don't remember her ever visiting, but she probably did a few times, as I have a photo of her holding me when I was three, in the garden of the Home. She looks very young and pretty and lively. I do remember she used to phone me sometimes. The matron would come along and say, "Louise, your mummy's on the phone," and I would cringe, because she wasn't a mummy to me. I didn't know her. She was a stranger, a strange voice. Looking back, I don't know why I loved The Carol so much, but it was just my home, where I felt at home. The staff weren't at all loving or even affectionate. We had a lot of church and Sunday school, and we were definitely looked down on in the neighbourhood.'

She looks back on the place with such a rosy glow of nostalgia, perhaps only because what came next was worse. 'When I go north, I still feel I'm going home, from my time at The Carol. I hope to retire to Gateshead, as it has such strong, good associations for me. I've been insecure and emotionally battered all my life, and I think I'd still find comfort there. Though of course the home has long since been closed. It's an ordinary family house now. Well, we were all illegitimate children there – I suppose that's why we were looked down on. And illegitimate children don't get put in homes any more, do they? Their mothers keep them, or they get adopted.' The very word 'adopted' brings her up short, and makes her pause. Adoption, as she experienced it, was more like the hi-jacking of her baby daughter on false pretences at a time when she was too weak and vulnerable to be able to do anything about it.

When she was seven years old, her mother married, and she and her husband decided to take Louise back from the home. 'It was costing ten shillings a week and my new step-father said he couldn't afford it, which was rubbish.' She remembers standing in this court room for the adoption hearing, as her mother and husband applied for legal adoption to 'legitimize' her and give their married name to this illegitimate child.

'I cried and cried when I left the home. I didn't want to go with these people who were strangers to me. I remember my mother saying, "Now kiss your new father," and he had an awful hard rough face to kiss.' He owned a small business, which he conducted from a converted farmhouse outside Rugby, with a small factory at the back. 'He was very successful and made a lot of money.'

They lived over the business, and Louise's mother had two more children, both boys. 'I was jealous of them, and I felt I was very much the poor relation who didn't fit in.'

From time to time her mother and step-father sent her back to The Carol. 'I was so happy when that happened. I loved going back, and I always begged them not to take me away from there. But they always did. I was sent to a kind of finishing school, on the south coast when I was fifteen, and then to a secretarial college in Hampstead. I should have stayed in London then. The school offered me a job there as I came top of my year. But my step-father insisted that I went back to work for him in his office. I was weak. Why was I always so weak? Why did I always give in to other people?'

She was worked hard by her step-father. 'He was a ruthless business man' – and supervised strictly at home. 'I was never allowed boyfriends. My mother was so suspicious of me she used to go searching around in my underclothes drawer.'

Through friends at a Rugby table tennis club, she heard of a chance to work in Norway, when she was nineteen. She and her friend decided to go. 'We had a wonderful time, the happiest time of my adult life. I should have stayed there. I really should have. Why did I come back?' She meant to come back for a short Christmas holiday. But while she took a brief temporary Christmas job at the post office, she met a man there, and fell in love with him. 'I believe you only ever fall in love once. I've never ever loved anyone else. So, I decided not to go back to Norway, and we had a long affair. He never said he'd leave his wife, but he never said he wouldn't. He gave the impression the marriage was unimportant, but that wasn't true.' She had been with him for six years when she became pregnant. She says there was no thought in her head of doing such a thing on purpose. But then she did think it might precipitate him into leaving his wife. 'He was very kind and supportive at the time – but not with real help or money. He was a weak man, and unscrupulous but he was the only person in the world I loved.'

Social services sent her to a mother and baby home in Rugby, which doubled as an old people's home. 'I never for a moment thought I'd have my baby adopted. I didn't even contemplate the thought of it. I thought that either the baby's father or my mother would come round to the idea. My mother had a large house and plenty of room to take me and the baby in. I waited to see what would happen.'

The baby was born, a daughter she named Gillian. 'She was perfect, beautiful, and I loved her more than anything.' She returned to the mother and baby home, but her lover did not come to see her or the child. Her mother did visit once, and made it clear that she and Louise's step-father thought the child should be adopted. Her step-father said, 'She'll have others later.'

'A woman from Chiswick in London came to see me,' Louise says. 'I don't know who called for her. Maybe she went the rounds of certain mother and baby homes. She had arranged over 500 private adoptions already.' Louise finds something sinister about her, thinking back. These mysterious private adoption fixers keep cropping up in people's stories, from the days when private adoptions were permitted. Those who speak of them always seem to think of them as little more than baby snatchers, whose interests lay entirely with the couples seeking children to adopt. They are sinister figures, driven by some inner need of their own, insensitive to the suffering of the mothers whose children they are taking, and with little thought for the ultimate well-being of the child. 'She had lost four children of her own, in four miscarriages. I am sure that had something to do with her whole attitude,' Louise says.

When her time at the mother and baby home came to an

end, Louise had to put her baby into a foster home while she decided what to do. She still hoped that either her lover or her mother would help, and she did not want to have Gillian adopted. However, the woman from Chiswick came back several times and kept leaning on her to give away the child. 'She said there was this couple living in Southwark in London, with a big house and garden, who wanted to adopt Gillian. They were the nicest people, very well off, who could give her everything she could want and need in life. Well, I didn't know anything about London, and I didn't know what sort of area Southwark was, so I had no reason not to believe her. By now I was beginning to see I would get no help. I went to see the baby every day in her foster home, but neither my mother nor the baby's father wanted to go near her. They showed no interest at all, so it was becoming obvious to me that I was on my own. I was very depressed and I just didn't see how I could cope.'

Something else happened too. She was so miserably distressed that she developed a lump in her throat and convinced herself she was going to die. She couldn't swallow and felt ill. 'I thought that my baby wasn't going to have a mother anyway, as I'd be dead, so that finally decided me to sign the papers. It was winter, and I had nowhere to live, nowhere to take her. I hadn't any choice, though I knew I would regret it for as long as I lived.'

She gave in to the constant pressure of the adoption fixer from Chiswick, who came to take her baby away. In a few months she signed the final papers, but because of the irregularity of the whole procedure, she did manage to catch sight of the name and address of the people who were taking her child in Southwark. She kept that engraved on her memory for years. Looking back now, she wishes she had insisted on meeting them first. Some of the better adoption agencies do now arrange such meetings – though always keeping the names of the adoptees secret to prevent future contact. Louise feels she was lied to and cheated. She doesn't know why the woman from Chiswick did it, but she was not told the truth about the family taking her child. She feels now, rightly or wrongly, that if she had struggled on she would probably have ended up giving her daughter a better home herself.

Later, when she was looking for her daughter, she wrote a sad account of the whole experience for the newsletter of Norcap – the self-help group that tries to help mothers and adopted children to find each other again:

'I have never got over losing my baby and would never recommend adoption. Nothing can take the place of a natural mother's love and no one should have to part with their own flesh and blood. How can you "start again" or "pretend it never happened" when you have been robbed like this, and what a price to pay for falling in love.

'I have been back to the spot where I last held my baby eighteen years ago, several times, and stood forlornly looking around asking myself why didn't I run off with my baby instead of standing there having my photograph taken holding her for the last time, which I have carried around with me ever since. My thoughts have been with her over all the years and I have "looked for" and "seen her" everywhere. Birthdays and Christmas are particularly poignant times and for me it has been a living nightmare which still goes on now.'

Once the baby had gone, Louise went back to her lover. 'I was so heart-broken at losing my baby, and he was the only person who ever showed me any love. I knew he was hopeless, and he would never help or support me, or leave his wife, but at least I think he did love me. His marriage was fine, by all accounts. He and his wife had three children during the time I had an affair with him.' She adds that last thought with some bitterness – the children her lover could keep, while she had to give her own away.

Did she mean it to happen again? It is hard to think that she didn't. It is so common for women who have had babies taken away to want to replace them quickly that it seems unlikely it was pure accident. She is an extremely intelligent woman, even though she may not have been good at organizing her own life. 'I thought it was the safe period,' she says rather lamely. There are a hundred good/bad reasons why women may want to get pregnant and it seems to me unlikely that greatly improved sex education or propaganda from the Health Education Council will have much effect. I have come across many women who having had one child adopted, found themselves pregnant quite soon afterwards. The drive to fill the empty cot was too great. It may be one reason why adoption is rarely the right answer for the mother giving up her child.

Once she discovered she was pregnant again, she decided to leave Rugby and her whole previous life behind. Her mother, when she discovered, went straight round to her lover's wife and told her. 'I cannot think why she did such a thing. I don't know why I still see her now. She has some kind of hold on me.'

She fled, leaving behind a letter for her mother, and a letter for her lover, whom she never saw again. Her only contact in London was, ironically, the adoption fixer in Chiswick, who was of course delighted to see her again, and to find her expecting another child, ripe for adoption. She went to stay with her for a while. 'She was a very strange woman indeed, very Victorian in her outlook. She talked a lot about the children she had lost, the children she could never have.' She fixed Louise up at a nearby hospital, and told her to tell the doctors that this was her first child, and that the father had emigrated to Australia. She found Louise a flat with another girl who had just given up her baby for adoption.

She got a job working in a pub, together with her new flatmate. Behind the bar was an older widower, Henry, who befriended her. 'He saved my life. He decided to protect me, once he knew I was pregnant. He used to drive me up to the ante-natal clinic. He gave me the courage to decide that for certain this time I would keep the baby.'

When her son Simon was born, she put him in a foster home for a month while Henry helped her to find her a flat of her own, and a day nursery so she could go on working. 'I didn't know about the social services. So I never got any help at all from them. It just didn't occur to me that I was eligible for anything. I had a very hard life, when I got Simon back from the foster home, but he was such a lovely baby that it helped to keep me going.'

She was never in love with Henry, nor was she his lover, but he continued to help her. 'It hasn't had a particularly happy ending,' she says wryly. 'I feel very much obliged to him, but now I'm stuck with looking after him, and I'd really rather not.' He persuaded her to move down to Margate, where his mother lived.

'I cried when we left London. I'd kept hoping I'd see Gillian there and I felt I was leaving her behind.' She got a council flat eventually, for herself and Simon, then aged ten, and Henry moved in too. 'He likes an easy life, with me doing his cooking and washing. We sleep in separate rooms, and he is very dependent. When his mother died, leaving him this big Margate house, he kept saying he'd do it all up, and we'd all move into it. Or at least he would move out and move into it. But he does nothing about it. That house stays the way it was the day she died. It is starting to fall down now, and I don't thnk he'll ever do anything about it. It defeats him to think about it. So he stays living here, and I suppose I shall have to care for him for ever. I'm soft-centred. Because he did save me from that Chiswick woman, and if it hadn't been for him, I might never have kept my Simon. But if it hadn't been for Simon, I'd never have got myself into a state of having to owe so much to him. I wish he'd go. He's an embarrassment, but single mothers with new babies can't be choosers, can they? My God, I've made a mess of my life.'

All this time she had kept a surreptitious eye on her

missing daughter. 'I found Gillian when she was three. I had her adoptive parents' name and address, and I checked it in the phone book. Then a friend offered to drive me over to Southwark to look at the place where she lived. I stayed in the car and he went in. It was not a large house with a garden. Not at all. It was a council tower block of the older sort, in a busy high street. He found the family on the sixth floor. He saw a little girl exactly my Gillian's age, playing around in the lifts outside her flat. It was a smelly, nasty place. Of course he couldn't be sure that was Gillian, but she had bright blonde hair, and looked three years old. I was horrified, and very angry. I used to comfort myself that I'd been through all that suffering at giving up my child, but at least I was giving her a better life by having her adopted. It seemed to me then I'd given her a worse life, and that was so bitter, so unfair. My Simon has had a better life, better prospects, a better upbringing, than poor Gillian in Southwark. I cannot forgive that woman for having lied to me the way she did. A wealthy family with a big house? Oh, I know you shouldn't say and think these things. Of course working-class people should have the same right to adopt children, but if the true facts had been told me – a shabby high-rise block – I wouldn't have given away my baby.

'Once I knew where she was, I kept my eye on her. I rushed for the new telephone directory whenever it was reprinted to make sure the Jennings family were still at the same address, which they were. I still felt how much I loved my daughter, although I hadn't seen her since she was tiny. Then, when Gillian was ten years old, the family's name suddenly disappeared from the phone book. I was desperate. I thought I might have lost them for ever, and I didn't know what to do. I knew I could do nothing until she was eighteen, then the law said I was supposed to wait until she tried to contact me. But then the law didn't know that I already knew her name.'

On Gillian's eighteenth birthday Louise started to search

in earnest. She wrote at that time in the Norcap newsletter: 'I feel excited yet anxious as a search is underway, wondering what the outcome will be. Will she want to see me? Will she forgive me? Will she understand? On the other hand my torment is, is she alive? Is she well? Is she happy?'

She didn't know how to begin looking, once the R. Jennings had disappeared from the telephone book at the old address. She wrote to the council and to the GLC to try to find their whereabouts, but could get no answer out of them. Then she read a newspaper article about John Stroud of the Hertfordshire Social Services, befriender of bereft mothers. He gave her some advice and offered to help. He pointed her in the direction of the electoral rolls, stored at St Catherine's House in London. Louise assumed, rightly, that the family would have stayed in council property in the same borough. The lists for a whole borough are enormous. 'They are listed in alphabetical order of streets. I was very lucky that the family had moved to a house in a street beginning with D – Dundee Road. It was a miracle. It only took me a quarter of an hour to find, and it could have taken days and days.'

Now her daughter was eighteen, she appeared on the electoral register, together with her date of birth, the date of official entry onto the register. But her name was not Gillian at all. That came as a shock. She was now Samantha – a name Louise did not like. But she wouldn't have liked any other name. It was quite definitely her own Gillian, for the date of birth was correct. She noticed something else, the father's name was not there. Had he left? Had he died?

'I wanted to go there, but I didn't dare. The law doesn't give mothers any rights, even once the child is eighteen. Most organizations and social services won't help mothers at all, because the law is so clear on this point. So I didn't like to rush in. I contacted John Stroud, and he said he'd act as intermediary and contact Samantha. Of course I had to force myself to think of her as Samantha now, but it didn't come naturally after all these years of thinking of her, and writing of her in my diary as my little Gilly.'

She was also in close contact with Norcap, and from their list of contacts, picked out a woman in South London.

'She was very kind and helpful indeed. I don't think the official Norcap organization thought it right that I was trying to contact my daughter, but this woman became a great friend, and did everything she could to help me. I was stuck in Margate, so she said she would go for me and scout around outside the house in Dundee Road, and tell me what it looked like. She went and said it was a nice road, and they had a very small house, two bedrooms, rented from a housing association. I was glad it was a better place than those horrible flats.'

Louise came up to London one day, and her new friend from Norcap drove her to the street. They fell into conversation with a neighbour and found out one or two things more about the family. He said that Samantha was a plump girl with lovely blonde hair, that she was unemployed, though she had talked of joining the police. 'We walked up and down a few times, trying not to be noticeable, hoping she might come out, or I might catch a glimpse of her. I didn't but I stared at every young girl in the area, and kept thinking any of them could have been my Gillian –or Samantha as I had to think of her now.' She discovered that Samantha had an adopted younger sister, half black, called Tracy.

Louise, knowing her precarious position under the law, waited for the social services to act for her, but by now, patience wasn't easy. Her new friend egged her on, and told her not to bother with formalities. She said she would telephone the family herself. Louise was worried that this might lead to trouble, or possibly outright rejection, but in the end she was persuaded.

Her friend called the Jennings' number one evening. 'Can I speak to Samantha?' she asked. Gillian's sister Tracy answered and said she was out. 'Would you tell her that some relatives of hers from Rugby very much want to get in touch with her. If she's interested could she call this number?' She left her telephone number. She said Rugby, as that was on Samantha's birth certificate – and she might remember. Then there was a long wait, for several days, during which Louise became anxious almost to the point of despair. Clearly Samantha did not want to know about her family, or her mother.

Then, eventually, a few days later, the call came. Samantha rang Louise's friend and asked tentatively who it was that wanted to contact her. 'Your mother, your real mother,' she said. Samantha said she thought that was who it must be. 'Would it be all right if your mother wrote to you?' Samantha said it would, and that she would write back.

'I was overjoyed. I had waited eighteen years for the chance to write this letter. I sat down right away.'

> Dear Samantha.
>
> It is wonderful to hear you are alive and well. Thank you for telephoning. I want you to know that I mean you no harm, and I have no wish to upset your family.

She wrote a little about herself. 'I am forty-seven, five foot tall, and a bit tubby.' Then she told her about her son, Samantha's full brother, Simon, explaining he was taking his O levels again.

Through their letters, they arranged to meet. Louise gives this version of that first encounter. To my ear it doesn't quite ring true – or at least it leaves out other conflicting emotions. It is also curiously out of character with Louise herself, who neither talks nor thinks like this in real life. She doesn't see the whole episode in this rosy light – but almost as a continuation of the tragedy. She looks at Samantha, and although she likes what she sees, she also thinks of all she could have been – or all Louise imagines she could have been, had she been brought up in a better home. And as for the gratitude at the end for Samantha's adoptive mother, that rings with a hollow note.

But this is how Louise described the meeting, which she called 'A Mother's Joy':

'On the journey up from Kent my mind was so full with everything that had happened since the day she was born (which seems like yesterday) that all I could do was to gaze vacantly out of the window not really seeing anything: after all the years of pain, anguish, regret and sorrow I was to meet my daughter Samantha....

'I suddenly turned round and saw this lovely smiling face rushing towards me and I just knew this was my daughter.... I could hardly believe this lovely young person was my daughter. We spent a day together and the time went by all too quickly. There was much to be said but everything was kept on a happy friendly basis. Samantha kept pointing out similarities between us such as how we held our knives and we both parted our hair in the same fashion. Indeed she is the mirror image of myself – there is no doubting she is my daughter.

'When people ask how I found my daughter, all I can say is it was through a Mother's Love. I feel very humble. There are many kinds of love, but a Mother's love for her children is a most powerful force.'

What she doesn't describe here are those other feelings she also had about Samantha. 'Her background,' she now says, 'has certainly been very ordinary. I think she is very intelligent indeed, but she has been badly educated and she left school as soon as she could. She's unemployed, which is a pity. She has a boyfriend, who lives in Bermondsey, but he's out of work too. She doesn't get on very well with Tracy, her adopted sister. She says her mother favours Tracy. I feel I can say things to her that a mother ought. I said I hoped she was on the Pill, since it was obvious she and her boyfriend were quite serious about one another. I don't want what happened to me and my mother before me to happen to

Samantha. She *is* on the Pill, thank goodness.

'She is a very lovely girl, very sweet and very bright. I really feel her as my own, my very own daughter. But she does smoke like a chimney, and so does her boyfriend, and her whole family. I don't know how they can afford it. And they drink too. I don't drink or smoke. I think Samantha has led a very sheltered life in a way. She doesn't seem to have been anywhere. She's very uncertain in finding her way around London, although she's always lived there. Her letters are really very good. I think she might have a talent for writing. I did say to her that she should think of going back to a college, so she could get some qualifications and maybe get a good job. But I'm afraid she wouldn't even consider it. Well, never mind. I'm just happy she's alive and well. She does speak with a very strong cockney accent. Somehow I hadn't imagined that. I wish I'd married someone with money so that I had something to give her. I have given her a gold and pearl bracelet which she loves. I'd like to give her so much more – nice clothes and books. But she doesn't like me to give her too much. Perhaps it's as well I don't have money, since at least it has kept me on a closer level with the way she has been brought up.'

She sighs deeply when she talks of her life. 'It's all "If onlys". I've been done in by men. I was a mistake, and my mother was done in too. My mother never loved me. I never remember her kissing me once. I sent her a photo recently of me and Samantha. I thought she'd be pleased to know I'd found her again. She sent it back to me saying she didn't want to have anything to do with Samantha. I've done nothing with my life. I've been weak and given in to others all the time. Although it's wonderful to find Samantha again, and she'll always know I am here if she needs me, I can never replace those eighteen years. I can never get back what was taken from me. She *is* my daughter still, but at the same time she isn't.'

Louise has met her daughter five times now, yet they have

never talked about important things. Samantha has asked no questions, and Louise had told her nothing about her father or her beginnings. 'I hope she forgives me in her heart for having given her away. I hope she understands me and knows why I did it. I don't know how it is that we don't talk. She's keen to see me, but then teenagers are very wrapped up in their own lives. They aren't good at imagining what other people are going through, or what other people's lives have been like. But I hope the time will come when we can talk.' Samantha has now met Simon, her brother, but they were both somewhat tongue-tied. 'They eyed one another with great interest,' Louise says, smiling.

She is now passionately opposed to all adoptions, except in the most unavoidable circumstances. She feels people pay too little attention to the real ties between a mother and a child. Even if they think adoption is best for thc child, they too easily discount the lifetime of misery imposed upon the mother. 'To meet her again, to know she is on the end of the telephone, that has helped. It has healed part of the pain. But all the same, I have been deprived of so much of her. She isn't the same child she would have been had I kept her with me, and nothing can ever fill the hole she has left in my life.'

As we were parting, she turned with a sad smile and shook her head. 'I'm not a very cheerful person, am I? But to be quite honest, apart from the joy of my Simon, I haven't had a lot to be happy about, have I? They say these things go in cycles. I only hope to God none of these ever happens to Samantha.'

8

Sandra

Sandra is a slim, beautiful girl, with a mass of brown curls, and a misty look in her eyes. As she talks about her life, in her soft west country lilt, her voice is full of longing for someone or something beyond her grasp.

The day I first met her she was in a state of raw, exhausted emotion. The words tumbled out of her. She kept shifting direction in conversation. She alternated between bitterness, and a kind of wild romantic love for a mother she had never seen. Her loves and hates were pronounced, her resentments deep though sometimes undirected. She veered between sounding like a Mills and Boon heroine to a violently vengeful villainess. She saw herself as a disturbed woman, with all kinds of problems. She could trace them back to her childhood, she could talk about how emotionally immature she was for her twenty-eight years. She could identify what the lack of love in her life had done to her character and her destiny. But none of that self-knowledge helped to calm her feelings. She was still like a highly intelligent but helpless and perplexed child, a victim lashing out in all directions at once, knowing yet not knowing.

It was hardly surprising to find her in such a turmoil. In three days' time she would meet her mother for the first time, a meeting she had waited and longed for all the years she could remember. 'I can't believe it. I just can't believe it,' she kept saying, shaking her head. 'I am going to walk up to Her door. I'm going to see Her.'

Sandra now lives in a crisp and pleasant council flat in Epping, with Mike, who is not her husband, and their three-year-old son Darren. She feels, she says, as she has always felt, deeply insecure. She wishes Mike would marry her, after all this time together. He just says he might, and leaves it at that. She wishes he was more demonstrative, and knows she makes too many demands on his love. 'I can't stop myself doing it. He says he feels suffocated sometimes, but I have to hear him saying he loves me and that I mean everything to him. He tells me I'm too insecure, and I know it, but what can I do about it?' She says she's always been like that. She put the same pressure on all her boyfriends when she was younger, and on her first husband. 'I always said I loved them right away. I needed so much love, and of course they couldn't really give it to me. Or not the love I was looking for, the love of parents.'

Sandra's adoption was not, according to her, a success. She finds it unnerving that she does not really know exactly when she was adopted. She needs to focus on every small event of her childhood and infancy, things that would seem insignificant to most people – but she has little information. Her adoptive mother refuses to talk about it, or when she has told Sandra things they have often turned out not to be true. It has made Sandra suspicious of everything and everyone connected with her adoption, and certainly there were some mysteries surrounding it.

Her adoptive mother always told her she was adopted at a few weeks old. Later she found out that she was fostered first and she doesn't know why, or how long for. It seems likely that she was just a victim of a policy that used to be the general practice with adoptions. Babies were put out to professional foster parents, who were used to caring for scores of such infants a year for the first six weeks.

Sandra has a recurrent memory, which is also a dream. She is lying in a cot in a shabby front room, a room filled with other cots. Somewhere in the background is a man who is frightening. Her adoptive parents come and stand by her cot and stare down at her. She is crying fiercely. But this doesn't deter her adoptive parents 'We'll choose this one,' they say. She is not clear, in this memory of hers, whether this is good or bad news, but the atmosphere surrounding the place and the scene is terrible.

Sandra is now sure that all this is not a memory at all, but either a dream that keeps coming back or an invented memory she has imagined to fill in the known facts. Like so many other well-intentioned adoptive parents, hers kept telling her, 'We chose you. Out of all the other little babies in the world, we chose you.' It is a thought that sounds, at first, generous – as if the child had been promoted, selected. In fact, as some adoption agencies now well recognize, it is far better to say, 'We were chosen to care for you, out of all the parents who wanted children.' That implies that the baby is unique and special, not merely one of an unwanted bundle to be picked over. It means the parents were the lucky ones, not the child – and is far closer to the truth. 'We chose you' means in code, 'And you should be very grateful for being such a lucky girl'. Far better to make the parents the lucky and the grateful ones.

She thinks she probably wasn't told of her adoption until she was eleven. Her adoptive mother claims she always told her, but Sandra has no memory of knowing, or if she 'knew' then the words had no meaning for her. Not until children at school made the meaning crystal clear. 'My mum had grey hair, and she didn't mind much about her appearance. The other mothers were young and attractive compared to her. She must have been in her late thirties when she adopted me. The other children said she looked old and horrible. Then they said, 'She's not your real mother. You weren't wanted by your real mother. She gave you away.'

She was, she says, the butt of bullies, a weakling in the playground. 'They used to taunt me. They said, "Your mum and dad don't have sex, that's why they can't make their own babies. That's why they had to take you from someone else."'

She was a persistent bed-wetter, until she was fourteen – and worse, she used to wet herself at school, for which she was persecuted. She was so disturbed that she never spoke a word until she was four, when her mother took her to specialists to find out what was wrong. There were three adopted children in the family – two boys and Sandra, who came between them in age. She is not close to either of her brothers.

True or not, Sandra has it firmly fixed in her mind that her mother was cold and ungiving. She much preferred the boys, and Sandra feels she had it in for her. Perhaps just being a girl, she thought all Sandra's real mother's supposed evil was bound to come out in her. She kept Sandra under strict control, to prevent any of that evil bad blood seeping out. Right from the start Sandra says she never seemed to show the children much affection. 'I can't remember ever being kissed or cuddled by my mother,' Sandra says. 'She was so strict – and she was terrified of anything to do with sex, or bodies. She thought it was all disgusting and dirty.'

Sandra suffered and still suffers severe and recurrent nightmares. She used to sleepwalk as a child and caused considerable damage when alseep, pulling down curtains and knocking things over. Once she awoke to find herself in her younger brother's room with her hands around his neck, half throttling him, with him screaming and shouting for help. She used to peel the wallpaper off her walls, and gouge great holes out of the plaster and lath underneath, picking and burrowing obsessively with her fingers.

Her father worked very hard to keep the family. For forty years he worked nights, just to see that his three adopted children had everything money could buy. 'They really did try hard. I had ballet lessons, tap lessons, piano lessons. I had my own room which my dad decorated beautifully for me. He made me lovely things, new toys. I really did love him. I do love him. I wish I knew how to tell him. But my mother always got between us. She'd call me away, or tell him to do something if ever we played games together, or if he told me a story. She wouldn't cuddle me and she wouldn't let him. I cried, I wet my bed, but I never got cuddled. All those damned lessons, all those damned toys – and not a cuddle, ever.'

Like so many other adopted children, Sandra found the secret of her birth with suspicious ease. In a box under her parents' bed, she found her baptismal certificate. Someone not her mother, not her adopted mother, had baptized her. Who? There too was her birth certificate with her mother's name on it – a name she never forgot – Denise Mary Curtiss. 'I realized I was a bastard then. I'd always guessed, but my mum and dad went out of their way to say I wasn't and that I had married parents. They never said why I had been given away. They never talked about it until I brought it up. The first time was when I was eleven, and being so bullied at school that I refused to go. Eventually I told them it was because the children said I was adopted, so they did mention the word then. But hardly ever afterwards. Even now, they won't answer questions or talk about it.'

She kept the knowledge of her mother's name secretively to herself, and thought often about it. In 1979 she needed a passport to go on holiday to Spain. Asking for her birth certificate made her think again. This time she decided to try and find her mother. The address on the certificate was a street in Chatham – Jubilee Road. She worked out how she might find out if her mother was still there, and telephoned the town hall and a library in Chatham. Was her mother still on the electoral roll for that address? The town hall told her that Jubilee Road had been pulled down in the late fifites. Much of the street had been bombed in the war, and it was an area due for demolition since the year that Sandra was born. With no help or support, no backing from anyone, no experience or information, she had no idea how to search further, and she gave up, sadly, yet still with the belief that somehow, one day, the reunion would happen.

The birth of her son left her in tears for several hours. 'It was sheer joy. Here he was, this little thing, all my own, the only relative in the whole world that belonged to me, my blood, myself. I tried to explain to Mike how I felt, but of course he couldn't understand. I was terrified that Darren would die, because I didn't expect to have anyone belonging to me in the world. I know I'm highly strung. I always have been, but I feel these things deeply. I don't think people who have blood relations understand what it's like not to have any. Having my son brought it all home to me.'

When he was still a small boy, first Mike, then Darren became seriously ill. Mike contracted viral encephalitis, and Darren caught the same virus, though mercifully, less severely. They were both in hospital, Mike for many weeks. Lacking any self-confidence or self-esteem and full of guilt, Sandra managed somehow to blame herself for all this. She decided that she was the carrier of this disease; she had given it to her son, who had infected his father – an unlikely chain of events, to say the least, but one which fitted perfectly with Sandra's confused sense of guilt. It was her 'bad blood', surfacing in her child.

Sitting alone at home between visits to the hospital she began to brood. She thought she might have some hereditary disease. She knew little about her rights to information as an adopted child, and decided to use devious means to find out anything she could about her natural parents.

She rang the Catholic agency who had arranged her adoption twenty-eight years ago. She claimed to be a social worker at the hospital checking to see whether Sandra Hayes (adopted name) Sandra Curtiss (birth name) had anything in her medical records to suggest hereditary disease. She spoke to a nun, who went away to dig out her file. Perhaps this wise old nun guessed that this was no social worker. No doubt adoption agencies get so many eliptical inquiries of this kind from uncertain adopted children, testing the water. In any case, she said kindly that she would send the file up to London, to a Catholic agency there, where if this Sandra wanted, she could go for counselling and be told what her file contained.

A week later she received a letter from a Mr Hall at a London agency, saying her file had been sent to him, and she was welcome to come for an appointment when he would 'extract the relevant information' for her. Being a naturally jumpy and sceptical person, Sandra did not like the idea of anyone 'extracting' what was 'relevant'. Only she could know what was relevant to her and she felt she should have an absolute right to see everything in the file.

When Mike was well and out of hospital, he drove Sandra and Darren to the London agency and sat outside the office, entertaining Darren, while Sandra went in to meet Mr Hall. 'At first from the general conversation, I could see he was trying to work me out, decide what to tell and what to hide.' He said there was not a lot recorded there, but tantalizingly he read out only parts of it, when she was hungry for every small crumb. She caught sight of a letter in her adoptive mother's handwriting, presumably applying to adopt a child and giving her reasons why. Sandra longed to see this, and felt she might be touched and reconciled to her adoptive mother by the tone of that letter.

On the other hand, should she be entitled to see private correspondence from her natural mother, and her adoptive parents, without their consent? Although it concerned her, it was in no way addressed to her. There might be things there neither woman would want Sandra to know, or things expressed so long ago which no longer seemed to strike the right note. I put these thoughts to Sandra, but she was adamant that she should have the absolute right to know anything that concerned her, from the moment of her conception.

Mr Hall told her to take down with pen and paper what he

was telling her. Often adopted people are so flustered that they forget much that they are told the first time. She was born, as she already knew, Sandra Rosanne Curtiss. Her mother was living in lodgings the other side of Chatham, not at Jubilee Road at the time of her adoption. She weighed 5lb 15oz at birth, and was six weeks premature. Her blood group was rhesus negative, group D. Her mother, Denise Mary Curtiss, was twenty, a shop assistant, a lapsed Catholic who had left school at fifteen, worked in a laundry and a factory. She was described in the patronizing terminology of such agencies at that date as 'a respectable working girl from a respectable working family'. Sandra had been breast fed for two weeks and then fed Full Cream National Dried Milk. Every detail was of interest to Sandra. She even wrote down Full Cream National Dried Milk, wasting not a shred of information about her lost origins.

Then came the shock. Her father's name was there, listed as Norman Hayes, age forty-four, travelling salesman. Norman Hayes! She was horrified and delighted all at once. Her adoptive parents' name was Hayes. Her adoptive father's name was Norman Hayes.

It seemed in some extraordinary way that all this time without knowing it, her adoptive father had really been her real father. For a moment she was ecstatic. She loves her father deeply, though finds it hard to tell him so or to talk to him. All her childhood, the happy times she remembers are with her father. It was he who did things for her, was kind to her, and her adoptive mother who stood firmly in the way, told him off, or sent Sandra away. Or at least, that is how Sandra sees it. So when she found that the same loved Norman Hayes was really her father after all she was delighted but also profoundly shocked.

She pulled herself together and challenged Mr Hall wisely. 'Surely that's a mistake?' she said. After all, she was not allowed to see the documents herself. 'You don't mean Norman Hayes is my real father, but my adoptive father?'

Mr Hall checked and checked again, but that, quite clearly, is what the files said. Denise Mary Curtiss declared on the forms that she met Norman Hayes at a dance. He was a tall, dark man, respectable, with good manners, a commercial traveller, but he was not local. 'Of course he was not local. My adoptive family, if it was that Norman Hayes, lives in Bristol,' Sandra said, as if it confirmed the point.

She left the office dazed. She knew very little about her mother, but everything about her father – except how on earth he, with his steady job working nights, had travelled from Bristol to Chatham to meet her mother, and then father a child, at the same time as being married in Bristol, with one adopted child already. The complexity, the unlikelihood of it all left her stunned.

Mr Hall promised that he would write to every Curtiss in the Chatham directory – there being six in all – to inquire about the whereabouts of Denise Mary Curtiss, who had lived in Jubilee Road in 1956. But that drew a blank. None of the Curtisses were related or had ever heard of Denise Mary.

Sandra took matters into her own hands. She telephoned the registrar in Chatham, and explained what she was doing. There is something about a child looking for its mother that often touches the hearts of officials. He promised to help, by checking to see if a Denise Mary Curtiss had been married in the town any time after Sandra's birth.

He called her back shortly afterwards to say that he had found a marriage certificate, and that he himself had officiated at the wedding, in 1960, between the said Denise and one Brian George Brockley. Sandra wept. 'I was shocked she had married so soon after giving me away. I would have been four years old then. How could she just go off and get married, as if I'd never existed?' Her reaction seems unfair. How long is formal mourning for an adopted child to last?

The registrar sent her a copy of the marriage certificate, and now she had a new name and new address to work on.

'I'm not particularly educated. I'd never done anything like this before,' Sandra said. 'But the funny thing is that you find if you really want to find something out, you think it out for yourself. You become a detective, and you get cunning.'

She tried the address on the certificate but the Brockleys had long since left and been forgotten. She tried the telephone directory for Chatham, systematically calling all the Brockleys, asking if they knew of a Brian and Denise. No luck. She turned to the electoral register, and plodded through that, but no Brian and Denise Brockley could be found.

It was then that she took out the marriage certificate again and stared down at it. A new thought occurred to her. At the bottom were the signatures of two witnesses. One was a Smith, small hope of finding him, but the other had a curious name, Ruby Spiggott. Sandra hurried again to the well-thumbed Chatham telephone directory. There was just one Spiggott there, an R. Spiggott. On the same day she was in London searching records at St Catherine's House – and there she found her brother, Jason. 'Well, he was a half-brother, but that meant a lot to me. I was very excited. It was fantastic. Someone belonging to me. I should have applied for his birth certificate to bring home, and of course there would have been an address on it, but I'd run out of money, and I didn't have enough to pay the fee for another certificate that day.'

Back home she waited until evening to telephone the R. Spiggott who might have been a witness to her mother's wedding. 'Is that Ruby Spiggott?' she asked, anxiously. The woman the other end had a curiously wheezy voice, rasping and breathless. She confirmed that she was Ruby Spiggott. 'I'm trying to contact someone I knew long ago, Denise, who married Brian Brockley, and I wondered if you could give me her address?'

Ruby was friendly and helpful, but she sounded to Sandra a little odd. 'I kept saying to myself, this woman knows my mother! This woman knows my mother! And I could hardly concentrate on the conversation. I couldn't believe I was actually speaking to the name on her marriage certificate.'

Ruby said that she hadn't seen her old friend for five or more years now. Denise had moved away to an estate at the other end of town, and they hadn't managed to keep in touch. It was the Holmead Estate, she said. She had given birth to two boys, Jason and Barry, but her husband Brian had been killed many years ago in a lorry crash. Brian was a lorry driver. It was only after imparting all this that it seemed to occur to Ruby that there was anything odd about this young woman on the telephone who claimed to be such a great friend of Denise's and yet who apparently knew nothing at all about her.

'Who exactly did you say you were? Why did you want to find Denise?' she asked, a little sharply, in her strange breathy voice. Sandra, still not having her mother's actual address, decided to take Ruby into her confidence. It was a dangerous thing to do. After all, her mother may have had good reasons for hiding the fact of Sandra's birth. It might destroy her life to reveal it. But then Sandra was desperate, and she could not wait. She felt, each step that she took, that she *had* to find her mother, and soon. She could hardly go on with her ordinary life until she had found her. So she told Ruby the whole story.

'Long ago, before she was married, Denise had a little baby girl. And she gave that baby away. That baby has grown up. She's a big girl now, and I am her. I am the baby Denise had all those years ago.' There was a sharp intake of breath down the line. 'Oh my poor love!' Ruby exclaimed. Sandra didn't know whether she or her mother was the Poor Love. 'I didn't know. Honestly, I didn't know a thing about it,' Ruby said. 'Look, I will help you all I can. I will try to find her for you. I think I know people who might have her address. I'll go over and see her, and tell her all about you. I'll call you back tomorrow.'

Sandra could hardly wait until the next day. She didn't sleep. She paced the house. But no call came and she imagined the worst. Her mother had refused to speak to her. Or Ruby was lying. Maybe Ruby wasn't right in the head – as she certainly sounded strange. A day late, Ruby did ring to say she was now going to the council to get Denise's address. Days went by and Sandra heard nothing. Her patience was wearing thin. She shouted at her small son, and Mike. She could think of nothing else. She cursed and berated Ruby to herself. Where was the woman? Why hadn't she telephoned? What was happening? A week went by, and relations with Mike got worse and worse. 'He said I was neglecting him. He couldn't understand. I was being difficult I know, but it was understandable. Wouldn't anyone be in my situation?'

Then, on Saturday afternoon, finally the call from Ruby came. There was that cracked and rasping voice, wheezing down the line. Sandra was so tense and overwrought: Mike was sitting watching the Saturday sport on the television, phlegmatic and uninvolved.

'I've been to see your mother,' breathed the voice. 'I've told her all about you. At first she wouldn't believe it, couldn't believe it. She asked what your name was. I said Sandra, and then right away she knew I was telling the truth. Sandra was the name she gave you, and the people who adopted you obviously didn't change it. She burst into tears, and she cried a lot. We talked for a long time. She was so thrilled, and yet so sad at what happened. She's over the moon about you, and she does want to see you.'

The tears pleased Sandra almost more than anything. 'She cried, she really cried for me?' she said. 'Then it did hurt her, like it hurt me. She did miss me, and hadn't forgotten all about me. That mattered a lot.'

Ruby told her more about their conversation. Sandra's real father was Denise's dead husband, Brian Brockley. He was an older married man when he first started having an affair with Denise. But when Denise got pregnant with

Sandra, he took off in a panic, suggesting abortion. It was only after Sandra had been given up for adoption that the two got back together. He decided to leave his first wife and children, and married Denise instead. They had two more children, two sons, and they never told a soul about the daughter of theirs they had let go to strangers, and would never see again. Brian died years ago – but Jason and Barry were fine.

If Brian Brockley was Sandra's real father, then why did the name Norman Hayes appear in the files as Sandra's father? Ruby had put that question to Denise. She answered that she made up the name on the spur of the moment. Brian was a married man and she didn't want to make trouble for him by telling the adoption agency who he was. She thought they might come knocking on his door for money. She had invented the name Norman Hayes. It was just a coincidence that the couple who adopted Sandra were called Hayes, and that the husband was Norman. Actually, she said, she couldn't even remember what name she had invented at the agency, but she'd been careful to say he wasn't from around these parts, and that she didn't know his address.

Sandra accepted the fact that Brian George Brockley was indeed her father. She needed and wanted to believe it, as it gave her a family, very nearly of legitimacy, respectability for her mother, and most important – two whole brothers. Ruby told her that Denise said the marriage had been a failure. He was a bullying brutish man. She was not in love with him any more by the time she married him, and she'd done it partly out of confusion at the loss of her baby, and partly out of bloody-mindedness to spite her family who were against him.

On the other hand, Sandra was distressed to think that she had been given away during a lover's quarrel. Just because her father had abandoned her mother for a few crucial months, she had been abandoned for life. How bitter that they should then have married too late to get their child back. Sandra is full of bitterness, and it floods over her from time to time. 'My own real family, living together, with two more children, and no reason on earth why I shouldn't have been there with them! But I was alone and far away. No one else knew I existed. My brothers were never told that once they had an older sister, but she had been given away. Perhaps they wouldn't have understood. Why should they? It wasn't understandable, and it still isn't, not to me.'

But of course Denise and Brian didn't actually marry until four years after Sandra was born. That seems a long time. Was he really Sandra's father after all? There is room for some doubt. But Sandra scans the photograph of her dead putative father and seeks out resemblances in herself – a cleft chin, for instance, the 'Brockley chin' she calls it, keen to establish this definite identity that carries back through the generations in the shape of a dimple.

Sandra pulled all the information she could out of Ruby. Did her mother have skinny legs like her? How tall was she? Was she attractive looking? What colour were her eyes? Did she cry again? Every tear was precious to Sandra. Yes, she cried and cried, and could hardly stop herself. 'That sounded good,' Sandra said, pleased that her mother cared. Ruby described how after their long conversation, they had gone out together to buy envelopes, writing paper and a stamp, so that Denise could sit down and write to her daughter. Denise didn't feel able to talk to Sandra on the telephone quite yet. She would prefer to start by writing to her – but she would post the letter that very day, once she had calmed herself, and collected her thoughts.

That was how Ruby had left her, sitting down to write. Sandra had for years longed for the time she could write to her mother, and at the start of her search she had made a special trip to Debenham's to buy herself some particularly beautiful writing paper. She fingered it from time to time, and thought of her mother. Now all she had to do was to wait for the letter.

But the letter didn't arrive the next day, or the day after, or the day after that. From Monday to Friday Sandra waited with increasing desperation. She called Ruby again and again, but all Ruby could tell her was that when she left her mother, she was sitting down to write, with a stamped addressed envelope all ready at her side. What then did this mean? Did her mother just pretend to Ruby, to save face, that she would meet her child? Had she changed her mind? Did she find, when it came to the point, it was all too much for her?

Sandra lost the little patience she had. She decided that she no longer trusted Ruby. Anyway, who was this Ruby? Maybe she was a mad woman? Maybe she'd never even seen her mother at all? Or maybe she just hadn't dared tell the truth after all, which was that Denise didn't want to see her daughter. Sandra had to find out for herself, and by now she didn't care what she did to whom or who got hurt on the way. She was going to force her way to her mother. Her mother had been warned.

But she hadn't got her mother's address, only the name of the estate on which she lived. She decided that every estate has a community centre of some kind. A woman with two sons growing up on the estate was likely to have touched base with the community centre at some time. She called directory inquiries. Yes, the Holmead Estate did have a community centre. She called the number. A woman there finally said yes, she thought the name Brockley rang a bell. Jason? No. Barry? Yes, Barry! A nice boy, used to spend a lot of time hanging around the place when he was younger. Of course he'd be nineteen by now. But yes, maybe in the card index there would be some record of an address for him. And there was. The Brockley family lived at number 22 Nelson Way, just off Columbus Street. Sandra thanked the community worker profusely, couldn't tell her how important this was, and how grateful she was. 'I was speaking to a woman only streets away from Her!' Sandra said.

But what now? If her mother was disinclined to write letters, there was not much point in writing to her. But her mother had no telephone. 'How I wished I could have got on a train and gone straight down there. It would all have been so easy. But if you have a small child, no money, no transport, and you live miles away, what can you do? I felt so helpless. I really felt my situation then, being dependent, no money, no chance to take off and do what I wanted to do. Right from the start if I'd had the money to go to Chatham, stay in a hotel, and search over a week, I could have found her easily.'

Now she hit on the idea that her mother's neighbours might have telephones, even if she didn't. She called Chatham and made inquiries about the electoral register. Could she have the names of the people living at numbers 21 and 23 Nelson Way? The names were given her. She called directory inquiries. Yes, Mrs Wagner, at number 21 had a phone. She called Mrs Wagner. 'By now I'd become so good at creeping and crawling to people down the phone, I was on my knees. So polite, so apologetic. Could she please give a message to Mrs Denise Brockley next door?' Mrs Wagner was a very old lady, but friendly. She went at once next door and knocked to see if her neighbour was in. Sandra heard the knock and the fierce barking of a dog inside. 'Sorry love, but she's out. She'll be back at about four. Always comes in then to get her son Barry's dinner. She's at work before that, you see. She's a dinner lady.' Mrs Wagner promised to give a message, so Sandra left her name, and said she would call again at six.

Now she had to wait the rest of the day until six. But at six, she might actually speak to her mother. 'I couldn't wait. Literally, I couldn't sit by the phone and wait.'

So she took the thing one step further, rather than wait the rest of the day. A dinner lady? That was a new clue. She called the education authority to find out which schools were in the Holmead Estate area. There were three. She called the first two, and asked if they had a Mrs Brockley among their dinner ladies, but drew a blank. At the third school there was a waspish school secretary who said sharply, 'Why do you want to know? What do you want her for? Who are you? Why are you ringing her at school?' She admitted they did have a Mrs Brockley, but made clear her deep disapproval of anyone having the effrontery to telephone a dinner lady without a good official or emergency reason. Sandra panicked and put the phone down. But she knew her mother would get to know someone had called, and she might guess who it was. By now she would feel thoroughly encircled. Wherever Denise turned, at home, at work, old friends, neighbours, Sandra was everywhere. There was no avoiding her. There was no escape. Or that's how Sandra saw it, with some relish. Part of her was so incensed by not receiving the letter she had been promised, that she had become reckless about the effect her approaches might have on her mother and her life. Sandra had gone far beyond reason for a long time now. 'Waiting and waiting, and no bloody letter! I kept bursting into tears all the time.'

Six o'clock came. She called Mrs Wagner's number, but a different voice answered. A younger voice, not the croak of the frail old lady. This woman sounded as if she had a cold, her voice was quaking and shaking. 'This is Sandra. Could I please speak to Mrs Brockley?'

'Yes, my love, this is Mrs Brockley,' said the voice. 'This is your mum.' Sandra had not expected this. 'Are you? Are you really?' was all she could think to say. 'This is me, this is me,' her mother said. Sandra burst out at once, 'But I haven't had your letter? I've waited and waited until I couldn't wait any more, and I had to ring you like this!' Her mother protested that she had sent the letter, right away on that very day Ruby came to see her. 'Then where is it?' Sandra asked in a state of agony. Calmly they compared addresses. Ruby had given Denise the wrong address. Not 8 Brampton Road, but 8 Broughton Road. No wonder it had never arrived. Sandra kept saying, 'Oh, you don't know how I've been waiting for it!' and her mother just said soothingly, 'I know, I know, my love.'

Sandra shakes her head as she recalls this conversation. 'It was like a mother cooing and comforting her baby. It was so lovely, so beautiful.' She says, after all those years of longing for a real mother, the first few words she had from her felt like balm pouring in all she had never had. Sandra was determined to feel these things, to claim all that lost mothering. She might have drained it out of almost any words from her mother that day. Could a mother and child, twenty-eight years after, bond in seconds down a telephone line, the way they are supposed to bond in the first moments of infancy? Sandra says so – the superglue effect worked at once, she claimed, before mother and child had even set eyes upon one another.

'Have you been looking for me long?' Sandra remembers her mother saying. The way Sandra reports it, it sounds like the words of an archangel, greeting a new arrival at the gates of heaven. It has a mystical quality. 'But the phone can be so frustrating. This was not the way I had imagined the scene. Not at all. I didn't want to be talking to her now, like this. I wanted to be with her, looking into her eyes.'

Her mother described in that first call how she and Sandra's father had tried to get Sandra back. They had returned to the adoption agency, but it was too late, far too late. The papers were long signed, and the child had vanished for ever. 'Ever since 1975, when they changed the law, I have been hoping and waiting for a knock on the door,' her mother said. She said she had just told both her sons about Sandra, after the day Ruby came round. They were, she said, thrilled. They'd always wanted a sister, and they wanted to welcome her into the family at once. Sandra said she wanted to come down this very weekend, tomorrow. Her mother said No, she needed a little time to think. Maybe the week after would be better. They could write to each other, and in the meantime, she would give another telephone number, of a better friend, for Sandra to call if she wanted. 'I've turned you away from my door once, and I won't ever turn you away again,' her mother said, and she started to cry. 'I'm not ashamed. I'll walk down the street with you and tell the whole world you are my daughter, and I'm proud of you!' They promised to write and exchange photographs.

Sandra put down the receiver. She had told no one about this call. Mike, she said, would have been furious. He would have said she had no right barging in on her mother, and risking ruining her life. But underneath, Sandra knew he was jealous. She was in a kind of stupor when he came home from work. She lied and said her mother had called her, and then she burst into tears. 'He couldn't understand how I could be so upset when I ought to be happy. He doesn't believe in what he calls soppy stuff. He says my real mum gave me away and I shouldn't think about her. My mum and dad are the people who brought me up. My heart rules my head, I know, but then he has no heart. He's been so cross and bad-tempered since then. He accuses me of not paying enough attention to him – particularly not wanting much sex at the moment. I can't explain to him. I know he's jealous, but he'd die rather than admit it.'

Sandra and her mother exchanged letters at once. Also Sandra called her almost every day, when Mike was out at work. 'You know how it is when you are so much in love that you want to be with that person all day every day? I had to keep ringing her up to make sure she was still there. I kept saying I want to be with you. I want to see you soon.'

The first letter from her mother arrived promptly, with some photographs.

Dear Sandra,

I received your letters and the photos this morning. That is when my tears came, but I feel much better now I have had a cry. You have grown into a very lovely young lady. I think you favour your father, although I can see Jason and Barry in your looks. I also see myself in you, when I was younger.

Have you got my other letter yet? I am enclosing more recent photos of Jason, Diane (his wife) and their baby. Barry already refers to you as his sister. It is strange but when he was at school he always told his friends he had a sister who he called Victoria. I do hope you can forgive me for having you adopted. It was the most hardest thing I've ever had to do. I am not going to make lots of excuses but it was for your sake more than mine. I only hope you have been happy with your parents. Darren is a lovely little boy.

Really I think you should write as it costs quite a lot to talk on the phone. I am enclosing a photo of your Dad, taken at Jason's christening. Don't take any notice of me, as when I try to smile in a photo it always comes out as if I've got a nasty smell under my nose.

Well, Sandra, I must close as I wish to get this letter posted so as you will get it.

All my love, 28 years of it,

Mum

PS I wear glasses. So looking forward to seeing you. Hope you won't be disappointed. Bye Bye.

Sandra said the letter was 'Lovely' and 'Beautiful', and 'Perfect'. She didn't like the sound of a daughter-in-law especially when her mother said, 'I treat her like my own daughter. She replaced you in some ways,' and that made Sandra angry.

Sandra stared at the photograph of her father and decided, if she hadn't decided already, that she didn't like the man. 'Doesn't he look arrogant? He looks a bully. He was jealous and possessive and horrible. And, worse, when he heard my mum was pregnant with me, he wanted to abort me. To abort me! Then he abandoned my mother and left her on her own, so she had to get me adopted. She shouldn't have married him.'

She wanted to test her mother on things that were important to her. She wanted to find out if her mother lived in a nice clean flat, or if she had let herself go. She hadn't asked Ruby, and anyway she didn't know what Ruby's own standards might be. Sandra's own standards of cleanliness and tidiness are high. Her flat is spotless, and she does without if she can't afford to get exactly the right thing to match what she already has. She asked her mother straight out on the phone, 'Do you enjoy cleaning and housework?' Denise answered, 'Oh yes. I'm a Virgo like you, and we all enjoy keeping things clean, don't we?'

And then there was the phrase in the letter suggesting she should not call so often. Was that straightforward concern for her telephone bill – or did her mother feel pressured? All her life Sandra had thrown herself at people, squeezing love out of them. People don't like to feel squeezed, and perhaps her mother was daunted by the urgency of Sandra's needs and demands, pouring down the line from Epping to Chatham.

I sat and talked to Sandra three days before the reunion with her mother. She imagined the scene, rehearsing it over and over in her head. What if her mother said the wrong thing? Already she was quick to feel ruffled and offended by her mother. 'She has arranged for Jason and his wife, and Barry, to be there. But I want her all to myself the first time. Of course I'm longing to meet them, but I wish she had wanted to see me alone. What's she afraid of? It's as if she's using them for protection.'

Sandra mapped out the scene to me, as she imagined how it ought to be. 'At between 12 and 12.30 Mike will drop me at the end of the road, and drive off for a while with Darren. I want to walk up to her home all by myself, on foot. I see exactly how I'm going to approach it. Barry, who still lives at home, goes to the pub every Sunday until 2 o'clock. So I'll have her to myself until then. Then at 2, Barry, Jason and Diane all come round. My mum will be looking through the curtains at the window, looking out for me as I come down the road. She has my photo. She knows what I look like. All the neighbours will be peeping out at me too. They'll know who I am, the word will have got about. Then she'll open the door before I get the chance to knock. She has a big dog, I know. I heard it barking when I first called and I heard Mrs Wagner knock on her door. I'm afraid the dog may jump up at me. I'm carrying flowers and I'll give them to her. It'll be somewhere for me to put my arms, because I won't know what to do with them. I won't embrace her first, but I'll be very disappointed if she doesn't embrace me. I'll be very upset. I'd like a lot of physical contact with her right away. I'll say I don't want to come between her and her family. I'll want to know does she love me still. I'll say, "I've missed you for twenty-eight years and I want to catch up now."'

Would all this be more than one woman could manage? How can you turn on instant love, with the pain of the memory of it all, and the guilt? Perhaps she wouldn't be strong enough to cope with this grown woman, a mother herself, making such emotional demands. I asked Sandra if she thought her mother might find it difficult to give so much all at once, from the moment they met? 'Oh, I don't want her to look on me as a problem coming into her life,' she said. 'I'm just looking for the loving relationship I wish I'd had with her. I really believe in the bond between a mother and her child. It is a bond that never breaks whatever happens through all the years. It is eternal, everlasting. I will love her come what may, and I think she will love me too. I am from her, of her, from her very own body, blood and flesh. She is the only person in the world who can put things right for me, and give me what I haven't had. She is my very last hope. Bloody hell! She can't reject me now. I need her!' I admit I was afraid for Sandra and afraid for her mother – they might fail one another badly – Sandra wanted and expected so much.

The day came. I worried about it, perhaps more than Sandra did. I spoke to her next day, when she was back home, on the Monday, and she was floating on a cloud.

'I've just come back from the park,' she said. 'I've taken Darren there often before, but today it was different. I wanted to sit there on my own, and I did, on a bench for three hours, just thinking. Darren played, the sun was shining and I had so much to think about. My life is going to change now. Things are going to be different.' I was impatient to ask about the meeting, but I let her tell it all in her own way.

'I have decided I don't want to marry Mike. All this time I've been thinking that was what I wanted and it would make everything right. I've begged him and asked him, and he always put me off, saying Maybe, or Sometime. Well, I don't want it any more. He hasn't understood or tried to understand any of my feelings. If he had been going through all this, I'd have been so patient and helpful. He doesn't like emotions.'

She paused and thought: 'I'm not going to be stamped on any more. I'm going to be more my own person from now on. I'm not going to go around hanging onto people, leaning on them for support. Mike may not like the change in me, but that's too bad.'

What brought about this change? 'All my life I've been neglected, right from a baby. Looking for love any old place and never finding it. Well, now I have, and it's all I want and need. Down there in Chatham I've found my mother and brothers – three people who are ready to give me that affection, and that changes it all, doesn't it?'

The meeting was, she said, better and more important than she could ever describe. 'I waited a moment before I knocked on the door. I stood there. Here I was, knocking on my mother's front door. I was holding a rose tree for her to plant in her garden, so that every time she looked at the roses she would think of me – so that it would grow like our relationship. Cut flowers die.'

The door opened and her mother was there, just like the photographs. She looked young for forty-eight, and well dressed. She had a pretty oval face, neatly done hair, with a touch of blond highlighting, and glasses. She had been to the hairdresser the day before to look her best for her daughter. 'There was someone who looks just like me. It was frightening. I felt very upset, just looking into her face. I couldn't cry, I couldn't move, I couldn't speak. I just stood and gazed at her. Then she put her arms round me and hugged me, so tight the rose tree was getting squashed. She just went for me, and she was crying and crying, tears all down her face, and I couldn't stop her. "Look," I said, "you'll crush your rose. Now don't cry, don't cry." Her mother pulled her into the house. 'I don't know why I wasn't crying too, but no tears came, and I managed to stop her crying so much.'

Her mother had planned out some of the things she wanted to say. They sat down together on the settee, Denise calmed herself, and they talked. Denise explained why she had given Sandra away. It had been for the best of motives. She felt she couldn't cope, couldn't give Sandra a good enough life, struggling alone in a lodging house. They went over and over the details of those events, filling out the bare bones of the story Sandra had already heard. 'She was . . . she was . . . well, lovely. That's all I can say. She put her arm round me. She hugged me. As if all those years had just never been.'

Denise did say she was concerned for Sandra's adoptive parents. She urged Sandra to tell them about their meeting. She said she felt she owed them a great debt of gratitude for bringing up her daughter to be such a lovely girl. Sandra had the forbearance and tact not to make it clear to Denise how she felt about them. She did not, at this first meeting, heap upon her mother sad stories of her unhappy upbringing. Perhaps she feared that the bitterness would bubble out of her, and increase her mother's guilt. And the bitterness might well become directed at her mother, who had abandoned her to an unhappy home. The time would come, it was clear, when Sandra would tell her. She is not one for keeping things back.

Jason and Barry, with Diane and the baby arrived promptly at 2 o'clock for lunch. 'They were so pleased with me!' Sandra said. 'They really liked me. I felt closest at once to Jason, the eldest. He has the same coloured eyes as me. He came into the kitchen, where I was and we were both very embarrassed and didn't know what to say. I wanted to study him, look hard at him, and he wanted to stare at me too, but neither of us liked to, so we sort of looked away. I wanted to rush up and hug him. He's so good-looking. I wanted to prick him to see if he was real. If I'd met him in a pub, I'd certainly have been very attracted to him. He'd have appealed to me. And there I might have been, going off with him, and me not knowing he was my brother all the time! I wanted to put my arms around him and hold him.'

She liked Barry too, and she even liked Diane, Jason's wife of whom she had at first been so jealous. 'A really nice girl, so friendly and welcoming,' she said, and she forgot that her mother had ever said she regarded Diane as the daughter she had lost. 'Three of us, Barry, Jason and me were sitting on the settee together after lunch, and my mum began to cry again. She looked at us all sat there, so close together, the family we should have been. All those wasted years.'

At lunch she had nervously asked Jason what he thought she should call Denise. She wondered whether to stick to Denise. 'She's your mum, so you call her Mum,' he said firmly, and everyone agreed. So now she has two mums: she calls them My Mum in Chatham and My Mum in Bristol.

Luckily Mike liked them all too, and talked football with Barry happily for hours. The two brothers had told all their friends about their missing sister's arrival. There were no secrets now. The boys wanted to tell the local press and get a picture of them all printed in the paper, by way of a formal announcement to all the world, all their friends and relations that there was now a new person in the family.

Sandra didn't want to go home when it was time to leave. She promised to visit again soon, and her family promised to come and stay with them in Epping, as soon as they could. But these plans didn't please Sandra. She didn't want to go back to her old life as if nothing had happened. 'I want to be with them now, all the time. I don't want to be here at all. I look around here and wonder why I'm not at my home in Chatham,' she said that Monday morning. She was already writing two letters to them – one to her mother, one to Jason. 'I feel I'm aching all over, aching to be with them.' If she could, she'd go there every weekend, but she and Mike haven't much money, and she isn't earning anything. 'It's so frustrating that just money should stand in my way. If I had money, I could be up and down to Chatham every week!' She has worked out that if she used her family allowance money, that will pay for her and Darren to go there once a month. Her family allowance money is all the money she can call her own.

'I talked to my mum about Mike. She said for heaven's sake not to do what she did, and get married for the sake of it. Think hard first, she said and I certainly will.' She was jumping from one thing to another. 'Do you know, she has exactly the same size feet as me?' And then, 'I think I would always have known she was my mother, wherever I'd met her. I feel it, deep down.'

The meeting had clearly been a great success. Sandra was certain now that her life would change, in many ways. But could all this last, at such a high emotional pitch? There was a danger she would come crashing back to the ground, disillusioned at finding it harder than she thought to build a real relationship, founded solidly on her own character and her mother's, rather than on an idea of the perfect bond between any mother and her child. After all, there are enough people around who feel virtually no bond of any kind with their parents once they are grown up. Sandra dismisses that thought. But when inevitably she begins to find that there are things about her mother that she doesn't altogether like, how will she cope with that? Does her mother have to be perfect for ever? And inside there is still a confusion of bitterness about having been abandoned. So many adopted children have an ecstatic reunion with their mothers, but the relationship falters and fades after that.

Soon after this I went down to Chatham to meet Denise myself. Denise's house is light and pleasant, painted a south coast pastel shade, with a garden front and back. The estate is some way outside the main town, part of a huge post-war rebuilding programme. She is extremely thin, and tall, elegant and young-looking for her years. She says she thinks the bone structure of her face is just like Sandra's, but I find it hard to trace. I think I detect a similarity in the way they speak, but it's hard to be sure. Sandra need never have worried about whether her mother was clean – the house is bright and spotless, with an air of each article being carefully in position. On the sitting room walls are pictures of cats and a weeping clown, the floor a bright swirling patterned carpet.

Denise had been living at home with her parents when she became pregnant with Sandra. She'd been going out with Brian Brockley for a while. He was separated from his wife and children, and of course her parents disapproved strongly. 'I didn't tell anyone I was pregnant until I was six months gone. I suppose my mother must have noticed but she never said a word about it. She wouldn't ever talk about anything to do with sex and she'd just have avoided it. I was very close to my nan and I thought she might befriend me, but none of them did. My father said, "You'd better go," so I did. I pretended to be cool about it, and just said I'd get a flat. My mother only worried about what the neighbours would think. I got myself a bedsit in a block in the town centre, and I made friends with a woman upstairs who was very kind. She was a prostitute, and the only friend I had anywhere. Brian decided to go back to his wife to see if they could make a go of it, so he was gone from my life.'

She never went to a doctor, an ante-natal clinic or to book in at a hospital. She kept on working as if nothing had changed. 'I thought that if I didn't think about, it would go away. I made no plans, I had no thoughts. I lived from day to day and didn't dare think about the future.' She had been profoundly shocked by her rejection by her parents. She felt herself to be in a curious state of suspended animation, away from home and friends for the first time, deserted by her lover.

'I knew nothing of the sorts of places you can go for help. These days everyone must know about the social services and all kinds of helpful people – but I knew nothing then. I went into labour, and called an ambulance. They treated me badly in the hospital, because I wasn't booked in and I'd never seen a doctor.'

Like so many young mothers in exactly this state of crisis, she has managed to forget many of the painful events surrounding the birth and adoption. She does not remember if the hospital sent along someone from the Catholic adoption agency, or if she herself had the idea and asked someone to come and see her. She remembers that no one in the hospital thought of offering her help or advice, or telling her where she might go for help. 'I must have approached them, don't you think? Or maybe not.'

She was released from hospital back into her cold, bleak bedsit. 'I sat in there and looked at this poor little mite and thought, "I can't give you anything, nothing at all. I've got no job, no one to look after you if I work, no money and no friends or family."'

The next thing she remembers is a woman coming to the bedsit in a car. 'I came down the stairs with her, carrying the baby. I got into the car with her, holding the baby. She took the baby from me and put it in a carry cot, and I got out again. The car drove away – and well, I just never saw Sandra again, or heard what became of her, or what sort of family she went to.' She sighed and her eyes were moist. She shook her head and said, 'I thank God I've been given another chance now, and she's come back again.'

She remembers signing the papers some time later. 'It was the second worst part of the whole thing.' She got a job in a laundry, and still saw nothing at all of her family. They knew where she was, but they made no effort to discover what had become of her or the child.

Only nine months after the baby had been driven away in the adoption agency car, Brian came back to her again. It hadn't worked out with his wife, and he wanted to come back to Denise. 'He insisted that we went at once to the agency to see if we could get our baby back, but of course it was too late. I knew it was. I explained to him I'd signed all the papers, but I don't think he realized it was something so absolute, so final. He couldn't believe it. Of course the agency said no, absolutely not.'

Brian and she settled down together. It was four years before they married, as it took time for him to get a divorce. After a couple of years her mother and father came round to see them, and she made a kind of peace with them. 'Years later, my younger sister who never knew about my baby, was amazed when Sandra turned up and I told her the whole story. She said, "How could you have forgiven our parents for doing that to you? It was their fault that you had to give your baby away." But in a way I suppose I did forgive, even my nan who I loved particularly. I ended up having my mother living here in the last two years of her life, nursing her when she was dying of cancer. She never once mentioned the baby and nor did I. To me it seems so strange that she could have done such a thing – her own grandchild. It was cruel.'

Denise didn't have another child for six years. 'I thought it was a judgement on me and that I was unfit to have any more as I'd given my first one away. But then I had Jason. He was two years old and I was pregnant with Barry when the accident happened. Brian was in the lorry, and it crashed into a tree. He was killed outright. He had Jason in the cab with him, only two years old and he broke his leg badly, but otherwise he was all right. Five days later Barry was born. It was a terrible hard time for me. To tell you the truth, although I wasn't religious at all – I'd been brought up Catholic but I never thought much about it – I thought I was being punished with all this, and that I deserved it, for giving my child away. Well, God must have forgiven me by now, as he has sent her back again.'

Though Denise always held herself to blame, she could see too that a small amount of help offered to her at the right time would have made all the difference. First there was her abandonment by her lover, later her husband. Then there was the rejection of her parents. Then there was the failure of any kind of authority to offer support. Lastly, there was the complete failure of the adoption society to counsel her or to suggest to her ways in which she might live and support her child. 'The agency didn't know me or care about me. They didn't bother to find out if I was the sort of person who would make a good mother, if I was responsible and sensible. All they saw was the chance of another baby to take away to a better home, among the lists and lists of people waiting to adopt. They were hardly more than baby-snatchers. They wanted my baby, and after that, they wanted nothing at all to do with me. Pregnant girls were just baby factories to them, providing children for respectable couples. I was a good mother to my boys, and given a tiny chance, a little help, I'd have been a good mother to Sandra too.'

I asked about her first meeting with Sandra. 'I was worried she might be coming to blame me. Then I worried she just wanted to come and look at me out of curiosity, and would go away again and not see us any more.' She described the first meeting much as Sandra had, full of emotion, as happy for her as it was for her daughter.

What does she make of her now she knows her better? 'She

does seem an insecure person. She hasn't had the love a child needs. That makes me so sad. I'd have given her more. She does love her father, but her mother is cold. Of course they are both rather old too. I thought she'd go to a young couple.' She has reservations about Mike, the father of Sandra's child. 'I'm afraid he's jealous. He doesn't understand what all this emotion is about. Or perhaps he does understand and doesn't like it. I think Sandra seems young for her age, in a way.' She stopped and chose her words with care. 'She missed out on so much, and she knows about it. All those wasted years and she could have been here with us! I'll try to give her all I can, that's all I can say.'

She paused and thought about the intensity of her daughter's needs. 'She's written me so many letters, lovely letters. But in one particular letter she poured out her heart to me, in a way that cut me, I must admit. She wrote, "Why, oh why did you give me away?" and a lot more like that. Goodness knows, I ask myself that often enough. I could only say to her that she must try to put herself in my position as I was then. Not here and now, with a house and family. I wrote back that I gave her away because I loved her, and I wanted the best for her and I didn't feel I could give it. Now maybe that was a mistake, but it was the honest-to-God true reason why I did it, and I hope that she tries to understand that. Thank God, I think she has forgiven me, even if she'll never quite understand why.'

I asked about the mysterious fact that the name of Sandra's father in the agency's records was the same name as her adoptive father. She laughed, 'I can only say it is one of those extraordinary co-incidences. I remember the name very well, Norman Hayes. I was sitting in that adoption agency car the morning they came to take Sandra away and the lady made me, forced me to give the baby's father's name. I made it up then and there. I was kind enough not to give Brian's name, as he'd gone back to his wife, and I didn't want to make any more trouble between them. I invented that name, Norman Hayes, and then it was an act of God that it was a man of that name who adopted her!'

The coincidence is so strange that it takes some believing. On the other hand, it is hard to imagine that Denise is hiding an even stranger tale that ended with Sandra being adopted by her natural father. How lucky, she agrees, that Sandra did not hurry home to her adoptive parents and challenge them with this information. It might have destroyed the old couple, the revelation of this secret that never was. But then adopted children live in a world so shrouded in mystery, where the law insists on absolute secrecy, that they often come to believe that anything is possible. Anyone, known or unknown, famous or infamous could be their parent. And why not a much-loved adoptive father? Luckily, it never happened. Sandra held back, and discovered her mother in time, who assured her it was not so.

Denise looked out of her window into her front garden. 'There, that's the rose tree Sandra brought me when she first came walking down the street and knocked on my door. I planted it right away, and there it flowers. I gave a part of myself away, and I never felt complete until I got that part of me back.'

9

Colette

Colette is a community nurse, married with a three-year-old son. When I first met her she was only weeks away from the birth of her second child. She is a round, cheerful, ruddy-cheeked woman with bright eyes and short blond hair. Apart from her husband and children, she is to all intents and purposes alone in the world. She has all but lost touch with her adopted family.

She was adopted at the age of four, having been in an orphanage until then. Her mother kept refusing to sign the adoption papers to free her, so she stayed there through her infancy in that limbo, though her mother never came to collect her, or even to visit. Eventually her case came up twice in court and twice her mother failed to turn up. In the end she was adopted against her mother's wishes and without her mother's consent. Her mother never signed the papers.

The family who adopted her were Irish, like herself. 'Very Irish!' Colette says with a laugh at the thought of her adopted mother. She describes her as a naturally secretive woman with a tendency to deviousness. 'When she wanted to say she thought I looked tired, she'd take a devious way round it and say, "I saw a woman on the bus today who said she thought you were looking tired." I'd say, "What woman? Where? Who?" I'd know there was no woman.'

The Hagans, who adopted her, had three children of their own already. Their youngest, a girl, was only eighteen months older than Colette. 'That was what created most of the trouble,' Colette says. 'Of course we were always compared all the time, and they could never bear for me to be compared favourably with their real child. Try as they might, Janey, their child, was always the good one, and I was always the bad one. I don't believe that families with their own children should ever be allowed to adopt. However much they think they can treat someone else's child the same as they treat their own, they can't and they don't. They'll keep comparing, and they'll keep believing that their own good character will come out in their child, while maybe some bad blood will come out in this stranger's child. My mother kept thinking I'd grow up to be a tearaway, like she imagined my real mother, so she was especially strict with me.' She was quite fond of her adoptive father, but it was her mother who dominated her life, as in most families.

'She certainly didn't want me to do better than my older sister. But I did. I became a nurse, while she only did typing. She's married now, doesn't work, and I never see her, I'm afraid.' Colette works part time as a community nurse, as she says couldn't stand staying at home all day every day. Her job is an important part of her identity and her self-esteem.

The fact of her adoption weighted heavily upon her as a child. Her mother always told her not to tell anyone at school. It was a shameful and embarrassing matter. 'She always talked of other children as babies, how much they'd weighed at birth, who they looked like and so on. But then, I didn't look like her children. People at school used to comment on the fact that we were so unalike. But I didn't say why.'

Her adoptive mother told her that her real parents were both dead. 'I asked once if my real parents had been unmarried, but she was absolutely adamant about it. I was a legitimate child, born in wedlock. She told me my father died when I was six months, and then my mother couldn't cope well on her own, and she died of tuberculosis when I was twelve months old. I never believed a word of it. It just didn't ring true. I knew they weren't dead.'

When at eighteen she enrolled as a student nurse, she was asked all kinds of questions she couldn't answer on the medical form. She began to think more about her natural mother and to wonder who she was. 'I heard my mum and dad whispering, and my mum said, "Did you tell them what your parents died of?" in a nervous way, because of course she knew they hadn't died of TB.'

She did think of going in search of her mother, once she had left home and was living in the nurses' home. But she still told none of her friends about it. 'I had once told a girl at school, and she used to threaten me with telling everyone else, so after that, I felt I had learned my lesson. My mother was right, and it was something best kept a secret. Of course that was ridiculous and I should have been brought up to be open and unashamed about it. But my adopted mother never saw anything as simple and straightforward.'

She didn't tell her present husband until she had been going out with him for eighteen months. 'Then one day he suddenly said, "Did you ever used to imagine you were adopted when you were a kid?" So it was easy for me just to say, "Actually, I *was* adopted."' After they were married, her husband encouraged her to go and look for her mother. 'He was almost as curious about her as I was.'

She already knew her real name – Colette Hannigan. When she was fourteen she found her adoption papers in her father's chest of drawers. Her mother had told her she never liked the name Colette, but she had been four when she was adopted, and it was too late to change it. She wrote off to St Catherine's House in London for her birth certificate, but before she could receive it, she had to go through the statutory interview with a local social worker.

He was kind and helpful, but had very little information. He gave her her mother's name – Bernadette. Her father was listed as unknown. She had been born in Wolverhampton, and her mother's address was there. The social worker gave her the usual warnings, though he had no idea how particularly apt these would be in Colette's case. 'Are you prepared for absolutely anything? Have you given it plenty of thought? Do you realize you may not like what you find?'

He promised to help her as much as he could. She knew the name of the orphanage where she had spent her first four years – Father MacGregor's Home in Wolverhampton – and the social worker wrote to them on Colette's behalf, asking for all the information they had about Bernadette Hannigan who had left her daughter with them twenty-five years ago.

A couple of weeks later the social worker called her. He had been contacted by an elderly worker at the orphange who knew and remembered her mother well. She would talk to Colette and tell her something about her mother, but there was a reticence there. She hoped she would dissuade Colette from seeking further.

The interview was not a success. Colette learned a great deal from this woman at Father MacGregor's Home, and yet she felt vital information was being withheld. Colette longed to see the file for herself, but she got no more than a glimpse of it. Clearly the woman at the orphanage tried to put as good a gloss as she could on the circumstances of Colette's birth.

'She told it to me as nicely as she could, but what I wanted was hard information. She told me my mother looked after me until I was eight months old. I was well cared for and fed when she brought me to the orphanage. I was a bit on the fat side and I had nice clothes. But it was winter and my mother lived in one cold room and had no money. She came to the orphanage for help, but she didn't want to have me adopted. She left me there just for a little while, hoping her circumstances would improve. She came to visit some Sundays, but gradually her visits tailed away and she didn't come any more. Eventually the judge signed the adoption papers in her absence and without her consent.'

Colette found out something about her mother's background too. She had left County Kerry in disgrace. For she had another child, six years older than Colette, a little boy called Michael who she had placed in an orphanage in Kerry. She had hurried away to England to escape the shame. She was twenty-eight when Colette was born. The orphanage had tried to be tough with her, pointing out that she was irresponsibly depriving her daughter of a good home by refusing to sign the papers. Colette was getting older and more unadoptable. But still her mother refused to sign.

The orphanage never heard from her again after the final court hearing, until 1973, when Colette was seventeen. The files contained a letter from her. It said that now her life was in order, she would be able to cope with taking her daughter of seventeen home again, and she would like to collect her. Either she had forgotten, or she had refused to believe her child had left the orphanage all those years ago and had been adopted away into another family. The orphanage wrote back a firm letter. They were used to feckless parents wanting children back when they thought they could be useful earners. Also, they were outraged at the idea the woman thought her child had been dumped there all these years, and she had never bothered to inquire or visit.

Colette sensed there was something else in the files, a strong word of warning, but she found it hard to decode. 'I don't think it will help you to go and find her,' said the woman firmly, and added mysteriously, 'She's always been a lady who liked a good time.' Colette thought she meant she was a prostitute. 'She has been in trouble with the police, and as a result she has changed her surname to O'Brien.'

She wouldn't give Colette an address. 'I don't want you to go tracing her yourself. It'd be a terrible shock, both for you and for her.' That was as much as she was willing to offer. Colette says, 'She didn't want to get involved with me or my mother, so I felt I couldn't ask any more.'

Colette went back to her local social worker, who was far

more helpful. He pointed out the address on the birth certificate as a good starting point. Colette and her husband drove over to Wolverhampton, but found the house demolished long ago. But again her social worker offered more help. He suggested checking the electoral register to see where she had been rehoused after the demolition. Meanwhile, he tried the probation service. If she had been in trouble with the police, then the chances were that she had also been known to the probation service.

A few days later he telephoned her with bad news. Two years ago her mother had been in hospital in Wolverhampton in a bad state. She was a well-known alcoholic in the district, and had been admitted very ill indeed, with a fractured femur. They knew her well there as she had been in and out of the emergency department often enough. But no one had seen her for two years. Those who saw her in the hospital two years ago thought it unlikely that she could have survived another two years in her condition. He added, 'I think you had better assume that she *is* dead. Maybe I could help you to find out where she is buried?' Colette burst into tears. She wondered if she had gone looking for her mother sooner whether she could have helped her, even saved her from a terrible alcoholic death.

But then, days later, checking again, she found her mother's name was there after all in the electoral register, with her address – indeed an address Colette knew well. When she had been a student nurse, she had walked past that door every day, and might have passed her mother in the street on countless occasions. The social worker found a probation officer who knew her mother well, and indeed knew well that she was alive as he still saw her regularly. Colette hurried over to see the probation officer right away.

The probation officer explained that she saw Bernadette O'Brien most Thursdays. 'There's nothing I can do for her, but she likes to come in for a chat. She's a likeable person, innocent in a way – but she keeps getting into trouble with the police, shop-lifting usually.' She explained that Bernadette's alcoholism was total and incurable. It had damaged her brain, she was partly mad too, and perhaps senile as well. She thought she had had about five children in all. Her life had gone wrong once she had the first child in Ireland. When she put it in the orphanage she had gone off the rails for a while. Life had been hard for her, and she had taken to drink. She went in and out of prison regularly, and that was the only time she was sober. She was hopelessly vulnerable and gullible, and full of regrets about all her children, whom she talked about incessantly, though she had brought none of them up. 'If you saw her in the street, you'd look away quickly, the way you look away from mad people,' the probation officer warned. She probably stayed alive because she couldn't afford the hard stuff, and stuck to cider. Also, she lived with another old drinker called Reg. He was fed up with her and wanted to turn her out, but he hadn't quite the heart.

Colette says, 'The probation officer definitely did not want me to go and see her. Not for either of our sakes. She said if I wanted to take a look at her, I could stand in the office on a Thursday, and watch her come in. Then at least I'd know what my mother looked like. But I didn't like the idea of that at all. All these people in the office would have known what I was there for, and they'd have been looking at me looking at my mother. I'd have been embarrassed, and I didn't want to meet my mother that way.'

Why had the probation officer been so against a proper meeting? 'For good reasons really, I think,' Colette says thoughtfully. 'If I introduced myself she would throw her arms round me as her long-lost daughter. But she's not a sensible, rational person. She would turn up at my house day or night, dead drunk, singing at the top of her voice or something. I'd never get her out of my life again. And if I tried to I'd hurt her, as she'd be so glad to have found one of her children. No, she said quite firmly that I was better off not knowing her.'

The next Saturday Colette's husband drove her to her mother's address, a run-down house in a seedy street. He parked a few houses down the road, and stayed in the car tactfully, waiting for Colette. He knew how much this meant to her, and it was he who had encouraged her in the first place to find her mother.

It was midday, and the curtains in the house were drawn. Colette had thought long and hard about this encounter, and had come up with a clever plan of action. She was wearing her uniform as a community nurse, a uniform that gave her an entrée and explained her presence. She knocked on the door, but there was no answer. An Indian woman came out from next door and looked at her. 'Are you looking for her next door? She's a right lunatic, I can tell you! She wakes up screaming at night. She rolls home screaming down the street late at night. But she's in there. Knock loud. They sleep all day in that house.' Colette thanked her and knocked again.

A man's voice shouted out from the other side of the door, 'Who's that?' Colette explained through the letter box that she had come to see Mrs Bernadette O'Brien. The door opened and Reg a tousled old man in a dirty singlet stared at her and at her nurse's uniform. 'I've come to see how she is,' Colette said. He grunted and went back to his room, where the door was open, and she could see a rumpled bed and a chaos of clothes and newspapers. He called upstairs. An old woman came down with thick matted hair, wearing a semi-transparent short nylon nightie in what had once been a luminous colour. She had a black eye and half her face was swollen. 'I didn't for one moment think this was my mother. I thought this was someone else,' Colette says. 'Although I had been told what to expect, for some reason I just couldn't believe it.' Colette stood and stared at her, this poor crumpled beaten creature who was indeed her mother. 'Are you Bernadette?' she asked. But by then she had guessed the answer. She peered at her face, looking for some similarity, some sign of herself in this human wreckage. Yes, she thought she did see some likeness there, the cheekbones perhaps, the tilt of the chin. This was her mother and she was determined to recognize her.

Bernadette was delighted to have a nurse visit her. She needed people to talk to, people who would listen to her. She led Colette into another room straight away, where there was another unmade bed, clothes everywhere, old plates, rubbish, and the curtains still drawn.

'I hardly said a word to her, not a word. I just stared. But she really liked to talk. She began to tell me the whole story of her life, right from the beginning. Maybe she does that all the time to anyone who will listen. I was a good listener for her that day. She had an idea people were after her. "They're all after me, all the time. For sex they all want me," she said.'

Then she launched into her life story. Perhaps, Colette wonders, it was some strange telepathy but within moments of meeting her, her mother began to tell Colette about a girl she had given away once, called Colette 'She was a lovely baby, a lovely child. I miss her, even now, I miss her.' She mentioned all her children, all five of them, but the one she kept coming back to was Colette. She had looked after her for eight months, and perhaps the others had been adopted at birth. She rambled on about how much she wanted to find her again, how the orphanage had refused to tell her where her daughter was. She remembered the name of Father MacGregor's. She remembered Colette's birthday. She talked a little of a daughter, Irene, who was younger than Colette, but said very little about her three boys.

Colette sat there listening, a part of her longing to lean across to her mother and say to her, 'I'm here. I am Colette, your missing daughter.' She could imagine the joy she would give her mother. But a more sensible voice kept warning her that this was not the time. Maybe there would never be a right time, but certainly not now.

She asked her mother a few questions, but was careful not to arouse suspicions, by seeming too nosy. Her mother was delighted to have such a keen and sympathetic listener. 'Who was Colette's father?' Colette asked. Bernadette was happy to talk of that too. She had met him one night in an Irish club called The Shamrock, and he was lovely, she said. She'd been out with him for three weeks, when he suggested a long weekend in a hotel. She said she took a fancy to him. She didn't go with men usually, not in those days, but he was special, and she loved him. She hoped he would stay and she'd keep him. She thought it would last, but after that weekend, he disappeared, and didn't want to see her again. That was how Colette was conceived. After she gave Colette away, her life changed. After that it was, she said, more or less any old man, and she didn't mind who – but Colette's father, well, he'd been something special. She kept saying that. She said maybe that was why she loved Colette best of all her children, maybe that was why it was Colette she thought of most.

After telling her story – interspersed with muddled and bizarre asides, she turned suddenly on Colette and began asking her questions. Was she married? Did she have children?

'Oh, if only she knew!' Colette was thinking, and several times could hardly keep the news from her. It seemed cruel not to tell, yet she restrained herself. Her husband was waiting outside. She wanted to stay longer but she had promised this first visit would not be long. She told her mother she would call again soon, in two weeks' time. Bernadette smiled and said how much she liked her, and she would look forward to seeing her again. Colette would like to have kissed her – but it might have seemed odd.

Coming away from the house she thought about her. 'I liked her at once. She was so pathetic, so sad. She so wanted someone to talk to. Being a nurse, I know people like her, and I've always liked them. It's a shame some people are frightened of people who are a bit mad like that. But I've never been afraid, and I find their innocence touching. Even their hopelessness. They're like children. I don't know how much she said was true. But I was glad that I seemed to be so important to her, even after all this time. She kept coming back to me all the time, her Colette. Of course, since then, knowing more, I know she's not always easy. She picks fights with strangers sometimes, and gets put in prison for assault. She goes up to people in the street and says, "What are you looking at me for?" and hits them. But I am glad I have found her, and glad too that I can be of use to her. She likes my visits, and I can help her a little.'

Two weeks later she brought her mother some clothes. She was taken in the back kitchen, where she sat down carefully on a battered chair that had one leg missing. Looking around, she could see the filth and the rubbish everywhere, and she helped to tidy the place a little. Her mother had gone beyond pride about accepting charity, and was pleased with the clothes, which she clearly needed badly. She sat and listened again to her mother's life story, and to more about how she missed her children. For this alone, Colette was willing to forgive her everything else, to take pity on all her other faults.

Reg, whose house it was, was surly, and less than pleased with Colette's visits. He grumbled that she gave him no warning, no time to clean up the place. He was ashamed to have it seen like this. Although Colette couldn't imagine him ever cleaning up however much notice she gave. She tried to make him feel that she was not criticizing the way he and her mother lived. She cleaned and tidied a little, but, she hoped, not in a way that he would regard as an open rebuke, or an act of disapproval.

The next time she called, her mother was back in prison for shoplifting again. Reg, for once, seemed glad to see her. He said his back ached badly, so she saw to him and listened to his grumbles. She asked him a little about her mother, but once she thought she saw him looking at her oddly. For a moment she feared he had recognized her and any minute now he would accuse her of being who she was, Bernadette's own child. Like so many adopted children, she was convinced that she and her mother looked so alike that any eye would spot it. But he didn't. He talked of how Bernadette used to help around the house, did the washing and the shopping, had been useful at first, when he had first agreed to take her in. But things had gone from bad to worse. He wanted to be rid of her, but didn't know how.

Last time she visited Reg opened the door and started shouting, 'That bloody bitch. That dirty cat! She messed herself again! I've had enough, enough of her and her filth!' But he was glad to see Colette. She came in and found her mother lying in her own dirt, drunk, disgusting, wild. It was lucky Colette was a nurse, already well used to scenes of this kind. How else would she have managed? When adopted children go in search of their mothers, it is not scenes like this they have in mind. Few would cope so well, with kindness and understanding.

Colette cleaned her up professionally, found her some reasonably clean clothes, and tidied the place again. Her mother had scorched her legs from sitting too close to the fire, so she treated those burns. Her mother began to ramble, mainly about sex. She said all the Indians down the road were after her, sex-mad, couldn't get enough of her, and so on. Reg said she'd been barred from all the local pubs now and the local shops. No one would have anything more to do with her. He was angry, and kept saying he'd had enough. He wanted to sell up the house and to escape from her. 'Don't you know of a home to put her in?' he kept asking her. Colette became afraid now that if he went to the authorities, he would discover that she wasn't visiting the house officially at all. She would be in trouble. Worse, they might guess why she had been visiting Bernadette and who she was. If he knew who she was, then he would dump Bernadette on her without a moment's hesitation. It would be a matter of 'You're her daughter, she's your responsibility, you take her in. You've got a nice house, it's your job,' and that was more than she could manage.

'I could have managed her if I was on my own,' she says nobly. I am sure she would, too, 'But with a husband and child to think of, I couldn't do that to them. I couldn't do that to them. I couldn't bring her into our lives without causing chaos and it wouldn't be fair. Otherwise I would have told her who I was and cared for her myself.'

So far, nothing has changed. Reg has not left, nor thrown out Bernadette. But Colette thinks it won't be long now before Bernadette is put into a home of some kind. 'If I knew she was safely in an institution where they would take care of her, and where she couldn't come looking for me at home, then I would tell her. I shall certainly tell her before she dies, because I know it will make her happy. She may wonder why I didn't tell her before, but she's fond of me now, and I think she'll be thrilled when she knows that I'm her daughter. I know I am always in her mind, and Irene too, her other girl. I'd like her to know I've done well, that I'm happy, and married, and she has a grandchild. I want her to know that she did the right thing when she let me be adopted. Even if it hurt her, it was the right thing for me, and that might make her feel better about it. I won't tell her that my adoptive family wasn't happy, and that I'm not close to them. I don't need to say that. Because I was far better off with them than I would have been with her, given the life she was living.'

She paused and thought more about it. 'I know what I found isn't exactly the perfect mother.' She laughed at her own understatement. 'In fact it's the sort of nightmare all adopted people dread when they go in search of their mother, isn't it? And yet I don't regret it, not a bit. I am so glad I found her. I feel much better than I did about her, although what I found wasn't good. It is a terrible feeling to know you have a mother somewhere out there, but you don't know who, or what or where. You don't know where you come from, or who you are, or what happened to you that made your mother give you away. There should be more honesty all along in adoption, no secrets, no mysteries. I'd rather know the worst than not know at all.'

It is lucky that Colette is such a strong and self-reliant character. Perhaps other adopted children less sane and well-adjusted would have found the shock of discovering that derelict mother too much. Perhaps for other children finding an identity such as that would have done more harm than good. But I have yet to meet a child who has found their mother and has regretted it, even for a moment, however difficult and painful that discovery might have been.

10

Conclusions

Time and again these adopted people reiterated the same theme. Different people brought up in different families and circumstances, and yet almost all were emphatic about one thing – blood is important. Kith and kin, clan and ancestors matter. Since every human civilization has held family and blood kinship in high esteem, we should not be surprised that adopted children often feel that they have been denied a part of their natural birthright.

In the old days it was not common practice to tell all adopted children of their true origins, as it has been now for at least a generation. If adopted children never knew that those who brought them up were not their real parents, perhaps none of this would arise. I doubt if many people would claim some special mystical bond between a mother and child, without either knowing of their relationship. There is no control group available of children who do not know that they are adopted, but perhaps if there were we might find that they rub along with their parents, some well, some not so well, just like the rest of the population. They would not have had any particular focus for their complaints against their parents. They would not have dwelt unduly on any differences they might have noticed. I doubt there is some animal instinct that would tell a child that these were not its parents. The fantasy, the fear, sometimes the wish that your parents are not really your own, is common to most children, if only as a passing thought, at some time during their childhood.

But adopted children, for better or worse, have to be told of their origins. Adoption agencies insist that parents tell their children at the very earliest stage, even before they can fully understand what they are being told. This is because previous experience shows that children almost always discover for themselves, at some point in their lives. Often they discover in some cruel or shocking way, and they are likely to feel that the world has conspired to deceive them. Everyone around them was in on the secret, all their 'relatives', friends, and parents' friends. It doesn't take much imagination to guess how shattering a blow it would be to discover that the rock on which you had based your view of yourself and your world was only quicksand. With so many people knowing of the adoption the child is bound to find out, usually from another child who has overheard the gossip of adults.

All the adopted children I met had been told at a young age of their adoption – but most had found this bare fact confusing and hard to understand. It is a word that stays in a small child's mind, but it can take until eleven or twelve years old for the full meaning to become clear, especially in those families who are reluctant to discuss the subject further. Parents say apparently reassuring things: 'We chose you, out of all the little babies in the world. Other people have to take whatever comes along.' Speculation about the child's natural mother is usually very limited: 'She did love you, but she couldn't look after you, so she had to give you away.' But what do those phrases mean to a child? How can a mother love you but give you away? Does that mean this new mother might give you away too, if she gets cross, feels tired or finds life hard? And what about this great pool of babies waiting to be 'chosen'? What if they don't get chosen? Can they be unchosen and sent back if they're bad? Or swapped at a later date for a nicer one?

Most of the people I talked to were brought up in families where they gained the very powerful impression that any mention of their adoption was not welcome. It was a taboo that never went further than those first stock well-prepared phrases, sentiments meant to soothe and reassure but which often raised alarming questions. If they did ask more, few got answers. Sometimes parents knew nothing at all about the child's natural mother, but often they simply would not discuss the little they did know. Often the parents embellished and altered the story beyond all recognition. Either they had put the true facts out their minds themselves, or they felt them to be too unsavoury to bear repeating to the child. Very few people setting out in search of their roots started out armed with anything like the truth.

But then the adopted children themselves were not good witnesses as to what they had been told by their parents. They had clung to a few scattered remarks, some made when they were very young, and possibly they had misunderstood. No doubt they had done a great deal of their own embroidering and altering since then. Most parents had said something placatory and reasonably kind about the child's mother, but some painted a grim picture, 'She was not a good woman', or 'She didn't much like children', in order to make a favourable comparison with themselves. But beyond these few hints, most parents seem to have made impossible any further inquiry, or shared family speculation. 'It was even harder to talk to them about my mother than about sex,' said one adopted child. Of course for many adopters, talking about the adoption is exactly the same as talking about sex – both in telling where babies come from, and admitting their failure to produce one.

That left the child alone to fantasize and wonder, to create an imaginary parent, often to search the faces of strangers in the street for some secret sign of kinship. Most appear not to have talked even to their best friends in childhood about their missing mother. Alone, they wove a web of mystery and desire, creating for their mother an aura of glamour or pitiful poverty, but surprisingly, always a positive, loving image.

In the early days after the passing of the 1975 Act, people feared that a whole race of vengeful children had been let loose on the world. Armed with their birth certificates, they would set out on a rampage of revenge against the cruel mother who had abandoned them to strangers. But this appears to be extremely rare, though some natural mothers fear it.

I have only come across one angry child, who happened to be a bitter, unhappy man, active in left-wing politics, who, by unlucky chance was one of the very few to find his mother in far better not worse social circumstances than his own. His mother and her husband were rich and Conservative county magnates. He made an angry, though pathetically ineffectual attempt to blackmail her, feeling she had abandoned him as a social inconvenience. However, even he was reconciled to her, and she to him.

But that was a remarkable exception. All the other adopted children were full of love, understanding and forgiveness for their mothers, rightly assuming their mothers to have suffered as much as they had, or more. Even those who felt their adoptions had been very unhappy still harboured an affectionate favourable idea of their mother. Some were more realistic than others about the sort of mother they might find, but all thought they would like them when they met them. With many, time and again, I found it a little eerie listening to them talk about their longings for their mother. They would in their conversation very easily regress to a childhood state of mind, dreaming to themselves of how their mother would love and comfort them, put all things right, soothe and heal the pain of years. There was quite a strong element of this infantile regression in many of those I spoke to. Though in every other way most of them seemed to be sensible, realistic adults, they turned suddenly into four-year-olds when describing their longing for their imaginary mother.

In the light of what these people say about their experience of adoption I believe that it is now time to reconsider the theory, practice and purpose of adoption. In the first chapter I described how present adoption practice was first devised, in order to protect the child from anyone ever discovering his illegitimate origins. But that reason for secrecy has, mercifully, all but disappeared.

Adoption now is said to be designed to graft a child onto a new family as firmly and absolutely as possible, just as the orphan lamb, strapped into the skin of a dead lamb, is sent to graft itself onto a new mother who mistakes it for her own dead offspring. Without such deception, the mother ewe would never accept the alien lamb. But these days there is not supposed to be any element of deception involved in adoption. The child is to be told, the relatives, friends, and schools are to be told. And now the child can even seek out his first mother once he is eighteen.

But if adoption is really supposed to be so open and publicly acknowledged, why does the first mother have to be cut out of the child's life so absolutely? Why should an adoption order sever all contact – at least until the adult child chooses to renew it? The first mother is seen as such a threat that she must, on an adoption order being made, disappear for ever and never know the destination or the destiny of her baby. The reason, I suspect, is that adoption is still seen as a kind of unconscious deception. The adopters are the ewes who might reject the child unless they are allowed to pretend to themselves that this child is indeed their own.

Cutting a child away from its mother in this way is now profoundly out of keeping with all other aspects of child-care. Years ago when a child's parents divorced, it used to be thought easier to make a clean break, and one parent, usually the father would often disappear for ever, and the child would never see him again. Nowadays, although that is still all too common, it is strongly discouraged by every agency involved in divorce. Fathers are encouraged to press for visiting rights, even in the face of bitter disputes and acrimonious legal battles with ex-wives. The parents are urged to put the interests of the child above their personal battles – and all agree that what the child most needs is to continue to love and be loved by both parents, even when they no longer live together. No doubt such meetings can be deeply distressing for the child, but it is now generally considered far better for a child to live through that than to suffer the total loss of one parent. Mothers sometimes complain that parental visits from the father make the child cry, disturb him, make him moody, but most psychiatrists believe that this is far preferable to the secret sorrow and fear of losing a parent altogether.

In the same way, when a child went into hospital in the old days, visiting hours were short and infrequent. Young children were often taken far from home for long periods of time to convalescent homes. Stern matrons made parents unwelcome on the wards as they disrupted routine and, worse, they upset the children. The children cried when their mothers left. The matrons claimed that if the mothers didn't visit, the children cried far less. It took a long, hard campaign to change the attitude of the medical profession, but eventually it was proved that children who may have behaved like angels in hospital, never crying for their mothers, often suffered psychologically from the long separation. Indeed, the long-term trauma was often more serious than the original physical complaint for which the child had been admitted to hospital. Now, in most enlightened hospitals, parents are encouraged, indeed sometimes bullied, into spending as much of the day, and even the night as they possibly can, to minimizie the separation.

When children are taken into the care of the local authorities, either being placed there voluntarily by their parents, or taken away compulsorily, good social workers and the staff of the homes often take enormous time and effort to try to persuade the parents to visit all the time. Keeping parents involved can make all the difference to the psychological survival of the child. When children are placed in foster homes temporarily, it is, under the best social workers, one of the prime duties of the foster parents to try to welcome the child's parents and to make them feel at home. Children need their parents beyond anyone else on earth, except in those few catastrophic circumstances where they genuinely need to be removed for their own good. Even if the mother only visits haphazardly, this is usually seen as better than nothing. If this contact appears to upset the child at the time, most social workers now recognize that this is a sign of the importance of the relationship, and is far preferable to the contact being severed, and the child left motherless.

Recently I visited a children's home where children who had been in care most of their lives were being prepared to be put up for adoption, at ages ranging from about five to fifteen. These were deeply damaged children, many of whom had suffered particularly harrowing experiences at some time in their life. But the social workers there felt that the most important lack in the children was having no history, no family. Each child, several times a week, was taken step by step through a family history session. The child would try to remember everything that had happened, and the social worker would take out his file and try to place that memory. Between them they would attempt to build up a picture of exactly where the child had been and when. He might remember a person, a place, an incident. But where had he been? Which home? Which foster parents? Or was that with his real parents? Together they wrote down a chronological account of where he had been cared for, and they would piece together his memories into a coherent history. Unlike those of us with family to remember, these children had no one who shared any of their memories, no one who remembered their infancy or early childhood.

Before they were sent out for adoption, these children also needed to know everything available about their own families and their backgrounds. How had they come to be in this place? For most of them, no one had explained anything. Their whole life was a shapeless, meaningless confusion. They had been bundled around like small parcels, on the instructions of other, unseen people, without knowing who or where they were. They had little sense of self and identity. When they went off to their new and final homes to be adopted, they would be taking with them at least as much knowledge and understanding about themselves and their previous lives as could be discovered by the dedicated staff of the home.

But children who are adopted at birth tend to be regarded quite differently. They are seen as mouldable putty. They have no memory of their first mother, so their history, and their ancestors are supposed to mean less. When the Hensons brought Wayne home and renamed him Michael, they were clearly determined to regard his life as starting then and there, and not before. Wayne was obliterated and they dearly hoped that Michael would grow up with only one identity – their own. Michael would have his Baby Book, as prescribed by the adoption agency. The single photograph of his mother would fade with the years. From the Hensons' present attitude, even so soon after so much counselling from the agency, it was clear to me that they would not welcome Michael's exploration of his roots. They said they hoped he would never seek out his mother, and in saying that, it seemed unlikely that he would be brought up in an atmosphere that would openly encourage discussion of his adoption and his origins. However hard adoption workers try these days to make adopters understand the importance of talking about a child's first mother, once a child is handed over, there is nothing they can do to see this actually happens. Indeed the whole system of adoption seems to encourage adopters to shut the door on the child's origins as soon as they bring him home, and to settle down to a near pretence that this child is entirely their own.

Adopting parents are now being given two quite conflicting messages. On the one hand they are enjoined by adoption workers to bring the child up as their own. Mrs Henson was told to regard herself as 'pregnant', while awaiting to see whether they would be accepted as suitable adopters. She was even told that if things didn't work out, then she should regard the 'pregnancy' as a 'miscarriage'. If by any great bad luck, the child were to be taken back to his mother once they had taken him home, then this was to be regarded as 'a death', like a cot death, and the child would be mourned in the same way. But then on the other hand, they were given very firm advice about undeceiving their new child about his origins. He had his Baby Book, his mother's picture, and even the photograph of himself being brought into the house for the first time through the front door. The child, they were told, was to be encouraged to talk and speculate about his mother – but the child, they were also told, was to be treated exactly as their own. What are adopters supposed to do? Most choose one course or the other, and most feel deeply impelled by their own needs to opt for pretending the child is theirs, and has no history of his own.

Having listened to adopted children describing their view of adoption, it seems to me that on the whole it does not work well. It fosters an air of secrecy, mystification and romance around the child's unknown, unseen mother. It can leave the child feeling it has no real anchors, no blood relatives on earth. Is eliminating the natural mother really in the child's best interests? It would seem to me healthier for an adopted child to be brought up more like the child of a divorce. Unhappy circumstances have forced upon him a complicated family life – but it is not made easier by artificially cutting away part of that complexity. Just as in divorce, it does not help a child to lose his non-custodial parent, however difficult and painful visits may be, so I doubt whether an adopted child's life is made better or easier by obliterating his parents and his roots. Wherever possible, the adopted child should keep some contact with his own natural mother. He should know exactly who she is, in order to know exactly who he is himself.

An adoption order, as at present, should guarantee custody of a child to the adopters – and there could be no questioning the finality of that order. The adoptive parents and the child would need that security, rather than live in a limbo of uncertainty where a mother might reclaim her child. But having once established that rock-like foundation for the relationship between adopters and child, then the child should keep up some contact with his natural mother. At the time of adoption, or at any time afterwards, a natural mother should be able, and indeed should be encouraged to seek some access to her child. If there were disputes or problems, this access could be agreed by the courts, depending on the wishes and the circumstances of all parties. It would be hoped to keep the courts as far out of it as possible, and the good offices of the original adoption agency would be used as the best means of making satisfactory visiting arrangements. These might vary enormously from family to family. In some cases a child might see his mother rarely, while in others, if all went well, he might see her often. Even if visits were only once or twice a year, a child would be left in no doubt as to who he was, where he came from, and why. He would live with no particular mystery surrounding his existence.

It would be asking a great deal of adopters. But I believe it is a challenge that most prospective adopters would be ready and able to meet. If it were standard practice, and an automatic precondition for embarking on adoption, I doubt whether many adopters would shrink from the task. After all, there is an acute scarcity of healthy, newborn babies, and those adopters who succeed in being chosen to take one of them know themselves to be extremely fortunate. For each baby placed, there are at least nine other disappointed couples. Indeed, any prospective adopters who could not tolerate the thought of allowing the child access to his mother from time to time ought perhaps to be regarded with extra scrutiny as to their motives and likely attitudes towards the child they are taking on. If the natural mother is such a dangerous spectre to them, the adopters might later on have equivocal and strange fears about the emergence of alien genes in their child.

Some people say that keeping in touch with his real mother would confuse the child. How could he accommodate this other person, this other mother in his life? But that mother is already in his life, willy-nilly, powerfully present in his private thoughts and fantasies, if not in his conversation. Those who say it would be easier for him to keep to just the one set of parents sound to me a little like those brisk hospital matrons who wanted to keep parents, and untidy emotions, out of the smooth running of their wards.

It would not, of course be the perfect upbringing. No one would choose to complicate a child's life unnecessarily. But like the children of divorce, death or other disaster, these children have no perfect option open to them. They have two identities, and it is not helpful to them to attempt to cover up the problem. Just as the child of divorce is torn between loyalty to two parents, so the adopted child knows himself to belong to two families, even if one family is invisible. It might well be that an adopted child would find meetings with his natural mother hard to deal with, difficult to accommodate in an otherwise orderly life. He may not enjoy the visits, they may unsettle him for a few days. But it may be better for the child to face the truth than to invent a fantasy he may never rid himself of for the rest of his life.

As I listened to grown people in their thirties, still pining after a fantasy mother they could not find, I felt this must surely be something we should try not to allow to happen to children, if we can prevent it. The child's natural mother may be far from ideal. Indeed he may value his adoptive home twice as much when he finds that his own mother is unsatisfactory. On the other hand, he may like and accept his mother, in which case the extra dimension in his life would be welcome and fulfilling. The evidence with children of divorce is that they can accommodate a remarkable diversity of relations and relationships, with step-parents, step-children, step-grandparents, if all goes well.

A very large number of children now have complicated sets of relations, and from present divorce rates, it seems unlikely that we shall return to the time when virtually all children had a straightforward two-parent family. In fact, it was only for a relatively brief time, since the turn of the century, that the two-parent nuclear family has been the norm. For death used to break more homes than divorce does currently. Throughout history children had half-brothers and sisters, and relations of dead parents, step-siblings and their families to contend with. Conflicts of loyalties, difficulties with different sets of antagonistic relatives have always been the stuff of family life. There is nothing so startling or new about the idea that an adopted child might be brought up with a second family in his life, and might have to contend with a measure of tension between the two, if the worst came to the worst.

In some cases, sadly, it might not be possible to keep the natural mother in the child's life. Some mothers die, others disappear and want nothing to do with their child. A few seem to regard adoption as the welcome end to a disastrously unhappy episode in their lives. Many, for instance, come to England from abroad to bear the child in secrecy, and hurry back home afterwards, losing all contact with the adoption agency. Some regard the child as evidence of their sin, and want to put it behind them for ever. No one could devise a system for forcing a mother to keep in touch with her child. Though I wonder how many of those who say boldly at first that they want nothing more than to escape, would come back and inquire after their child in future years, once they knew they had the right to do so.

In my research for this book, I found that every mother except two welcomed back their lost child with delight. They had suffered the separation keenly, and felt remorse and shame at having abandoned a loved baby through force of circumstance. Most had married later, some within a couple of years. They had other children and always felt the empty place at the table where their eldest should have been. Once they had established a secure home of their own, their reasons for having given up their child seemed, in retrospect, trivial. From their new-found position of happiness and security, they could not easily remember quite why it seemed so utterly impossible at the time to keep the child. Often they had come under heavy pressure from their families, or had been rejected by their families when they were young, afraid and alone in the world. Many appear from their descriptions of themselves to have been severely depressed at the time, perhaps owing to post-natal depression, or perhaps due to the shock of being abandoned.

Once they had made the gesture of giving the child away, few considered taking the baby back, during that three-month period of grace before the adoption order is made. The first separation seems to her final. Once she has relinquished the day-to-day care of the child, she seems to sink for a while into despair. She sees the world as having done this to her, she sees herself as hardly instrumental in what has happened. But the regret is often deep and permanent.

From the mothers' own descriptions of this time in their lives, there seemed to be a fairly consistent pattern. In the first year or two most said they suffered severe shock at having had and lost a child. They found it hard to come to terms with still being in some sense a mother, but a bad mother who had given her child to strangers. They describe a kind of numbness, and a kind of mourning. Later, as each sorted out their lives the shock wore off, but they still felt the loss keenly. They all said without hesitation that if it had been possible, they would have chosen to visit their child. Of course it was difficult for them to cast their minds back twenty years or more, and their memories were often coloured by recent first encounters with their lost child. But they all described a life in which they felt everything to be overshadowed by the awareness of a child out there, somewhere, belonging to them – almost like a dead child, except it haunted them more strongly as they gazed at children of the approximate age in the streets, and wondered which one was their own. They would remember at birthdays and Christmas time, wonder where they lived, if indeed they were still alive, and what kind of families had them now. They had accepted the terms of the adoption order without argument or dispute. They had signed the papers and they knew the baby would be taken away for ever. But as the years went by, they never came to accept the finality of that decision. Most said than when the 1975 Act was passed, they had prayed that their child would come looking for them. Some had contracted the adoption agencies straight away to leave letters on the files should their child ever come looking, with their address and a note to say they would welcome any approach.

Adoption workers say that times have changed greatly since the days when the mothers I spoke to gave up their children. There is no doubt at all that this is true. Many of these mothers felt the adoption agencies they went to were predatory, interested only in getting their hands on a new baby for one of their waiting couples. They were given little or no counselling, and more often than not, the mere fact of illegitimacy was enough to make the agencies try to persuade the mother to give up her child. They were given little information on the help there was available to them, should they wish to keep their child. The mothers felt they were conspired against, to urge them to relinquish their babies. This may be paranoia on their part, or they may be shifting the burden of guilt they feel onto the shoulders of the agencies. But many of their stories are so convincing that there seems little doubt that some of the agencies in the old days did see themselves as agents for the acquiring of children to give to barren respectable couples. Also, perhaps, they saw themselves as rescuing babies from illegitimacy, irresponsible mothers, and probable poverty, to move them up several social classes to a comfortable, secure, preferably God-fearing middle-class home.

Attitudes since then have changed considerably. Adoption workers do not sound so unequivocally certain of what they are doing. I doubt if they regard social engineering as a part of their work. They have lost the old moral certainties about finding the best possible home for the child. How do they know what will be best? The counselling offered to a natural mother is intended to make her think through all the options carefully. She is shown what help there will be for her, if she keeps the baby, but she is also told how hard it is for an unmarried mother to survive unsupported. At least the social stigma against single motherhood is more or less removed, but the physical problems of day-to-day survival remain severe.

It is a measure of the success of this counselling that so many more mothers now decide to keep their child. Half of those mothers who first say they want to give up their babies, now change their minds after the birth of the child. The number of babies put up for adoption dwindles each year. But because they are now confident that they provide a very good counselling service to mothers, many are unwilling to believe that these mothers may still deeply regret giving away their child in later life. 'We discuss it with the mothers so thoroughly that we really can be sure that is what she wants to do,' one said firmly. 'It is better for her to get over a period of mourning, and then forget about the child, pretend it is dead. That is what we advise them.' I am sure adoption workers need to believe that this is so. They need to think that neither mothers nor their children will suffer. It undermines their work, if all they have achieved is a grieving mother and an unhappily uprooted child. Most of the adoption workers I spoke to remained convinced that it was better for mother and child to make that 'clean break', and separate for ever.

Although there are many fewer of them, I very much doubt whether the mothers giving their children up today are really so different from those of a generation ago. They may be under more duress, they may have more acute reasons for doing so, and they may well be making the right decision. But I would guess that all but the deeply disturbed and the mentally subnormal feel the same emptiness described to me by this older generation of women.

There is a concept of adoption, known as 'Open Adoption', which is in very occasional use in the courts. The child is kept in contact with a parent or relative, even after an adoption order has been made. A new system called custodianship is shortly to be introduced which will give parental rights to custodians, which is less irrevocable than adoption, but more permanent than fostering. However so far this system is only being advocated for the older child, who already knows a parent or relative well. No one yet, as far as I know, has considered Open Adoption or Custodianship for newborn babies. They are still a race apart. But I believe it is time to start looking for ways to make Open Adoption the usual practice for all children. Custodianship would probably not be suitable for newborn children, since it does not give the necessary security of a permanent and irrevocable placement with the custodians.

I know in advance how much fierce opposition there will be to introducing Open Adoption for most newborn children. Following a television programme I made on this subject, I was besieged by letters on all sides. The angry ones came from adopters, who described their own very happy families. They claimed that their adopted children had felt no such longings for their lost mothers. They considered it malevolently meddlesome to undermine many entirely happy adoptions out of misplaced concern for a few neurotic adopted children. The more vigorously they protested that they knew exactly what their children did or didn't feel, the less I felt they were on secure ground. What parent ever really knows such things? All I can say to them, is that it is my firm belief that most adopted children do grow up with some loss of identity, and many with strong secret fantasies about their natural mothers.

Another batch of indignant letters came from adopted children who said their own adoptions had been very happy, and they had never wanted to seek out their mothers, nor had they ever had much curiosity about them. They regarded their adoptive family as every bit as good, or better than any natural family. As I said in the first chapter, after talking to several psychiatrists, I found it hard to believe that their natural mothers really meant nothing at all to them. The image of motherhood is such a powerful part of every human myth, religion and culture, that I find it unlikely that these people are immune to it. It is a theme that dominates much of great literature, the searching of parent for child and child for parent, the changeling, outcast, foundling. Can they really be indifferent to their true origins? Or does the very vociferousness of their protestations suggest they are eager to deny a feeling they have long ago hidden away as too difficult or too painful?

I had far more letters from adopted people who said they had indeed always felt a lack in their lives. They needed blood relatives, they said. They missed the mother they had thought about for so long. Many asked for information as to how to set out on the search, and what were their chances of success? I had to admit that their chance of finding their mother was not great. It was a matter of luck and perseverance, since women change their names when they marry, and often move from the area mentioned on the birth certficate. NORCAP is the biggest self-help organization for missing parents and children. Registering with them can help, but sadly, it is rare for NORCAP to be able to match up mother and child. They are, though, extremely helpful to those who do not know how to set about looking for a missing relative.

I also had many letters from natural mothers trying to trace their children. There was very little hope I could offer them, though many of their stories were tragic. Some were very old women whose one wish was to see their child before they died. But the law makes it quite clear that once the adoption order has been made, a mother has absolutely no right of access to any information at all. The chance of a mother finding her child, unless she already knows something of its adopters, is very remote. But a great deal can depend upon the attitude of the agency they turn to. As we saw in the case of Dorothy, the agency there was anxious to help her find her daughter, despite her claim that she only wanted the address so as to leave her possessions to her in her will. Judy's mother succeeded in finding Judy after years of searching, through the kind offices of John Stroud at the Hertfordshire Social Services. He has often helped mothers, mothers who live nowhere near Hertfordshire and who are in no sense clients of his.

When I have made the case for Open Adoption, people have protested, saying but what if the natural mother is impossible and unreasonable? What if she lays siege to the family? Probably that problem would arise in some cases. But it would be no harder to deal with than bitter disputes between ex-husband and wife over access to the children. It ought to be a lot easier to deal with, since the natural mother and the adoptive family start with no history of anger towards one another. The courts could, if necessary, make an order, and the mother would be under the same constraints as any non-custodial parent to keep to the terms of that order. It would be hoped though, that in such cases the court could be kept out of it, and that arrangements would be made via the conciliatory services of the adoption agency, if problems arose.

As adoption is viewed at present, there might be deemed to be a strong conflict of interest between the adopters and the natural parents. While the adoptive parents want to call the child their own, the natural parents are seen as interlopers. But we should not be diverted into thinking too much about the rights of either party. The first question must always be, what is in the child's best interests? Should he be cut off from his birth parents for ever, or should he be brought up with access to his mother, and some understanding of where he comes from? Of course the interests of the child are inextricably linked to the happiness of those who are bringing him up. The feelings of the adopters have to be taken into account, when considering what is best for him. But if I were interviewing a family who wanted to take in a child, I would question their suitability if they said it was quite out of the question ever to have anything whatever to do with the child's mother. If the very thought of the child's natural mother is so upsetting and displeasing to the adopting couple, they may well convey that sense to the child. If they are so eager to impose their own stamp upon him, they may be disappointed when like so many children, natural as often as adopted, he does not grow up in the expected and desired mould. I would be inclined to choose a couple who understand at the outset that this baby already has a history of its own.

Moving to a system of Open Adoption might help to change the atmosphere in which decisions are made about taking children into care, and the adoption of older children. Most adoptions now taking place are of older children. In 1982 2000 babies under a year old were adopted, whereas 7000 children between one and seventeen were adopted, the biggest single group being those between five and nine years old.

There is a wide diversity in the practice of taking children into care. All too often it still happens that parents lose all rights to their children, sometimes after having placed them into care temporarily of their own accord. Delays in court proceedings often mean that once a wrong decision has been made, perhaps on the advice of a social worker who may not have known the family long, or who may have made a mistake, it can take months for a mother to get her case heard in the Crown Court. By then the court may decide the child has been happily settled in a foster home and should not be removed. Often the mother has been given no access, or visiting has been made impossible. In these situations all too often an adoption order is thought to be best for the child, to avoid further disruptions, and the mother is cut out altogether.

But if all future adoptions were regarded as a 'Custodianship' or like a custody order in a divorce, in which the mother was expected to keep up some, however limited, contact with her child, then the way in which all care orders were approached might change. The mother would always be in contact, and only in exceptional circumstances would a child be cut off from her altogether. The difference between fostering and adoption would be less important, and the child would have a better chance of keeping hold of some of his roots.

At the moment the verdict of a social worker can be final and yet it may never be possible for any outsider, however well trained, to judge with accuracy how much a child is getting from its mother. The experience of the people interviewed for this book suggests that even a 'bad' mother has a great deal to offer a child, just because she is its mother. Too often in these tangled unhappy cases, where parents are clearly fairly inadequate, adoption is seen as a way out, a 'clean break' for the child. He will be placed in a secure, well-heeled family, and be cared for and loved. It may look like the best solution, especially where previous court orders have effectively severed the link between mother and child already, but the 'clean break' may also sever vital invisible bonds, unless the child is allowed to keep some access to its mother.

Before researching this, I had never given much thought to the importance of genetic origins. We all regard emotional and social background as vital to the development of the human personality. We do not know how much genetic factors influence us, or what the balance is between nature and nurture. But I am now quite certain that the *idea* of the importance of blood ties and genes is common to most people, and they feel profoundly deracinated if brought up with no knowledge of their blood origins.

Perhaps the people interviewed here would have had nothing special to report about their upbringing and their feelings about there adoptive parents if they had never known they were adopted. It was this knowledge of their rootlessness that disturbed them, the mystery surrounding their missing mothers. When mother and child were reunited, they both believed in a special bond between them, although they had not seen each other since the baby was a few days old. But they both found what they were looking for, and imagined all kinds of physical and psychological similarities to their great mutual comfort and delight.

The current debate about surrogacy, in vitro fertilization and Artificial Insemination by Donor should all centre around the needs of the children who are created by these methods. What the adopted children in this book say about their loss of identity shows how dangerous it is to confuse a child's origins. Adopted children are at least an accident, and deciding how best they should be brought up is not easy. But it seems to me that it would be a very alarming development to bring thousands of new children into the world on purpose who would be destined to lose their biological parents.

At the time of writing it looks as if commercial surrogracy may well be banned. How would a child feel to be told that its biological mother sold him? Surrogacy, though rare, has always existed, but almost always within close families, where a woman decides to bear a child for a barren sister. At least in those cases when the child is told the truth, it will find it still belongs to the same family and already knows its real mother well. At least the child was conceived for love and not for money. I asked some of these adopted people how they would feel if they had discovered that their mothers had only conceived and borne them in order to sell them, and they were shocked at the idea. It was difficult enough for them to understand that their mothers had parted with them out of poverty and necessity. They would, they said, have felt angry if they found that their mothers had sold them.

So far in vitro fertilization has been a miraculous new treatment for hundreds of couples without children. The Warnock report recommends limiting further researsh that will help to develop the technique, by curbing the experiments that can be carried out on embryos. It would be a tragedy if this research were to be stopped, because of pressure from 'Life' groups.

The real ethical questions arise, it seems to me, when doctors consider implanting the egg of one woman into the womb of an infertile woman. Medically, that is already entirely possible. New human beings would be created born of women who are not their genetic mothers. The children will have a genetic mother, and a mother that carried them in her womb. If adopted children feel confused about their origins, how much more perplexed and disturbed these children will be. Most of the adopted children I spoke to voiced strong objections to the idea.

For many years now there have been children conceived by Artificial Insemination by Donor. But at least these children have a natural, biological mother. From talking to adopted people, it appears that they are far more concerned about their maternal than their paternal origins. In America, though, there is a group lobbying for the right to know and trace their AID fathers. There is also much evidence to show how children brought up never knowing their fathers feel a strong curiosity and anxiety about their missing parent, and often set out in search of their father.

There will always be some unlucky children who lose one or both of their parents, and children who will need to be adopted. Luckly the number of children this happens to diminishes each year, as society encourages mothers to keep their children and families are increasingly willing to take in illegitimate offspring which they might have rejected a generation ago. But now, suddenly, we are in danger of deliberately creating thousands more children destined to be brought up without their genetic parents.

The number of infertile couples is growing every year, partly due to greater promiscuity, and the spread of venereal diseases that damage women's reproductive organs. Most people are brought up expecting to have children and there is no very clear role or place for the childless. The demands of unhappy, infertile couples for children are powerful and pressing. Some try to buy third-world children, some hope to hire another woman to bear a child for them. It may seem that the easiest answer would be the donation of an egg from another woman, to be implanted in their womb, a simple and painless procedure for providing many of them with a child. But I hope that the experience of the adopted children in this book will make people realize that it would not be such a simple solution at all. Although a child born in this way might be bound more closely to its artificial family, both the child and the parents would still know that this was not a genuine blood relationship. (I assume this, since someone else would be bound to tell the child eventually. Secrets are rarely kept for ever.) Parents who are not blood parents may watch for alien traits in the child, and the child may imagine a lack of love, exploring and exploiting their differences. The blood tie may not matter in itself, but many parents and children are unlikely to escape altogether the feeling that it does.

We all know how very different natural brothers and sisters can be, products of the same gene pool emerging as very dissimilar human beings, showing how random and arbitrary inheritance can be. And yet families time and again take pleasure in tracing supposed similarities sometimes stretching back several generations – 'Doesn't he take after . . .' 'Isn't she the spitting image of . . .' The cultural and traditional belief in genes is far stronger than the genetic messages it purports to observe. For these adopted children it is the idea of blood kinship that counts. A child has a place in the world from the moment of its birth into a family. It bestows meaning on the lives of older generations in the clan, and derives meaning for its own existence from them. It is another instalment in a family saga. Listening to the children who have none of that shows us how important it is, and warns us not to meddle with it unnecessarily.

* * *

Those interested in trying to contact a missing parent or child should contact NORCAP – The National Organisation for the Counselling of Adoptees and their Parents, 49 Russell Hill Road, Purley, Surrey CR2 2XB (enclose S.A.E.). Those interested in adoption and fostering should contact the British Agencies for Adoption and Fostering, 11 Southwark Street, London SE1 1RQ.

JILL GREATOREX AND NIGEL SMITH

MONEY GUIDE FOR WOMEN

This new and up-to-date book is the most comprehensive guide on money from a woman's viewpoint. Whether you are single, married, widowed, separated or divorced, you will find sound advice and all the facts you need on:

- spending and borrowing
- saving and investing
- social security
- cutting out bank charges
- getting a mortgage
- taxes and allowances
- children and dependants
- earning money at home
- protecting yourself from risks
- separation and divorce
- widowhood

Get the best possible value from your money – whether you are earning it, spending it, investing it or finding it difficult to make ends meet. Written in clear, accessible language, **MONEY GUIDE FOR WOMEN** is an indispensable handbook of practical advice and information.

BRIAN MASTERS

KILLING FOR COMPANY

'Probably the best thing of its kind since IN COLD BLOOD... a classic study in criminal mentality'

Colin Wilson, *Yorkshire Post*

On February 9th 1983 Dennis Nilsen was arrested at his Muswell Hill home, after human remains had been identified as the cause of blocked drains. Within days he had confessed to fifteen gruesome murders over a period of four years. His victims, all young homosexual men, had never been missed. Brian Masters, with Nilsen's full cooperation, has produced a study of a murderer's mind which is unique of its kind.

'KILLING FOR COMPANY must stand as one of the most remarkable and accurate accounts ever written of the singular relationship between a mass murderer and a society. Brian Masters, in the writing, has achieved the impossible. Though dealing with sensational and horrific matters he has managed, God knows how, to treat his material with such objectivity and restraint that what we have is not a penny dreadful from the Hammer House of Horror, but a bloody masterpiece'

Beryl Bainbridge, *Observer*

CORONET BOOKS

ANDREW TYLER

STREET DRUGS

Prescribed, trafficked or stolen, drugs are swallowed, smoked, sniffed and injected at all levels of society. Patterns of use and abuse change and change again. Yet accurate information and level-headed advice are hard to come by.

Instead we are bombarded by a succession of panic headlines as scare follows scare. Even medical opinion reverses: yesterday's wonder prescription is today's killer. Fact and fiction are muddled. The law and government policies either limp along behind reality or become sidetracked by moral crusades. History is ignored and lessons never learned.

STREET DRUGS is a much-needed guide to the whole range of drugs – legal and illegal – in use today. Effets and side-effects, trade names and street names, history and geography, methods and fashions, benefits and dangers, are all clearly described.

STREET DRUGS is for drug workers, drug users, teachers, parents, for everyone who needs or wants to know about drugs and drug taking in the Eighties.

CORONET BOOKS

EILEEN EGAN

MOTHER TERESA: SUCH A VISION OF THE STREET

Mother Teresa's life and work among the starving and the sick of Calcutta is now known and honoured worldwide. Formal recognition has included the Nobel Peace Prize and, although she is not a British citizen, the Order of Merit.

Through television and the press she has become loved and admired as the embodiment of the best in humanity. In a world where suffering and destruction seem ever more widespread, she gives us hope for the future – all our futures: a standard bearer in the fight against our descent into callous despair.

Yet now, through that very publicity, there is a danger that we might lose sight of the human being behind the inspirational image. Here, in the only full-length biography authorised by Mother Teresa herself, written by a woman who has known, loved and worked with her for many years, is the story of someone who may stand out among humankind but never stands apart from them.

'The full, detailed, wonderful story'
Malcolm Muggeridge

'We know that this is the only full-length biography which Mother Teresa will authorise in her lifetime, so it is unique, and the author's insights into her aims and spirituality make this book one which we should recommend wholeheartedly'
The Co-workers of Mother Teresa

CORONET BOOKS

GAY SEARCH

SURVIVING DIVORCE

A Handbook for Men

When it comes to divorce, many men in Britain are getting a raw deal. Not only are they likely to lose their home and a large slice of their income, but, more importantly, they may virtually lose their children as well.

The annual divorce rate is over 150,000. Nearly 50% of children of divorced parents lose all contact with their non-custodial parent – and that usually means the father – within two years. Yet, while there are endless magazine articles, books and organisations for women, it is somehow assumed that men can cope alone. Most can't.

'At last, here is a book which explores all the implications of divorce for men with children. It offers guidance on all the problems likely to arise in connection with children, the home, money and the emotions caused by family breakdown.
There is plenty of advice here on agencies to use, what conciliation can offer, how to cope without a solicitor, the ins and outs of the law and how to handle your children's future. The best and most up-to-date book on divorce and the family'
Families Need Fathers Newsletter

'Abundant common sense'
Social Work Today

CORONET BOOKS